Sprayed

David Dabbs

ISBN-13: 978-1-964055-00-8

Any references to historical events, real people, or real places are used fictitiously. Names, characters and places are product's of the author's imagination.

Front cover image by the author.

"Hungry dogs run faster"

James Patterson's Grandmother

Contents

1. The Last Notice   1

2. Monday Blues   9

3. Gifts   16

4. Handpicked   25

5. The Loco Motive   32

6. A Raise   37

7. Mashed Potatoes   42

8. The Contract   49

9. Flat Tire   56

10. Checklist   65

11. Roundtable   68

12. The Full Plan   72

13. The Roaches Enter   78

14. Nap Time   91

15. Sprayed   102

16. Bloodloss   113

17. Headlines   126

18. Cat and Mouse   139

19. Rainy Day   150

20. Operation Dog Biscuit   162

21. Carry Jones Jr. Esq.   174

22. Search Warrant   184

23. Decisions   195

24. Aftermath   207

25. Lucky's or Unlucky   218

26. New Beginnings   226

27. Yard Bird   229

28. Common Enemies   238

29. Can't Beat Em, Join Em   247

30. Making Peace   252

Chapter One

The Last Notice

Jack peeled off his filthy work clothes and sweaty respirator behind his work truck. It was the last house call of the day. He put his backpack insecticide sprayer into his work truck next to all the chemicals and walked a few feet away to light up a cigarette.

A worn-out red bumper sticker on the back of the truck said, "no opn flme within ten feet".

Playing with the cigarette between his hands, he took a few puffs of smoke and blew it into the air. Another week down in the books and finally a payday. A much-needed one at that.

Finishing up the cigarette, he flicked it on the ground and smashed it with his boots.

Climbing back into the work truck, Jack headed back to the main office of Presto Pest Control to collect his paycheck.

Over forty work trucks were lined up when he pulled into the parking lot. The trucks' orange logos had an iconic roach symbol that was known to be the most popular pest control company in the city of Chicago.

Jack shut off the ignition after backing the truck in and heading into the brick building. The old carpets, like some of the light bulbs in the office, needed replacement.

"Ready for the weekend?" Jack asked the secretary who kept the paychecks at her wooden desk.

"Well, you are holding it up as always," replied Susan as she opened the drawer of her desk and handed over his paycheck in an envelope. She was overweight, impatient, and had faded blond curls. "You are always the last one back on Friday."

He grabbed the check, muttered, and walked out. Jack climbed into the cab of his faded red Ford Ranger. Opening up the envelope with his check, he saw the amount, crumpled up the envelope, and threw it against his passenger window. $1,280.

Stopping at the gas station on the way home, he filled up his Ranger and went inside to buy a carton of Marlboros.

"That will be $67.43, sir," said the cashier.

As he rummaged through his wallet to get his credit card, his phone rang.

"Yeah, hello?" Jack answered just before it got to voicemail.

"Hey, man! I'm off. Meet you over at Lucky's?" questioned the guy on the other end of the phone.

It was Donny, Jack's younger cousin who worked as a mechanic for his shop. They frequently gathered for Friday beers.

"Yeah, just finishing up with some gas and I'll head over in ten," replied Jack.

The two were close family. Jack was there for Donny three years back when Donny's mom passed. He was there for Donny when he got out of prison on an assault charge in 2019.

Fresh cigarette in his mouth, Jack left the gas station and headed over to Lucky's Bar and Grill. He pulled into the parking and Donny was already waiting in his all-black Shelby GT350 Mustang among just a few other trucks. The letter U in Lucky's red sign was flickering out on top of the dilapidated bar.

Donny got out of his car and threw a hard punch to Jack's arm.

"Cheer up, it's the weekend, man," said Donny in his low voice.

He was much shorter than Jack, and rougher around the edges. His right arm was covered in a sleeve of tattoos from skulls to pinups, and his clean beard made him look thirty-nine, not thirty-four.

Inside, they gave a nod to the bartender and pulled up two stools that scraped across the floor.

"What will it be?" asked the bartender who knew Jack and Donny from many Friday afternoons.

"Two buds and a better attitude here for Jack," replied Donny.

"Did you get a new haircut?" The bartender joked with Jack. Jack had very thin hair for what was left of his buzz cut. Although he had thinning hair at thirty-eight, his smile was infectious, and he grinned back at the bartender.

The beers clinked together and the two started to complain about the long workweek. It wasn't just that Jack had to complain about.

"I'm going to lose the house," Jack told Donny after getting out the weekly gossip.

Donny had a look of disbelief. Both were extremely hard workers. His look of disbelief started to turn to anger. Jack had a wife and two kids at home. He wasn't mad at Jack but with life.

"We work too hard for this," he said while finishing his beer, motioning to the bartender for another.

"We'll figure this out. Life owes us more than this."

A loud thud hit the bar top as the next two beers were set down in front of them. The guys went to grab a pool table over in a dimly lit corner of Lucky's. Donny racked up the balls and tossed Jack a cue from the wall.

"It's your break!"

Jack, usually calm and collected, lined up the white ball and smashed it on the break. There was a stiff crack as the balls flew in all directions and two of the solids went into pockets.

"So, what are we going to do?" Jack asked.

"I don't know just yet but we will figure this out," Donny replied.

There were no solutions by the end of the pool game. Jack couldn't pick up more hours and unfortunately, his wife wasn't working. Presto Pest just didn't pay enough.

Donny and Jack settled their bill and headed out of Lucky's. Under the darkness in the gravel parking lot, Jack's lighter lit up another cigarette and he blew the smoke up into the air. It mingled into Donny's icy breath as steam came out of his mouth in the cold air.

"You gotta quit that," said Donny. "It's expensive, you know?" He smiled jokingly.

"Go in Monday and ask for a raise. You've been there two years and made the same as when you started. Call me Monday and let me know what they say."

He got into his Mustang and waved Jack goodbye. The red taillights lit up the dark parking lot as he left. There was a feeling of darkness in the air aside from the night. The weight of bills over Jack's shoulders wasn't just heavy but rather crushing.

Jack drove back home in silence, all while contemplating if he could get a raise. In his mind, he deserved it. To say he was a loyal employee would be an understatement. Jack hadn't even used a sick day since he started.

Turning the Ford Ranger into the driveway he could see the lights on in the kitchen through the front window of the house. It was nothing special but an average middle-class home. Maybe one that stretched the budget a bit too much but Jack never thought that when they bought it. He just wanted a comfortable house to grow the family.

Opening the door, Jack was greeted by his youngest of two daughters.

"Daddy's home!" screamed the three-year-old Sofia running around the house with her bouncing brown pigtails.

"Hon, dinner will be ready in fifteen!" shouted his wife Jennifer from the kitchen that was up the stairs of the split-level entry.

All this yelling was the reason Jack stopped at the bar. A little peace.

Jack kicked off his work boots and went to see Jen in the kitchen. She was standing over a large pot, stirring while steam rolled up into her brunette hair. Jen was a few years younger than Jack, early thirties.

"Mail is on the table," she said and then kissed him. "Did you get paid?"

"Yeah, it should help the bills a bit," replied Jack before heading over to the table. Loud-pitched screams came from the living rooms as the girls played with their dolls.

"Do you think you can go watch them? I'm just finishing up. The mail can wait till after we eat," said Jen with a disgruntled attitude.

Jack went into the living room and played with the girls, then seated them at the dinner table.

"How was work?" Sofia smiled at the dinner table. She was pure happiness with a toothy smile.

"It was fine, sweetie," Jack replied while putting a small pile of pasta on her plate. Mary, Jack's other daughter, stuck her hand out for the spoon afterward. She was seven but tall for her age and had dark brown hair like Sofia.

They all ate and once done, Jack took over the dishes while Jen watched the kids. He wiped the sink dry and sat down at the table with a beer from the fridge. Opening up the first piece of mail, it was an electric bill for $263.44. Next, he opened a few spam pieces of mail, which he crumpled up into a ball. After that, he could see a red slip.

He tore open the envelope in frustration but knew what was coming. Notice to foreclose, it read. The fine writing said that they had two more months to catch up with payments or the foreclosure process would begin. His eyes drew to the overdue balance. $4,771.

Jack's stomach sunk to the floor of the kitchen. He finished his beer and went out back to their patio for a cigarette. The screen door slammed by accident behind him, making a loud thwap!

"Everything ok?" screamed out Jen from the living room. "Wait here, girls." She directed the children who were now at her hip as she went out back to join Jack.

He was pacing back and forth anxiously on the patio when she got outside.

"It came and we are going to lose it," Jack said with his voice shaking. "We never would have been behind if it weren't for the medical bills."

Just a year back, Jack had to get lower back surgery. Considering his health insurance was terrible, they still owed more than $12,000 on the operation, which they hadn't made a payment on in months. It all stemmed from the heavy backpack sprayers at Presto Pest. Jack even told the owner of Presto Pest, Mr. Granger, and asked for help on the bills. Mr. Granger told Jack it was just part of the job when you age.

"Don't worry babe, we always figure everything out," Jen told Jack while rubbing his back.

There was fear in her stomach though. Not being able to meet the mortgage again. When will they ever pay off Jack's medical bills? The list went on and she didn't have an answer. She had more stress than she let off. The foreclosure was at the top of the list but her mind always had to think about the kids and finishing her education. Between Jack and herself, she had better emotional intelligence, generally speaking.

"Let's leave it for now and we can talk about it after the kids go to bed." She walked back inside and left Jack to his thoughts, which crowded his brain.

"Why is it me in this situation?" Jack asked himself. "I don't feel worthy enough to even support my family." His hands were freezing and he snapped out of the thoughts. Jack tossed his cigarette butt into a flowerpot and went back inside. He returned to the living room to see his girls playing happily.

"You smell stinky Daddy." shouted the young Sofia as she jumped on him when he sat on the couch. Jack made a roar and picked her up into the air above his head. "It's bedtime for you two little ladies." He tried to keep a smile on his face, at least for them.

Jen and Jack worked as a team and got the girls ready for bed. Jen then headed to the kitchen, poured herself a glass of white wine, and returned to the sofa. Jack sunk in deeply next to her to discuss one of his most unfavorite things: finances.

She looked over the foreclosure notice and at least saw one positive.

"Well, at least we have some time to figure it out. We always do."

We actually might not make it through this one, she thought.

"I plan on asking for a raise on Monday," Jack told Jen. "Not sure what else I can do to catch up on all these bills. The middle class is dying, babe."

"We aren't even middle-class, Jack," she explained with logic and honesty. It was the truth.

"That's partially because you don't work," Jack said in his tired voice.

"If watching the girls, cooking dinner, and then studying in the evenings isn't enough for you, then what is?" Jen's voice was louder than the TV. Suddenly, one of the doors down the hall squeaked and Sofia stuck her head out. Jen got up off the couch in disgust and went down the hall.

"Go to bed, sweetie. We are headed to bed soon too." She smiled at her daughter who had a blanket and teddy bear in hand.

Back in the living room, she stared at Jack once she sat down. His face spoke of his tiredness through the bags under his eyes.

"If you get that raise on Monday, we can put most of this behind us. I only have six more months of studying for nursing school. You have to help me here." Jack felt the weight of the world on his shoulders but Jen arguably felt just as much, if not more stress. Between the two of them, they had never felt so much strain in their relationship.

Jen got up to get ready for bed. "I'll be out here for some time to think," Jack said while wishing her good night. He sat there on the couch hunched over with hands folded between his knees.

Everything was causing him pain. Mental stress beyond belief and as Jack thought, "For what? We work so hard but money is just paper with perceived value. All this stress for paper? The risk of losing a house due to bills from, paper."

Still in his work clothes, Jack adjusted himself to lie down on the sofa. He looked up to the blank ceiling watching the fan spin around him like his life before him. He didn't even want to think about the options for where they would live if their house was foreclosed on. While he didn't sleep well, that was the last thought on his mind before going to bed.

The next morning, Jack awoke to Jen making coffee in the kitchen. The smell lofted from the dripping black brew straight to his nose.

"You shouldn't sleep on the couch in those dirty clothes. Ever." She greeted him as he came in for a cup. "I'm making pancakes for the girls. Sit down at the table and I'll get you a plate."

Tired, he sat down and looked at the Saturday newspaper Jen had already put on the table. She had laid out the jobs section on top of the rest of the newspaper.

"Maybe there's something in there for you," she said with a smile as the plate clinked down on the old wooden kitchen table. She heard him rustling through the pages while sipping on his hot coffee.

Jack's eyes were caught by two immediately. An ad for a truck driver with a $3,000 signing bonus if employed for six months and a construction job offering significant overtime that was the night shift.

"I could easily do Presto and a night shift if it would save the house," he thought. Stuffing another pancake in his mouth, he tore both out of the newspaper.

The girls emerged, running out of the hallway and to the kitchen table.

"Slow down!" Jen yelled at them with no patience left. "Hon, did you find anything in there?"

"Yep, surprisingly." He held up his two squares from the classified ads. "I'll give them a ring first thing Monday."

He slid out of his dining room chair across the floor and went down the hall to finally shower.

Turning on the hot water, he got in and washed off layers of grime, bug killer, and cigarette smoke from the day before. The brown-shaded water dropped off of him into the bottom of the shower. Standing there, Jack knew that come Monday, it could be the start of a new beginning.

Chapter Two

Monday Blues

Beep, beep, beep! Jack reached over and hit the alarm clock for the second time in the morning. He rolled over groggily, got out of bed, and got dressed. He buttoned up his gray Presto Pest short-sleeve button-down and looked in the bathroom mirror. Checking his cheeks, he knew a shave was needed before meeting his boss.

It took him a minute, but he built up a nice lather of soap and started to shave. Rushing to finish up and get to work he nicked his neck and couldn't stop the sudden bleeding. Putting some toilet paper on it, Jack rushed to the kitchen where Jen had already set out his lunch.

"Good morning sweetie, you look great!" Jen said in a positive tone.

Jack smiled and kissed Jen before grabbing his lunch and heading out the door. There was an ominous chill in the air when he stepped outside. He put the key in the ignition of his Ranger and it sputtered. Swearing up a storm, his hand twisted the key again and the motor turned over on his failing truck. As Jack backed up his truck out of the driveway, he rolled down the window and lit up a cigarette. A puff of smoke blew out the window as he tried to calm his nerves before reaching the office.

Pulling into the parking lot and parking his truck, it was early. The lot was full of Presto Pest trucks except for two which were already out on jobs.

Jack climbed out of his truck and saw that Mr. Granger, the owner of Presto Pest was already at the office. Susan was inside too as he saw her older car parked next to Mr. Granger's shiny Mercedes. Walking on the concrete sidewalk, he tossed his cigarette butt onto the back window of Susan's car as he built up his courage to head inside.

Mr. Granger was known to be a penny pincher, abrasive and nonsensical at times which was most likely why he hired Susan to work under him.

Jack opened the cold metal door handle to see that the office was nearly empty. He walked past the receptionist and down the hall to Susan's desk. Off to the left was a call center for scheduling but none of the ladies were in yet.

"Susan, happy Monday!" Jack used the nicest tone he could find.

"You are late on Friday and early on Monday. What do you need?" Susan replied with her typical attitude. She took a sip of her coffee and adjusted her glasses to look at Jack better.

"I need to meet with Mr. Granger this morning," he said.

"Did you book time or just expect time?" she quickly replied. Then she started to check through a paper calendar. "He has time tomorrow afternoon."

Mr. Granger's office connected to Susan's and Jack could even see the light on through the closed door. He walked over to look in. Sitting with his back towards the door and his feet propped up on a bookshelf, Mr. Granger was on an early morning call.

Jack gave a loud knock on the door.

"What do you think you are doing?" Susan shouted at him. "I told you, tomorrow."

Unapologetic, Jack knocked again, this time louder.

Mr. Granger could be seen waving his short right arm in the air to stop the knocking while holding the phone with his left. Susan slid out of her office chair and stood in front of the door with her overweight aged body as a shield.

"Out!" She pointed to the hall.

Jack turned around and took a seat in the hall waiting chairs just outside her office.

It felt like ages as Jack watched the hallway clock across from his seat but it wasn't more than fifteen minutes until he heard Mr. Granger's door open. He could hear Susan's high-pitched voice talking to him.

Just then, the short chubby man with his balding head popped his face out into the hall. "Jack, I have ten minutes before my next meeting. Step into my office."

Hopping up out of his chair, Jack followed Mr. Granger back past Susan who gave him a glaring look.

"Have a seat! What can I do for you this morning?" asked Mr. Granger as he pulled the large wooden office door shut behind Jack. He walked behind his desk and stayed standing with his short stature as Jack sat down.

"I want to thank you for my time here..." Jack started.

"So you are quitting?" blurted in Mr. Granger. He picked up a die-cast Presto Pest truck from his bookshelf and played with it in his hands.

"No," responded Jack in a firm tone. "I've come because I need a raise."

"Look here, Jack." Mr. Granger went to his window and lifted the blinds so they could see out over the parking lot of trucks. "I'm sure Hector and Paul want raises as well. Why should I pay you more? You've been with us now, one year?" questioned Mr. Granger.

Jack saw the two guys getting their trucks ready to go out on their jobs. He liked them both as coworkers but it didn't make a difference.

"Two years actually. I need a raise because I can't even afford to live on this wage. My house is going to get foreclosed, I have back medical bills and my truck struggles to get me to work. I just need a bit extra to stay on top of everything."

Mr. Granger checked his watch and saw it was five minutes till eight.

"We all face problems. It's hard not to say that you have created a lot of yours. I never told you to buy an expensive house, have kids or drive far to work. You'd have more money if you didn't drink, smoke or make frivolous purchases as well. Don't you think all employees want more pay?"

"I'm sure they do, but I am in a time of need. I have been a loyal employee of this company and never missed a service call." Jack replied.

Mr. Granger set down his die cast car and rechecked his watch.

"I'll tell you what. Let me sleep on it tonight and I'll see if I can work something out. Anyway, it's eight, and I need my office back. Thanks for voicing your concerns." Mr. Granger opened the wooden door and Jack thanked him while walking out.

Jack could only hope that Mr. Granger could make some adjustments to his pay. Any sort of increase to help. He mentally gathered himself and went back out to the lot, grabbing his company truck key at the receptionist's desk on the way.

Taking his lunch out of the Ranger, he threw it onto the passenger seat of his work truck. Taking one quick look in the back of the truck for all his chemicals, Jack slammed the doors shut and climbed in the driver's seat.

He headed to his first address of the day, a residential job for an older lady customer, the tablet said. Arriving thirty minutes later, Jack pulled up to a well-manicured gated community. The guard let through his Presto Pest box truck and Jack found the small but quaint brick house. Unable to park in the small driveway, he pulled it up next to the curb, put on his hat, and went up to the door.

Jack spent the next two hours spraying inside and then outside the house. He always kept the outside for last as his shirt was soaked from excessive sweating when he was done.

Wiping the sweat off his brow, hat in hand, he grabbed his tablet from the truck and took the bill up to the homeowner. Finally, with his morning job out of the way, the thoughts of the morning meeting were still in his head. Jack walked back to his truck, past perfectly growing daffodils on the sidewalk.

The bright cheery spring day was nothing compared to the thoughts of not getting that raise. Jack grabbed his peanut butter sandwich from his brown paper bag on the passenger seat. Still parked in front of the house, he exhaled a long deep breath. Everything was perfect in the little gated community except him.

Jack scrolled through his phone and knew he had to make a call.

"Hello? What are you doing calling me at this time of day, man?" The voice on the other end of the phone was muffled by automotive shop noises in the background and loud metal music.

"I spoke to my boss today and it doesn't seem like I'm going to get anywhere with that guy," Jack replied speaking quicker than normal.

"Slow down a bit. Alright, don't you worry. We will figure this one out. Give me some time to think and we can catch up at your daughter's birthday but at least we have something to celebrate." Donny always tried to keep it positive, knowing Jack was hurting on the inside.

"Anyway, I gotta go buddy. We'll catch up soon and sort this out."

The two exchanged goodbyes and hung up. Jack crumpled up his brown paper lunch bag and threw it at the passenger window glass in frustration.

Just then, his tablet lit up with a notification of his afternoon job. Jack put the truck into drive and pulled out to head off. He turned out from the community, back onto the main road, and arrived at a light. Sliding his hand into his pocket, he pulled out his two newspaper clippings. Then he grabbed his phone from the passenger seat and dialed the first number.

"Hello? J&Js Trucking." An old lady's voice answered the phone.

The light turned green and the traffic went into motion.

"Hi, I was calling about an ad in the paper. It looks like you are hiring a driver there." Jack got right to the point.

The lady on the other end of the phone asked the one question which would sink Jack's hopes.

"We are! Tell me about your trucking experience. Is your commercial driver's license current?" she said, shifting the conversation onto Jack.

He went on to describe his time at Presto Pest and that he had a clean driving record to date. Praising himself as a model employee but then got to the topic of the commercial driver's license.

"Yeah, so my CDL is currently in progress," he said. He lied through his teeth as he hadn't even started.

"That's great. Well, it sounds like you'd be a perfect match for us once you get that complete. Give us a call back and we can speak then." The lady hung up.

"In 700 ft, turn right onto Cardinal Avenue." the GPS narrated. Jack tossed his phone back onto the passenger's seat and turned into an apartment complex after following the GPS instructions.

Pulling in, he parked next to an old Lincoln town car with a flat tire. It looked like it had been sitting there for years. Jack took his backpack sprayer and navigated past children's bikes strewn on the lawn into the brick complex.

Two hours later, he was all done. It was one of the dirtiest complexes he had been to in a while, with more roaches than usual. Jack packed his truck back up and started to make his way back to the company lot.

Jack picked up his phone but this time called his other newspaper advert that he had ripped out before.

A rough-sounding man answered the other end of the phone with audible jackhammers in the background.

"Yeah?" he shouted.

"Hi sir, I was calling about the job you posted in the paper," Jack said.

"Well, I didn't post it but my boss did," the foreman of the construction company sharply replied. "We have had a ton of interest. Go down to our warehouse and fill out the paperwork if you are interested but I'd be surprised if it's not filled."

"Oh right, ok. Well, thanks for the advice." Jack hung up.

What the heck is this crap? The two most likely matches in the newspaper, seamlessly dead ends.

The Presto Pest truck rattled off the ground as Jack hit the deep pothole that had been sitting in front of the company lot for years. He whipped the truck into the parking space and turned it off, exhausted from yet another taxing day.

As he walked back to his Ranger to drive home, fear set in. The thought of telling Jen about his day put chills in his spine. At least he had the possibility of Mr. Granger still raising his pay, but it was a long shot.

Jack and his old truck slugged home under a gray and dreary sky. Unfocused on his truck mirrors, he saw a flicker behind him.

Red. Blue. More red and blue. Jack pulled to the side to let the cop car go by him but it slowed down. The black and white cop car with its flashers came to a stop right behind Jack.

"Good afternoon! License and registration please," the tall state police officer requested.

Jack opened his glovebox pulling out a bird's nest of papers, flipping to find the right one. He handed it off to the officer who took it back to his car.

Not wanting to come home smelling like a box of cigarettes, he still had to light one up while waiting to calm the anxiety that was going through the roof.

The officer came back to the side of the window and handed back Jack's documents but no ticket to his surprise. Then the officer pulled out a separate paper.

"So I just want to explain this to you," the officer said while pointing to a citation. "Your back left taillight is out. There is no fine today but you have thirty days to get it repaired and take it to a police station to get this signed off. Otherwise, there is a $250 fine."

More bills... Why is everything against me?

He handed it to Jack who had a stoic look on his face. The officer went back to his car and waved Jack out when the road was clear. Only for him to have a few more streets and be home in the driveway.

Why can't I catch a break?

Smashing out his cigarette butt in the center cup holder, he put the citation under the radio in the center console and sat there for a few minutes. The feeling in his stomach reminded him of when he had to face Mr. Granger for a chat, but now his wife.

Chapter Three

Gifts

Saturday came quicker than expected around the house. Jen was easier going than Jack thought when discussing his dead ends the past Monday night. She had bigger things on her mind as a mother.

"When you finish with the streamers, be sure to clean off the grill grates before the guests arrive," she instructed Jack. "Also, make sure Sofia's present is hidden away and the cake has four candles."

Jen and Jack were running around in tandem, checking off chores before two. Then the doorbell rang.

"Hon, what time is it?" yelled Jack from the kitchen.

"1:22! But I'll grab the door!" She called back from the living room with the two girls.

She looked through the glass of the wood door and opened it quickly.

"Donny! You're so early," she said while welcoming him in and kissing him on the cheek.

The girls lit up in the living room.

"Uncle Donny!" They screamed while running over to him. He squatted down on his knee in his jeans and a black hoodie to give both girls a squeezing hug.

"Jack is just out back finishing up. Beer is in the fridge. Holler if you need anything." she said while smiling at him. "You look good, by the way!"

"Beard oil," he said as his dark beard was shining.

Donny walked into the kitchen and grabbed two beers from the fridge. Then headed out to Jack.

"Hey stranger!" he shouted when opening the door to the deck. "Got you something." He handed Jack a beer and they clinked the bottles together.

"Thanks man, but I have to finish up these final tasks from Jen before everyone gets here," Jack said while getting back to scraping the grill. Donny sat down in a patio chair, with weathered fabric and made small talk. It seemed like in no time, Jen was sticking her head outside to let them know guests were arriving.

The guys headed inside to be greeted by young kids running through the house. Aside from Sofia's grandparents, a herd of moms sat around the living room. They couldn't be interested if they tried.

"Man, let's just go back outside. She can only hound you so much." Donny said while laughing at Jack.

Jack motioned his cigarettes to Jen for a smoke break. The two guys then went back outside and sat in the beat-up patio chairs on the deck. A puff of smoke came out of Jack's mouth.

"How'd the job search turn out?" Donny asked straightly.

"Nonexistent," replied Jack. "I doubt a raise is coming at Presto, so just scraping by to make ends meet."

"I hear you, man. I told you I'd think about what we can do." Donny leaned in closer. "Crime always pays. So, listen before getting on me. Let's do a bank job."

"What are you talking about, man?" Jack laid back in his chair. "Are you saying to do pest control at a bank, work there, or rob the place?"

"Well, yeah, we'd borrow some money and not pay it back." A devilish smile flashed from Donny. "I've thought about of a bunch of ways to get you and myself on some firm financial footing. We do something small like stealing cars. I'm not going back to prison, so that's why I'm saying we do a bank and we're set. Just think about it. No need to decide today but it would take care of all your problems. That foreclosure on the horizon, you can turn that thought into a new house."

"There's no way, man. I don't need to think about it, so give me another idea." Jack stood up and went to the small cooler near the grill and grabbed another beer.

Click, click. His thumb pressed in the propane ignition to preheat the grill. Walking over to the wooden deck railing, he leaned on it. Donny looked at him staring off into the distance. A mindless gaze. He let him be.

Donny went inside to the high-decibel excited children. He pulled open the fridge door, peered inside, and grabbed the plate of raw burgers. No chef but always willing to cook something into a masterpiece.

The metal hinges of the grill made an achy creek as he lifted the lid. Throwing on two rows of burgers, the sizzle began. Then smoke and flames kissed the meat.

The fresh char-grill smell overpowered the secondhand smoke in the air.

"So you couldn't think of anything legal?" Jack asked Donny in an annoyed tone.

"Well, it's not illegal unless you get caught." Donny grabbed the spatula to flip the burger.

"There's plenty we can do. But if you want to make money fast, we have to be creative."

Creative and Jack were two words not to put in the same sentence. Donny gave him other ideas. Chopping cars, running tobacco over state lines, and even growing cannabis. Things Donny knew all too well and too familiar from his friends from the slammer.

Just a few years back, one of the most lucrative schemes he heard of was running tobacco. It wasn't instant money though and he knew Jack needed the cash immediately.

Donny carried the mountain of burgers inside with Jack following behind. Jack smelled of cigarette smoke but at least Donny smelled of grill smoke.

"Burgers are ready!" shouted Donny from the kitchen into the living room.

A single file line of children, followed by their mothers came through the kitchen to make their plates.

"Just look at this mess," Jack said as Jen came through grabbing her food. The burger pile had been decimated. The plate of tomato and lettuce looked like a rabbit had gotten into it.

Jack looked out into the living room and even saw some of the couch cushions on the floor being used as seats.

The guys tried to clean up the kitchen as best as possible before everyone finished eating. Jack grabbed the cake from the fridge.

"Looks nice, man," Donny said while peering over Jack's shoulder as he put it on the table.

The cake had pink frosting, Sofia's favorite color. Rummaging in the kitchen cabinet, Jack found 4 candles and a lighter.

"Hey, we're all set in here, hon!" Jack shouted to Jen. There was always shouting going on in the household. For such a small house, the couple never just walked to the same room.

The group gathered around to sing Happy Birthday to the young Sofia. Jack stood next to her putting a tiara on her brown hair to make her a princess for the day. She went ahead and on a loud count of three, blew out the candles.

Donny and Jack went into full production mode by cutting and plating the cake.

"Teamwork." Donny gave Jack a fist bump after cutting the last piece. With all the guests in the living room, he pulled out a white envelope from his front hoodie pocket. "Just a little something for Sofie in here," he said, while handing it to Jack.

Jack's eyebrows raised as he pulled out the card and opened it up. Not just because of the thoughtful words.

"Man, that's too much. I probably don't want to know where this came from, but thank you." Jack counted twenty-five $100 bills inside the card.

"Make sure that's for her college fund," Donny laughed. "And not for your cigarettes."

It was more money at one time than Jack had seen aside from his two-week paycheck when he started back at the company.

"Let's go join the rest of the party." Jack placed the envelope and card on top of the fridge and walked into the living room with Donny. Sofia was opening up the last of her gifts. She tore the wrapping paper off a soft oval object and revealed a pink stuffed bear. A toothy grin lit up her face and she gave it a big hug.

The hand on the clock was a quarter after six and the sun got lower outside. One by one, the moms left with their children. Only to leave the living room to look like a tornado went off.

"We can clean it tonight Jack, let's just get Sofie washed up and tucked into bed," Jen instructed Jack.

"Well guys, that's my cue too," Donny said as the last child and parent left the house. "Jack, let me know later this week! Love you guys." He gave them both a hug and walked out the door.

The exhaust of his Mustang fired up in the driveway and shook the front house windows as he left.

"Did you have fun, Princess?" Jacked asked Sofia who was playing with her new toys.

"Yes, Daddy!" she said, smiling back.

"Let's get you cleaned up." He swooped her up and took her down the hall for a bath. Followed up by tucking the birthday girl into bed.

"You're next, Mama," he said to Jen, leaning in for a kiss in the kitchen. "I know you are tired but I'm going to stay up for a bit more and watch the Cubs game."

"Sounds good, hon." Jen went down the hall and off to bed.

Jack, still standing, clicked on the TV and tuned in to the game. Already the fourth inning. He walked into the kitchen and opened the fridge for a beer. After twisting off the top and tossing it in the garbage, he paused.

The cold bottle touched his lips and the peace of being the only one up was blissful. Jack reached back on top of the fridge and grabbed the envelope. He took it to his recliner and sat down.

Half of his beer was gone before he even got settled in the chair. Taking the envelope, he flipped it upside down and poured the cash out on his lap. The $100 bills were laid out like it was $10,000. Jack relished the thought of having so much physical cash.

He hadn't felt this rich since, well, he couldn't remember. All his hard work for such little paper. The thought pained his brain. Flipping the bills between his hands, he was mesmerized.

"Three two count... here comes the pitch... home run!" the announcer shouted, breaking Jack from his trance. His hands frantically tried to find the TV remote in his seat to lower the volume.

Jack had an itch with all the cash. Take it to The Sapphire Casino and see if couldn't double or triple the money fast. He finished off his beer, letting the thought sink in. If Jack wasn't smoking then he would love to be gambling. The only issue though, he never had the money to embrace the hobby. Until now.

His mind dreamed of the thought of going on a big gambling streak and sharing his winnings with Jen. Just a few hours could make enough to pay his debts. The ball game finished up, Jack turned off the TV and tucked the envelope under the seat cushion. He shut the living room lights and went to join Jen in bed after a shower.

The next morning, Jack rolled over in bed to find it empty. He turned his groggy eyes towards his alarm clock and saw he overslept. His head was pounding from the birthday party and frankly, he couldn't even remember how much he had to drink. He remembered his last thought of the night though.

Out in the kitchen, he kissed Jen and the girls were already eating breakfast at the table.

"I need to run over to Donny's shop today and get some work done on the truck," he told Jen.

"On a Sunday? I was hoping we could have some family time," she replied.

"Yeah, I gotta get these brakes fixed before running to work all week. Might change the oil too." Jack said while grabbing a piece of toast popping up from the toaster. He took a loud crunching bite and went to greet the girls.

"Do you feel older?" he asked Sofia.

"Ha. Nooooo." she laughed.

Mary looked up.

"Well, she's not going to feel older after one day, Dad." she snidely remarked and then continued to eat her cereal.

Jack grabbed the newspaper off the kitchen table and went to sit in his living room chair. He sat there for a minute, flipping about the pages. Having a clear view of the kitchen and dining room, he saw everyone was preoccupied. Sliding his hand down onto the seat cushion, he pulled out the white envelope and put it into his pants pocket.

After flipping to the last page of the paper, Jack folded it neatly and put it on the table next to him. He grabbed his keys and smoky coat next to the door and let everyone know he'd be back later in the day.

Excited, he got into his truck and put the envelope in the glove box. He put in his key to lock it, remembering the lock was broken and wouldn't turn.

Jack didn't have a history at casinos but was a regular gambler when he could be. The occasional sports wager with friends or raffle when he could get his hands on a ticket. He took to the interstate which had light traffic for a Sunday morning.

Drinking a cup of coffee in his thermos, he listened to classic rock over the low-grade speakers. It was quite the drive but worth it in his mind. On the side of the road, as he got closer and closer, more colorful billboards for The Sapphire were popping up.

Taking the next exit off the highway, Jack got the light and could see The Sapphire closely off in the distance.

The bright blue neon letters could be seen off in the distance and the famous gem logo. Jack pulled into the parking lot and saw the sign for free valet parking. He took a turn and went to put his truck in the far corner of the parking garage instead.

Putting the wad of $100 bills in his pocket, he made a beeline for the cage. A chubby, short, bald guy finished up in front of him.

"Next!" yelled the cashier.

Jack handed her the wad of cash.

"Any preference for chips?" she asked.

"No," Jack replied while his eyes were distracted by the stacks of chips piled up behind the blonde lady.

She gave him a rack to hold the chips and slid it under the metal bars.

Taking a loop around the large casino floor, Jack surveyed the games. The bells of the slots could be heard behind him as he made his way to the table games. Eager to put down some chips.

There were only two games Jack really wanted to play. Roulette and blackjack. He stood behind the Roulette wheel and studied the last colors the ball had landed on. After three blacks in a row, it was time.

"Twenty-five on red, please." He said while handing over his first bet. The other players placed their bets and the gentleman placed in a ball.

It spun around and around. Seemingly forever. It popped and skipped from red to black. With one final hop, it settled in red.

"Winner!" The employee doubled Jack's chips and slid them across the table.

Too easy, thought Jack. Thirty seconds and he had made more than his hourly wage. He flipped the chips between his fingers and felt a high. It was a rush better than nicotine.

Standing out for the next round, he lit up a cigarette and observed again.

Once there were three reds in a row, Jack put down another $25. This time on black. The ball spun and landed on red.

"Double it up!" He put down $50 on black.

Sure enough, it landed on black.

He played the same strategy for the next two hours. His chips rotated in and out of his rack. Occasionally going up, and then back down. Only to be ahead.

As the chips multiplied into his rack to over $3,600, Jack did something different.

"$1,000 on red." He slid the chips across.

The ball spun and landed on black.

"Double it up."

The metal ball went around and around again. It landed on black.

It sent Jack's heart rate up as his chip stack went down. He knew he had about one spin left in him.

He put down 2,000. Still red.

Fixated on the wheel, the ball dropped in. It spun around and on its last few hops kicked into red. The wheel was still spinning. It took one last hop to black.

The employee cleared the chips off the board and Jack was stunned. Six black in a row. The odds had to be impossible, he thought.

He took his remaining $600 in chips and cashed them out back at the cage. Inside, he was angry, frustrated, and annoyed. It's always the big guys that win, never the little guys, he thought.

Jack stopped at the gas station just a turn outside the casino and filled up his truck using the cash. Afterward, he headed to an auto parts store just across the street to get his replacement light bulb for his truck.

Defeated, Jack got back on the highway to make the commute back home. His truck hit the rumble strips and his mind was drifting off into thought. He knew a call to Donny had to be made sooner than later.

Chapter Four

Handpicked

It was just another Monday to go back to work for Jack. He contemplated ringing Donny, but held off. The mix of the lack of sleep after his casino loss and the Monday blues didn't help.

Jen, back at the house, was vacuuming and heard her cell ringing on the table near the front door. She quickly shut off the vacuum to pick it up on the last ring.

"Hello?" she answered.

"Hey! How's the day going? Donny asked cheerfully.

"Not too bad. Jack is at work. How can I help?" Jen said.

"Well, you see, the other day at the party, I accidentally left an envelope behind. Can I swing by tomorrow to pick it up? I need it back," he said.

"Sure, but I don't know where Jack would have put it. Let me ask him tonight and I'll get it set out for tomorrow," she said.

After dinner, Jen was washing the dishes and Jack came into the kitchen for a beer. He opened the fridge and Jen mentioned that Donny called.

"He was looking for some sort of a white envelope that he accidentally brought here," she said.

Jack's eyes drifted to the top of the fridge and then over to her at the sink.

"Oh, that envelope? I put it in the truck to run it back over to Donny. Don't worry, I'll take care of it with him tomorrow." Jack told her.

"I'll just drop it by after work and have him replace my light bulb anyway."

Jen finished up the dishes and sat down at the table to open the day's mail. Standing behind her, Jack rubbed her shoulders as she opened it up. Charge card statements and more bills.

"Did your boss ever come back on a raise?" she asked, while flipping through a small stack of bills.

"No, it seems like a lost cause. I don't think it's worth even revisiting the subject." He stopped rubbing her shoulders and went into the living room.

The two relaxed for the rest of the evening before calling it a night.

Jack went about his normal routine the next day. First a morning job, then lunch. He rang up Donny to let him know he was going to swing by the auto shop after work and to get him to work on his truck light.

He went to his second location of the day. It didn't take him long to spray inside the small Chinese restaurant. Afterward, he headed over to Donny's shop.

"What's up, man?" Donny said enthusiastically, seeing Jack walk in.

"I gotta get this light fixed but we also have to chat," replied Jack.

"Jen said you were calling about the envelope and need it back."

"Yeah, man. I need the cash back but didn't mention it to Jen. It was more than I could give." Donny wasn't joking but it was like him to renege on his word.

"Well, I can't give you that money back. Let it be a lesson, Don." Jack said sternly.

"What do you mean?" The tone of Donny's voice was much louder. "I told you to not spend that money."

He pushed a finger into Jack's chest.

Jack immediately shoved him back into the side of his Ranger.

"I couldn't help the bills I need to pay," Jack shouted at him.

"You think you are the only person with bills?"

Jack let go of his collar but Donny's words cut deep.

They stopped quarreling for the time being and Donny went on to repair Jack's light bulb.

"Alright, you're all set. No charge," Donny said while wiping his dirty hands. It was the cleanest and quickest job he had all day.

He turned off the stereo in the shop and the two guys then went to sit outback. Two rickety lawn chairs were set by a fire pit. The light creeped out into the night from inside the shop's roll-up doors.

Jack sat down in the cheap chair and put his feet up on a car tire. Donny handed him a beer and sat down next to him, looking up into the sky.

"It's been hard, man," Jack muttered. He had a sip and turned to Donny. "The more I think about it, we can change our life in one day."

"See, that's what I'm telling you." Donny looked over. "We deserve more than this."

Donny finished his beer and tossed it from his lawn chair into a burn barrel set up in front of them.

"I know a guy," said Jack.

"Oh, you know a guy?" Donny got a laugh. "Well, I'm thinking we do the Central Bank of Chicago," said Donny when he was finished laughing. "Y'all do the pest contract for that bank if I'm not mistaken."

The tension rose in the air as Jack wasn't the same type of man as Donny. He had never stolen anything, let alone even been convicted of a crime.

"I've never had a better plan, but we just need the right people." Donny knew he had to convince Jack. "We can pull off the entire heist with no weapons and no one getting hurt. This would be retirement-style money."

Jack was immediately a bit more intrigued as his ears perked up. He shifted his chair from facing forward to looking at Donny.

"Ok, go ahead."

Donny described the plan in detail. It wasn't something he had just made up. To be fair, Donny was a mastermind when it came to plotting illegal activities and even Jack knew this. He just never wanted to be associated. Until now.

"So we're going to hit it on St. Patrick's Day?" Jack had Donny clarify.

"Yep, that's the plan. While the city and cops are focused on the drunks, we will be in and out." Donny smiled.

"I'm thinking we will need two more people though. Between you and me, we need some muscle and a smooth talker."

Jack nodded in agreement. Thinking of smooth talkers, no one popped into Jack's mind quicker than his childhood friend, Tommy.

The guy could sell a no-name baseball card for six pieces of bubble gum vs the standard two pieces at recess. Tommy was always a hustler. The concern was spilling some of the plan to him and getting him to be on board.

Donny listened in as Jack pitched Tommy to him. Jack then propositioned two other guys who could be a fit.

"No... Tommy sounds like the one, if you can convince him," said Donny.

"For the other, I have someone in mind."

Donny had done time before. He had connections from his time in prison back in 2017. Lock pickers, con men, muscle, drug dealers, you name it. His assault charge had him locked up for two years when a customer hadn't paid for months. He strong armed the payment. A decision he never regretted. Good behavior got him out earlier than he should have.

"I'm going to convince my friend Ray. He was in prison for armed robbery."

"Yeah, I've met Ray. I thought you just said we won't use weapons?" Jack got frustrated.

"Don't worry, the plan doesn't call for them. We won't." Donny reassured him.

Jack was anxious but it was like putting a carrot in front of a rabbit. He couldn't turn down a life-changing payday and frankly, it was the best option to solve all his problems.

"We gotta reach out and get them on board with the plan. St. Pats is less than twenty days away."

Donny stood up to pet one of the shop dogs who had wandered over to his chair. He had two Rottweilers that roamed the ground. It slobbered on his messy jeans as he stood next to it.

The night had drifted late and Donny's shadow was cast by the almost full moon.

"So you really think we can pull this off?" Jack sounded unsure.

"Yeah, I'm confident. Plus, I've put more time than you know into thinking this thing out. This heist, it's going to solve all our problems."

"So what's the next steps after tonight?"

"Catch up with Tommy and pitch it to him. I'll go down to the train yard to pay Ray a visit." Donny replied.

"We gotta get these guys on board to sort out the last details of the plan. I'm telling you, I've put a lot of thought into this. "

Jack walked inside the shop, grabbed a bottle of lighter fluid and came back out. He soaked the dry trash, sticks, and debris in the burn barrel, then tossed in a match. The radiant heat warmed his face in the chilly night.

"My only concern is if we get caught or the wife finds out," Jack said while huddling in close to the fire.

"Well, let me be honest with you," Donny looked him square in the eyes. "You don't have too much to lose."

"The worst scenario is that we get caught and locked up for a bit. The kids will be there when you are out but think of everything you can provide for them."

Jack didn't disagree. He took it as food for thought.

"I guess that's fair. I do just want the best for them."

He pulled his cell phone out of his pocket and checked the time. Another hour had gone past and it was almost ten.

"Alright man, I gotta get going," Jack said as he started walking back to his truck in the shop. Donny packed up too and they let the burn barrel go into the night.

Turning on the lights to his Ranger, they were both working as Jack pulled the truck out of the large roll-up door.

"We're gonna get you a new one of these too." Donny smiled and smacked the side door of the truck with his hand. He pulled down the roll-up door behind Jack as he left and shut the shop down into the darkness.

Jack made it home and pulled in as quietly as possible. The house was pitch black. He slowly opened the front door to the split-level stairs and could see the flicker of the TV from the living room.

Putting his keys down, he walked up and saw Jen still awake on the sofa. She was sitting in her pajamas with a glass of wine. Her face was disappointed.

"Every day, it feels like you get home later. All night to change a light bulb?" she immediately snipped at him. All she wanted was a bit of help around the house and time with him.

"Well, you know, once Donny gets talking and time starts passing," Jack replied. He wasn't in the mood to argue late at night.

"I've been doing everything. Don't you see? Who do you think cooks the girls' dinner? Cleans the house. Puts them to bed."

Jack stood in the doorway between the kitchen and the living room looking at Jen. He knew it wasn't easy for her but it's not like she was working a job, he thought to himself. His mind reflected some more and he knew he messed up. Jen was his rock. Kind, caring and frankly ran the house. He was lucky to have such a good woman.

She got up off the sofa, left her wineglass, and went to the bedroom. His stomach sunk.

The stress was just too high in the household. Jack needed money. He sat down at the kitchen table and wrote down a list of numbers. The house, kids' future college fees, and retirement. Although he had never been good at math, he tallied it up. For a grown man, he was struggling to control his emotions, but as the head of the house, he didn't want to stress Jen. An argument was one thing, but he didn't want to put the stress of the bills onto her. He tried to keep the entire situation from her as much as possible.

All he needed was to get into the vault for five minutes and fill a backpack with a million dollars. Just one backpack of cash could take care of all his needs, he thought as his mind wandered.

"Fair enough. I can do this." He told himself.

Chapter Five

The Loco Motive

The coffee pot beeped in the kitchen as the aroma drifted through the apartment. It smelled like decent beans, but it couldn't be further from it. Donny drank coffee for the caffeine, not the taste. He took it black, with no cream or sugar, and didn't care if it tasted like dirt mixed with burnt hair.

Wiping his groggy eyes, he checked his alarm clock. He only managed to get about six hours of sleep since the late night before. Eight to ten was usual.

Donny took a sip of his black coffee and the caffeine hit him! He could almost feel the hair getting thicker on his chest from the thick black brew. It was exactly what he needed for the mountain of a day ahead of him. He went back to his bedroom and threw on a previously worn pair of jeans and a gray hoodie.

Taking his phone off the charger, he saw there was a new text. Ray had replied to the message Donny sent before going to bed.

"Come to the yard at 12:30." It read.

He slid the phone into his pocket and finished up at the apartment to head off to his auto shop. It wasn't the first time he had been down to Union Station to catch up with Ray. Ray generally knew in advance something serious required a chat near the tracks. The guys used the ever-moving train yard to muffle the volume of their conversations in the past. Steel wheels on steel tracks could cover the voice of the loudest man in Chicago.

Donny locked up his apartment and took his Mustang down the street to the shop. Although he still had an hour till the shop opened up, there were cars behind the metal building in Donny's storage lot that were calling to be worked on. Instead, he went into his office, took out a notebook, and sat down.

He listed down three rudimentary phases in his notebook.

- Getting into the bank

- The heist

- Escape plan

Inside his desk drawer, he pulled out a layout to the bank. It stretched all across his messy desk which was stacked with auto part invoices. Donny's eyes narrowed in on all the entry and exit doors. He took a yellow highlighter and marked each one. Next, he took his pen and circled the delivery area to the bank. Donny was aware there was always a guard letting the trucks in and out. The guard didn't concern him though. Getting a truck did.

Donny rolled up the floor plans and tucked it back into the desk, along with his notebook. He locked up his office and went to pull in the first car for the day.

It wasn't long before his other mechanic showed up to work in the other bay of the shop. They both had vehicles above them but Donny could only think of the heist.

"Hey!" shouted Donny to get his other mechanic's attention.

"I gotta run downtown but should be back in the late afternoon. Keep an eye on everything."

Donny could see the skyline driving in. The city could be easy to get into but hard to get out.

He navigated his Mustang over the bridges and down to the rail yard. Pulling in across the street from an automatic gate for the workers, Donny waited.

A few minutes later, he saw a rather built figure in a gray train company shirt approaching. Ray was in his early fifties but was in good shape from all the walking along the tracks and working in the yard. His biceps showed through his short-sleeved shirt. The sun hit off his right forearm which had a tattoo of a rifle.

"Aren't you cold in that?" Donny asked as he got out of the car in his hoodie.

"Nah, man. One of us works all day!" Ray jokingly said.

"Will my car be ok here?"

"Yeah. Of course. No one bothers anything down here." Ray led Donny back to the tracks where the sound of moving train cars over the tracks filled the background. Other men worked on pieces of track and cars that were out of service.

The guys kept walking away from the station and out into the yard.

"I don't see you often, but when I do." Ray paused and smiled.

Donny laughed. "Well, I have a big one, but a good one in store for us this time."

The last job the guys worked together was chopping cars. They did that for a few months after they both got out of prison but then Donny's shop got hot and they stopped.

"We're gonna do the Central Bank of Chicago on the Saturday after St. Patrick's Day."

"Whose we?" replied Ray. "Surely not me." He laughed. "I didn't enjoy our time in the pen. Maybe you did, but that's an interesting idea."

"I need your help on this one. For me and my cousin. The take should be about a million a piece, at least."

Ray turned and looked at Donny. Now he was more intrigued. They both turned their backs to the tracks and a train car came whooshing by. This wasn't small potatoes like their odd jobs before.

"Yeah, you heard me right. A million each. More, if you can stuff it in your backpack. That's enough to get your kid through college and keep paying your ex-wife's child support." He joked.

"What do you need from my end?"

"We need you to be the muscle but no guns."

The look on Ray's face was perplexed.

"You wanna do a robbery with no guns? You are asking to get caught. I ain't going back inside the system. Nothing will make me."

"No. We have a plan. Plus, the bank will only have four workers on Saturday after St. Pats, something we can easily deal with."

"I'm not sold, but I'm interested," said Ray. He had never had anything go wrong doing a job with Donny and no reason to doubt him.

They had reached about half a mile up the tracks and the trains of Union Station were small off in the distance. Graffiti covered the buildings near the tracks and broken bottles littered the ground.

Ray checked his watch and still saw he had a bit of time. "My biggest concern is who we are doing the job with and it's a valid concern."

"Yeah, it'd be you, me, Jack, and his close friend."

"See, I know you and you know Jack. I know of Jack. The guy has never robbed anything in his life."

Donny gave a nod. "But it doesn't mean he isn't up for it."

Ray knew Donny's former charges. He had even been in fights with him in prison. There was a brotherly bond, unspoken.

Ray and Donny turned around and started going back towards the station.

"So what else is new, man?" Donny asked Ray. "Kids and wife are all good?"

"Yeah." He laughed. "Now that you ask."

"And that's the only reason I'd even consider doing this job. For the little one and the wife."

The guys passed by a group of guys working on a signaling sign. Ray and Donny's conversation went silent. It wasn't long and they were back to where all the tracks met together.

"I'll call you in the coming days." Donny turned to give Ray a hand-shake and then a hug.

"You need anything else from me in the meantime?"

"No, just your help, so have a think."

Chapter Six

A Raise

"Jackie boy, what's up lad?" the Irish accent on the other end of the phone questioned.

Tommy had known Jack since grade school and they spoke on the regular. Their two lives were just different. Jack with kids, Tommy more carefree. He was always about making money, chasing women, and working. Over were the days for Jack to leave a pizza box on the coffee table for three days like Tommy in his bachelor pad. He was a real connoisseur of takeout food.

"Let's catch up for food, lunch tomorrow? We haven't been to Riverside Pie in about a month."

"Yeah man, that sounds good. Twelve thirty?"

"Cool, perfect. See you then." Jack hung up.

Riverside Pie was one of Jack's favorite pizza places in the city. Tommy would argue that he had a few favorite pizza places, but if pushed, Riverside was near the top of the list. Just alongside the river walk, Jack found it to be one of the best lunch spots for people-watching.

Businessmen in suits often hurried by at the same pace as some of the joggers. He'd seen younger kids and it reminded him of when he used to come in his teens, a long time ago. His favorite stuff to watch was the water traffic and the tour boats motor by.

The next day rolled around and Jack showed up early. He grabbed a seat on the water on the river walk. The small storefront only had four outdoor tables.

"Classic deep dish and two waters." He told the server as she came over to take his drink order.

It wasn't long and a tall, lengthy guy walked towards the table. He had a buzz cut and looked much younger than Jack but in actuality; it was only by a few years. A combination of pale Irish skin, no facial hair, and no wrinkles kept him looking ageless.

"Tommmmmyy!" Jack got up and embraced him. It was a heavy hug as Jack patted him on the back. "It's been a minute."

"Order yet? I'm starved." Tommy was skinny but Jack knew he could put away some pizza. He had seen that guy eat two full-sized deep dishes in a sitting and not put on a pound.

"Yeah, I got ya the usual."

"Good lad!"

"How's the job?" Jack asked.

"Shite as per the usual. We're pouring the foundation for a new building off 5th and 7th."

For construction, Tommy had no muscle. The guys on the job site knew he was reliable and fairly witty when it came to work. His best trait was being hard-working Irish. It also made him a great drinker. On Fridays, when Donny couldn't catch up for a drink, Jack often called Tommy. The inseparability of Tommy and Jack made Tommy perfect for the heist in Jack's eyes.

The guys continued to catch up on everyday monotony as the city of Chicago moved by on the riverwalk. It was an endless bustle of people. Sitting still in the middle of the city hustle almost seemed to stop time.

"One large classic deep dish." A brunette server interrupted their conversation. She must have gotten all the free pizza she could eat, thought the guys by looking at the size of her.

"Thanks, mam...You're the man," Tommy said to Jack as he quickly grabbed a slice with the pie server. Smells of tomato sauce and fresh pizza went straight to their noses. The bright red sauce leaked all over Tommy's plate as he cut into it. Jack threw a piece on his plate and grabbed the red pepper shaker.

"I don't know how you eat that stuff," Tommy said, referring to the hot pepper flakes. He would never dare put anything else on a pizza.

Just as Jack went to shake some on, the top came off and a pile of red pepper flakes covered his slice. It made a mountain of pepper flakes.

"Got enough?" Tommy laughed. The server was setting down pizzas at the table next to them and flashed a look over that said, "Was that intentional?"

When no one was walking by, Jack took the piece and threw it in front of him on the river walk. Three seagulls swooped in to attack the mushy slice of pizza as Jack grabbed a fresh slice.

He cut up a piece and stuck it in his mouth. "So there's something ..." he took another bite, "I have to pitch to you."

"Would you be interested in never working construction again?"

"What kinda question is that? I'm not leaving it to spray for bugs if you have a job opening." Tommy said directly. "I can't imagine you are even making the big bucks there."

"No no, I don't mean that and it's nothing like that. I'm gonna take a bank for a few mill." Jack said while lowering his voice and leaning over the table.

"Man, what are you talking about?" Tommy first let out a short laugh but then his face turned to a confused look. "Are you ok?"

"Yes, I'm ok. And I mean, I am gonna rob—" Tommy cut Jack off.

"I think you are losing your mind. Plus, don't say these things here. Let's finish our meal, check the time, and we can walk over to Millennium Park. Then tell me whatever you want in the open space."

The server came back around to fill the waters which were drained empty. At least she wasn't one of those servers who leaves your glass dry all meal, Tommy thought to himself.

"You guys want a box?" she asked over the sound of the ice clinking into the water glasses.

Jack pulled one of the last three slices. "No, we're good. Just a check will do. Take one or two of these things, would ya?" he asked Tommy to help finish up which was simple work for him.

The guys split the bill and started walking over to Millennium Park. It was a short walk to the park. The weather was great, so if that was where Tommy wanted to chat, it was fine with Jack.

"So, what have you lost your mind about these days?" Tommy's thick accent wasn't difficult for Jack to understand but many people struggled.

"I haven't lost my mind. Only my house." Jack said. He wasn't even so much depressed anymore as rather angry.

"I'm serious. The Saturday after St. Pat's Day we are hitting Chicago Central Bank. I want your help."

Tommy had never committed a robbery before, let alone a big crime. He had experimented with a few drugs growing up but other than that, he was a pretty straight guy.

"That's way beyond my league. I've got too much to lose."

The guys crossed a crosswalk and dropped the conversation. Taxis were lined up at the light and ready to carry people through the bustling lunchtime rush. Finally, the guys were in an open area of the park where they could speak.

"What's going on with the house, man?"

"Already got a few notices and now it's in foreclosure," Jack explained. "I know Jen is hurting inside and I just want to do the best for her and the family."

Far off in the distance behind them, the famous bean provided a shiny backdrop. The crowds gathered for pictures around the sculpture.

"But we have a good plan, man. As I mentioned, you could be done with construction forever. Think retirement."

"Want one?" Jack pulled out his pack of cigarettes and offered one to Tommy. He took one and lit it up.

"Man, you are going crazy. I've known you for a long time but this is way out there. I like to see you as a brother, Jack but I'm not sure I'm the guy you can count on."

"You'd be thinking the same thing if you were in the situation I'm in."

"True. Well, how much money are we talking about?"

"Everyone should take at least a million."

"That's it?" Tommy asked, as his voice rose.

"What do you mean, that's it?" Jack replied.

"I'm only kidding," Tommy said. "Morally, I'm against it. Money-wise, I need it too. I could help my mom who is aging, pay off my vehicle and buy a house. Honestly, I think I could live a good life with that money but I need to know more about the plan. I'll help you as long as it is as low risk as possible. None of that half-assed planning that leaves five gaps in a job."

That was the thing about convincing Tommy. Jack knew it wouldn't be the hardest task because Tommy, he was a down for anything type of guy. Between trusting Jack since childhood and a promise of a better life, that's all Tommy needed to hear. It's not like he had done anything too impressive with his life up to this point. He could turn that all around.

Tommy checked his watch and saw the time was drifting into the afternoon. It felt like he walked off the pizza because his stomach was starting to grumble again.

"I can show up late to work, but not too much later. Gotta start heading back."

"Gotcha." Jack turned around to walk back to their cars. "Well, I can tell you that St. Pat's Day is one of the days with the least number of bank employees working. The bank closes at noon for a half day. It overlaps perfectly with the crowds outside."

"Makes sense." Tommy was in a deep state of thought. "Once you figure out the final details, let me know. I'm an eighty percent yes."

At the next street corner, the guys departed separate ways and Jack felt a small win inside.

Chapter Seven

Mashed Potatoes

"I don't care what's on your schedule. Make yourself free and be over at six thirty tomorrow night." Donny hung up his phone. He stopped at the liquor store on his way home and grabbed a six-pack of beers. Budweiser, the only beer Donny swore by.

Back at his apartment, he kicked back in his recliner, put a basketball game on his small TV, and worked through the bottles. He lined them up one by one on the table next to his recliner and fell asleep in the second half.

The next evening, his doorbell rang. A sizzling noise ripped from the cast iron pan on the stove with steaks in it. The butter and fat were splattering all over the cooktop. Behind the cast iron, the rumble of boiling potatoes was on the back burner.

"Come in!!" Donny yelled. The only noise was the grease of the steaks popping on the stove. No one came in.

"It's unlocked!"

He quickly flipped the steak which had a brown crust on the first side. There was a pile of three other steaks piled up on the back burner, resting.

The doorbell rang again.

"Oh, what the fuck? Come on, man." He walked over to the door quickly from the kitchen and opened it up.

"What's up, man?" Jack asked, with beers in hand.

"It was unlocked, you idiot. Just come in."

As Donny shut the door behind Jack, the potatoes started to boil over on the stove. He saw the bubbles coming out of the lid. The water hissed as it hit the stove. Donny ran over and pulled over the lid with his bare hand.

"Ah! Damn," he yelled, as he threw the lid on the counter. "See, you shoulda just walked in."

"My bad man. Smells good in here though!" Jack said, while checking out the steaks. He put his beers in the fridge and opened one up. One thing Jack hadn't had in the last year was a proper steak, money was too tight.

"I didn't even know you could cook."

"That's just because your wife does all your cooking," Donny prodded at Jack. We're not all as lucky to have a talented lady as you do.

The plates slammed together as he pulled them down from the cupboard. Donny threw a steak on each and then slopped a large ladle full of mashed potatoes.

They took a seat at the table and Donny muted the Cubs game on TV as they said a quick prayer.

"... and we give thanks Lord, Amen." Donny blessed the food, family, and friends. The door bell rang again.

"Come in!" Donny yelled.

Ray walked through the door, followed by Tommy.

"See, that's how you make an entrance," Donny said. He got up to welcome the guys. "Y'all drive together?"

"Nah, just happened to pull up at the same time," Ray replied. His meaty hands were holding a six-pack of beer on each side of his body. Donny took one and put it on the kitchen counter.

"You know me too well!" Donny said, seeing they were both Budweiser as well.

"Seeing as how we spent what felt like a lifetime together in prison, the least I could do is remember your favorite beer."

"Tommy, good to see you. I haven't seen you in a minute, man," Donny said. "Ray, you get a chance to meet the kid?"

"Just now, yeah," He said, looking over at Tommy.

"Well, this might very well be our crew. At least I hope so and I know Jack does too. So, I invited you guys over for a little hang out of sorts. I've made some food, we've got drinks and we can even do some poker in a bit if y'all are keen."

"If you want your money wiped, we can play," Tommy said. Ray laughed. He used to be young and cocky, like Tommy. It never really got him anywhere in life.

The guys fixed plates in the kitchen, opened their beers and joined Jack at the table. Jack grabbed his steak knife and started sawing into his meat. It was a perfect medium color.

"Where do we stand, Tommy?" Donny looked up from his plate. He cut right to the point. In his mind, he knew if he could invite Tommy over for a dinner and a chat, he could peer pressure him into the job.

"I'll tell you guys this — This would be the biggest thing I've done in my life. Like a lot of you guys though, I could really use that money. Shit, I feel like I need it worse than Jack and that guy's house is getting foreclosed on. That's why I came over. Just look at my savings and there are only a few hundred dollars in it. I don't want to live my life, slaving away. If this is my punched lottery ticket to put me ahead, I'm in."

Donny lifted up his beer to cheers Tommy.

"Ray, you want to make your announcement?" Donny asked.

"Well guys, I spoke to Donny before coming over tonight. It's safe to say I'm in. This is my last job though. Jack, I want you to know that Donny speaks highly of you and if it wasn't for all the time I spent with him in prison, then there would be no chance that I'm in for this job. This is the last bit of crime you'll ever see out of me and you guys have my word on that. One final job."

"To Ray!" Donny raised his bottle and had a swig. Every inch closer to committing a heist, Jack felt like he was breaking down a barrier. He couldn't believe he had three guys willing to help him on a bank robbery. Or was it three guys helping Donny?

Donny stuck a spoon in the mashed potatoes to take a bite. They were as thick as cement. Not enough milk or butter.

"How's the steak gents?"

"It's perfect," Tommy replied.

Jack had eaten over half and Donny was still getting his second bite in his mouth.

"Look, we have a good crew. I know you and Tommy are the least experienced but we're going to get through this thing. I've been studying the layout of the bank, and the streets around it and this is going to be easier than you imagined. Plus, there is going to be a lot more food like this in the coming months once we are done."

"Well, give me some more of the details." Jack was supposed to be in the know. Every day felt closer but the plan didn't feel clearer.

"Alright. Calm down." Donny went to the kitchen and pulled out the notebook he had brought back from his shop. It was hidden under his trash can bin liner.

"I have it all laid out here." He stood in front of the three guys and gave a presentation. Pointing to the first page in this notebook, it was full of bullet points. The next page had sketches on it and lists of possible rendezvous points after the heist. Another list was the possible scenarios that could play out and the risks to consider. He turned the book to face Jack and slid it across the table.

Jack's eyes finally peered at the plan.

Second bullet, day eight - "Switch the insecticide contract."

Fourth bullet, day fifteen - "Steal the truck and outfit for the heist."

"Who is gonna do all these things?" Jack asked. "A truck, the gear?"

"Well... You and me. Mainly you. I've got a shop to run. The less we can pull Tommy and Ray into this at the beginning, I think the better. You need the money the most and I don't think there needs to be more cooks in the kitchen trying to get everything together before the heist. That's a recipe for disaster."

Tommy was quick to nod in agreement and Ray didn't have much to say. He committed to the heist, not to prep for it.

"Isn't day eight on like Monday?"

"Exactly!" Donny replied while picking up Jack's plate and going to drop it in the sink. It was completely cleaned off.

"Time is ticking. We need to flawlessly complete these first items so we are all set when the day comes," Donny shouted from the kitchen. He then came back and went on to explain the plan for Monday.

"So it's only me?" Jack was frustrated by the lack of help.

"I'd help you son, but I gotta be down at the train yard," Ray said.

"Jack, look — I'm in on the plan, but yeah, if you can do most of the prep work, I can help on the day of. I can't be out of work and stuff for this," Tommy chimed in.

"There isn't much else we can do to help, so for phase one, yeah, it's you. Plus, if you can't do that, then we shouldn't be doing the bank job anyway."

Donny went over exactly how Jack was to execute phase one. There wasn't a question that Donny couldn't answer, he just couldn't be there during the execution. Jack flipped the pages of the notebook and looked over three possible escape plans for the heist, including the locations. He paused for a minute.

"One and two look good but the third idea ... no way."

"It's fine. Nothing's set in stone. Plus, we have to be flexible on the day." Donny leaned back in the wooden kitchen chair and propped his arm up on the chair next to him. While there was uncertainty for Jack, Donny was calm and collected. The experience of being a thief wasn't accumulated over just one job in the past.

"You gotta trust this guy," Ray chimed in. "I promise you he's a real professional. You young guys, leave it to someone with experience."

Jack closed the notebook and slid it back across the kitchen table to Donny. It was a lot of information to process but at least the food was good... well, the steak.

"Feeling better about it all?" Donny questioned.

"A little bit not much. To be honest, I'm nervous. Not sure if I'm up for it. I have mixed feelings." Jack finished his drink. "If it's not the house, then it's the job. If not the job, then the heist. These gray hairs are only getting grayer." He brushed his hand through his salt and pepper hair.

Tommy and Ray had moved to the couch so it was a good thing they didn't hear that come out of Jack's mouth.

The stress, just in the last few months had taken a physical strain on Jack. He smoked more than ever before. His teeth were yellowed from the cigarettes and black coffee. Even his weight was down to one of his lowest since college. Donny could see it from when he saw Jack six months ago. At least he was a bit more vibrant and outgoing then.

The chair scraped across the floor as Jack slid it out from the dinner table. He went down the hall to take a piss. It was evident that if the heist was a success, Donny needed to upgrade his apartment. The once gray carpet floors had marks from Donny's work boots. When Jack lifted the lid to the toilet, it had a ring as if it hadn't been cleaned in weeks. A true bachelor pad or just a mess. Some would say they were the same.

The water swirled around the bowl like Jack's life washing away. He skipped the soap at the sink and walked back out.

"So what do I tell the wife?" Jack asked Donny, who was still relaxing at the table.

"Tell her dinner ran over."

"Not about tonight. I mean the heist."

"You don't need to tell her anything since we will be back before dinner. Trust the plan." Donny reassured him.

Jack joined the other guys on the couch and Donny took the living room chair to watch the rest of the game. The Cubs were down three runs in the bottom of the fifth and never pulled back.

"Poker gents?" Donny asked. "We've got a lot of beers to finish."

He cleaned off the table and took out a poker set from a metal case. Tommy split the chips out into four even stacks.

"So, what are we putting on the game?" He asked.

"Y'all know I'm broke," Jack said,

"Yeah, he's not in the best position to gamble. Shall we play for fun?" Ray suggested.

"Buy in is twenty thousand," Donny said, dealing out the cards. "Everyone is going to have way more than that from the bank soon."

"Fine by me," Tommy said.

"I'm telling you, Jack shouldn't be gambling right now," Ray said.

"No, you know what —. I like the idea. I'm in for twenty," Jack replied.

Over the next few hours, Tommy proved to back up his big talk. He ended the night up just over ten grand with money owed to him by the three other guys. Jack put himself in a further hole by owing money to Donny and Tommy. The guys called it a night around one in the morning.

Tommy left in a better mood than he arrived. Ray thanked Donny for hosting and told him he'd see them soon.

"Keep in touch. We have work coming up." Donny thanked Jack for stopping by when he saw him out the door. Little did Jack know of what stress was to come.

Chapter Eight

The Contract

The vibration of Jack's cell phone on his wooden nightstand woke him up. 3:53 a.m. on Monday. He swiped it off with his finger and he could barely see the time. He quietly slid out of bed, not to wake Jen, and headed to the bathroom. If he woke her, he'd hear about it, rightfully so. Getting her up by accident was one of her biggest pet peeves.

The toothpaste came out in a large glob, which Jack stuck on his mouth. While looking in the mirror, he saw a man. The man he saw was himself but he knew he needed to put his family on his back. It all started today, he told himself.

He took his bags under his eyes with him to the kitchen. Grabbing a brown paper bag lunch that Jen made him on Sunday evening, he headed out the door.

Thank the lord for a great wife.

Knowing the mission for the day, Jack's palms sweated on the steering wheel driving to work. The air conditioning couldn't cool off his nervous or overheated hands. Not that his truck put off decent AC to begin with.

Off in the distance, a neon sign lit up the early morning sky. The old truck shook as he turned it off the road and pulled in for some gas. A scratchy piece of paper covered the pump with writing in a blue marker that read "cash only". That didn't affect Jack, who couldn't open a credit card in his name.

The metal bell rang on the door as Jack walked inside and up to the counter.

"Let me get a pack of cigarettes and the rest pump seven," he said while opening his wallet and handing the cashier all his money. A twenty-dollar bill. Jack put the empty wallet back in his jeans pocket and cigarettes in his shirt pocket.

"That will be $8.50 on pump seven. You're all set." Enough to get Jack back and forth to work for a couple of days.

Jack let the traffic free up on the road and the bald tires on the truck squealed as he put it in first gear. He took a detour on the way to work and pulled into a small brick building. Squad cars were parked throughout the parking lot.

"Next!" a black lady yelled behind a safety window in the lobby. Jack stepped up, bent down, and put his mouth close to the opening in the window.

"I need to see an officer to clear this violation on my vehicle." He handed across the yellow slip. The lady behind the counter pointed him to wait by the door. It wasn't long before an overweight officer dressed in a dark blue uniform with a buzz cut came out. Jack led him out to his truck where the officer had him demonstrate all his lights.

"Alright, looks good. Follow me." The officer signed his slip and led him back inside.

"Stand over there." He put Jack at the back of a line of people. The clock seemed to move fast as the line crawled along. The little detour was now surely going to put him late to work.

If it's not one thing, then it is another. Can they go any slower? I better not need this job in the coming months.

"Next!" He was back at the same counter lady, forty-five minutes after the first time. Even though there were four windows, the station only had one lady working. Typical, Jack thought to himself. After getting a receipt, Jack finally sorted out his truck light.

He headed into work and got on with his normal routine to start the rest of the morning. The first location to spray wasn't far from the office and Jack knew he had to be back by lunch to execute the start of the plan.

After finishing up at a small apartment complex, Jack saw there was an hour until lunch. He knew he had to kill some time but still be at Presto, right at a certain window of time. Deciding to go back to the office and wait, Jack parked the Presto truck back in the lot and waited. Checking his watch every few minutes, his heart rate increased. 11:55, he told himself.

Jack closed his work truck door behind him and started walking down the sidewalk to the front doors. Grabbing onto the door handle with his sweaty palms, he went inside.

He walked right past the receptionist on the phone and past Susan's desk to the office break room. It was at the end of the hall with only a few white plastic tables and chairs. His peripherals were stunned to still see Susan in her chair. At noon, Jack's expectation was for her to be at lunch as she generally left the office.

He waited.

All Jack could do was sit and wait. Twelve-fifteen and her loud voice was still carrying down the hall from being on the phone. Not much longer and it was silence.

She must have hung up, he thought. Taking a chance, Jack popped his head into her office with pure conviction.

"Do you have thirty minutes to talk benefits, or are you grabbing lunch?" Jack asked Susan. He didn't imply it but she needed to leave.

"You can't come to me mid-lunch and ask to go over benefits." Susan snarled back. She started to pack up her purse and grabbed her keys.

"It's fine. We can talk benefits tomorrow then. Is Mr. Granger around for a quick chat this afternoon?" Jack dug for more information. He wasn't afraid of Susan's repercussions. It was clear to him that they would never get along.

"You can't come in here requesting high level people's time. You need to give notice. We're not all just bug sprayers with free time."

The stigma didn't bother Jack and he had the information he needed. Armed with knowing Susan was just about to head out for lunch, he retreated to the break room for the time being.

His window of time shrank. The clock hands were almost at a quarter to one. While he knew Mr. Granger was out and likely to not return before then, it was still uncertain.

Jack left the dingy break room, which was never updated to improve employee moral. He was probably the first person to have used it in months. The hall opened up to Susan's office and Jack immediately went behind her desk. She had boxes behind her desk with files, a three-tier organizer on her desk, and even files in the drawers of her desk.

His mind was racing about where to start. First, he rummaged through the organizer on the desktop. It was current bills and invoices. Next, Jack opened the bottom desk drawer. The color-coded folders were arranged chronologically.

Pulling out the previous year's folder, Jack frantically flipped through, looking for a bill to the Chicago bank but couldn't find one. The folder bumped into the computer mouse which slid across the coffee-stained mouse pad as he went to put it away. The computer lit up.

Jack stared at the lock screen trying to think what Susan would use for a password. It could be anything, he thought. He scanned her notepads on her desk and then saw the sticky on the side of the monitor. That brazen lady left it out in plain sight, he thought to himself.

His fingers and palms were sweating as he tapped the keys to key it in. Suddenly, he heard footsteps coming down the hallway. Jack looked to put something in his hands to make him look inconspicuous.

Grabbing a notepad off Susan's desk, he stared down at it hoping the person would walk past the office. Instead, they came through the doorway.

"What are you doing in here?" the younger-aged brunette receptionist asked him kindly. She was in her mid-thirties, slightly overweight, not as bad as Susan but always had a great personality. Jack was instantly relieved to see it was her.

"Just dropping off some health care paperwork." He pointed to the three-tier filer on the desk. "I just need to use her desk for a minute and review this last form." He picked up the top sheet of paper from the filer and held it close to him.

"Oh well, I'm sure she won't mind! Can you just add these papers to her stack as well?" The receptionist handed a stack of mail across the desk to Jack who put it in place. She thanked him and headed back to the front of the office.

Jack felt as if he had dodged a bullet and resumed keying in the password. Relieved, he was in. He knew there was scheduling software on the computer from seeing Susan use it before. Searching on the desktop, he opened it and scrolled down to the Central Bank of Chicago. It was scheduled for the 19th of April and had the bank manager listed as the contact.

It felt like it could be any minute before someone else walked in but Jack picked up the phone and dialed.

It rang.

It rang some more.

"Mr. Phillips speaking," an older but stern voice answered the phone.

"Hi, this is Thomas Miller from Presto Pest. I just wanted to call about the scheduling for your upcoming treatment." Jack hid behind the bogus employee's name on the call. "Our teams can't make it out on the 19th of April. Susan wanted me to follow up and suggested we come earlier in March."

"Hi Thomas, to be honest with you, we generally always schedule through Susan. Additionally, we had this date booked pretty far in advance."

The nerves built up and Jack could feel knots in his stomach but he looked to sell it. "I completely understand, sir. What if we bring it up to March twentieth?"

"I'm not really in a position to make that judgment over the phone without checking my calendar for the bank. Also, isn't that Saturday the St. Patrick's Day parade?" Mr. Phillips inquired.

"It is. Are you headed over to the parade? We would be looking to spray when the bank closes but there are still a few employees of course. How about I write you down for 1 p.m. and you can call back if you need to change it? The spray won't take more than two hours at most."

"Ok. That should work. It can't go later than 3. as the workers are looking to attend the parade. I'll call Susan back if that day doesn't work. Otherwise, see you then." The call ended.

Stunned, Jack couldn't believe he had got the date switched. He put his hands on his head in disbelief and stared out the window behind him.

What if he calls back?

His daze broke. An Oldsmobile was pulling back into the parking lot.

Jack rushed to shut down the software and log out of the computer. He took a final look at the desk to make sure it appeared orderly and walked into the hall. As he approached the front of the office, Susan was just coming through the doors. She had her large blue purse and waddled in back from lunch.

"You're still here? Shouldn't you be out on an afternoon job?" Her voice was seemly always a moan to Jack. There wasn't a more annoying voice in the office.

"Headed out just now." He smiled and almost bumped shoulders as he quickly passed her.

Back in his work truck, Jack reached into his shirt pocket to write down Mr. Phillip's name. He patted his pants. Then checked his truck's cup holder. "No. I left it on her desk."

It was an orange Presto Pest pen, so it shouldn't tip her off but it was out of place. There was nothing he could do now except leave it.

Jack drove to an office park for his afternoon job. Inside the shiny new glass building, he had to spray in all the first-floor tenant's offices. The only two noises were people on the phones and the pumping of the spray canister.

"Sir, you can't do that with employees in here. We're getting concerns from the employees," said a middle-aged lady with a short haircut that only went down to her shoulders. She had walked over quickly to get him to stop spraying.

"Thanks for your concerns ma'am but this is already cleared with property management." Jack pumped the hand sprayer. "It's odorless too." He continued to spray as the lady took off to find someone so she could complain further.

After wrapping up his rounds in the office, Jack headed back out to the truck. The roll-up door slammed loudly to the roof of the truck. Jack set the sprayer inside, closed it, and climbed into the driver's seat. Grabbing his cell phone from the passenger seat, it had four missed calls. "Can't he ever wait?"

"What do you need, man?" Jack questioned.

"Hey! Good to hear from you too. So how'd it go?" Donny asked eagerly.

"It couldn't have been more stressful, but I did it. The date is moved and we are good to go."

"What? You are the man! I knew you'd get it done. Why didn't you call me? The excitement in Donny's voice wasn't hidden.

"I'm working ... but yeah, I was going to call you on the way home of course and break the good news. We have two hours, 1 to 3."

"Hold on one second, would ya?" Donny set his phone down but he could be heard shouting to one of his mechanics. "Well, awesome job man, but hey I gotta go. I'll catch you in a few days for phase two."

Jack tossed his phone back onto the passenger seat and headed back to Presto Pest to grab his truck.

So this really is happening.

Chapter Nine

Flat Tire

She never noticed that extra pen on her office desk.

Days passed since Jack made the call to switch the date of the bank. The new date was approaching faster than ever now. There were only nine days left until the seventeenth.

The Ford Ranger pulled into Donny's shop. With the sun setting and it just past seven, only one shadow of a figure could be seen inside on the shop floor. Jack turned his truck off and walked in under one of the bay doors, his keys poking his leg in his jean pocket.

"If it isn't my favorite criminal cousin." Donny set down a wrench on top of a red toolbox, greeting Jack with a fist bump.

"Not a criminal yet. I haven't robbed anything," Jack interjected, as he was kinda offended.

"Well, that call you made wasn't exactly truthful." Donny laughed. "I'm only messing with you. Relax. So tonight we will go out and scout a few places where we can steal a box truck. Then hopefully go back and hit it tomorrow night."

"Sounds like a plan, the plan." After making the call, Jack wasn't going to disagree with stealing the truck.

"But we gotta take your truck tonight. It's more inconspicuous than the loud Mustang rolling down the street."

Jack rolled his eyes and the guys locked up the auto shop. A little smoke came out of the tailpipe of the truck into the cold air. The two rolled down the street, scouting the area. Being on the industrial side of town, Donny suggested driving behind a local brewery, bakery, and some retail shops.

Being just minutes from Donny's auto shop, the guys turned into the Happy Toad Brewery first. The tall metal silos greeted them on the side of the building towards the road. It was quiet.

All the lights were off and just a few employee cars remained in the parking lot. Back around at the loading docks, they saw a few vehicles. There were two delivery vans parked that had the green Happy Toad beer logo on the side. One box truck sat off to the side but the front right tire was deflated flat into the ground.

"That one there looks like just what we need." Jack pointed to the box truck while turning around in the Ranger.

"It's a possibility but changing the tire and getting away with it is risky," Donny replied while surveying the rest of the brewery.

They looped the truck around and chatted further as they pulled out of the parking lot. Cameras in the back of the brewery looked to be working but didn't seem to pose a hurdle.

The next stop on the list for the evening was a large commercial bakery. A large metal fence surrounded the perimeter of the shipping dock and yard. Tall bright lights shined down on the razor wire that sat on top of the fence. Jack took a right on the street when they reached the end of the brick building and arrived just as the train crossing sign came down in front of them.

Stopped at the tracks, it took a few minutes for the train to pull into the bakery and the guys were able to continue making their lap around the outside. They were now on the side of the train and their view was blocked to the shipping yard. Jack made the last right turn so they could see the loading docks through the fence.

"Pull over to the side here so we can have a look," Donny instructed Jack. "Get out and pop your hood."

Jack pulled up next to the fence and shut the truck off. The hood sprung open a bit as he pulled the release lever down near his leg. With his head under the truck hood meddling around, Donny looked out his window to assess the possibilities.

A few minutes later, Donny put his head out the window. "All good, let's go."

"What'd you think of that one?" Jack asked while navigating through town to the final business.

"Looked like the fence would be a doozy." Donny rolled down the window and put his arm out to get some air. "There was a blind spot though with the cameras and one of the yard lights was out. There seems to be a good movement of trucks going in and out but they all have to pass the guard gate. The only camera at the guard gate points at the license plates."

The chilly wind whipped across the cabin and hit Jack in the face.

"Roll that thing up, it's like forty degrees out." He complained.

The last location was just across down in a local strip mall. Super Buy Electronics trucks couldn't be missed whenever one of the bright yellow trucks rolled down the highway.

Jack drove behind the strip mall and saw three of the box trucks parked behind the store near the dumpsters.

"It looks promising," he said, while driving to the other end of the alley behind the strip mall.

Just as they were turning out of the alley, a man in a white shirt and name tag that shined under the lights appeared. Donny gave him a wave and a head nod as they pulled out. The security guard took a left and did a check down the alley.

"Well, that location is a bust now. That security guard had a clear view of my face." Donny wasn't happy. "Those were going to be the easiest ones to lift."

Hitting the highway, the guys went back across town. They couldn't meet a consensus as Jack liked the brewery and Donny was keen to hit the bakery. Rolling back into Donny's garage just past midnight, the guys called it a night. They knew they would have to pick one or the other tomorrow.

***

Jack showed up the next night around ten at Donny's shop. It was pitch black out and the Ranger was the only truck out in front.

"Hey, boy." Jack petted the dog as it approached him outside the shop.

Inside, Donny had his black Mustang up on the lift. The front wheels were off to the side as he was changing the brake pads. The bright red caliper was dangling off.

"Damn, that's hot!" Jack shouted as he walked in with the dog following by his side.

"You finally made it." Donny turned his head around. "Grab yourself some liquid courage out of the fridge." A beer bottle was near his foot.

Opening the fridge, Jack grabbed one out and walked back over to watch Donny. There was a beat-up old office chair for spectating. Leaning back, he put his work boots up on a stack of dirty tires.

"How much longer till we head out?" Jack asked, as Donny was focused on the task at hand.

"I have to do the rear brakes but I was thinking like one in the morning," Donny replied.

"Alright." Jack continued to scroll on his phone.

Time drifted by as Donny moved from the front wheels to the back. Greasy rags piled up behind him while working through the job. The shop air had a mixed smell of oil and rubber. Finally, he put the last tire on the Mustang and let the lift down.

Its exhaust rumbled the metal on the building as he reversed it out of the shop.

"I'm almost ready." Donny came back inside and tossed a sling bag to Jack. Put these on and then we can go.

The bag had a long-sleeved black shirt, black pants, shoes, a mask, and black mechanics gloves. Donny went to change in his office while Jack put on the new clothes.

"You look good. Hard to see," Donny said when he came back out and saw Jack. Jack had his mask in one back pocket and gloves in the other.

Donny grabbed two screwdrivers and some pliers. He threw wire cutters in the back of the Ranger's truck bed. They made a loud smash against the rusted metal truck bed.

"Let's do it." Pulling out the key and locking up the shop, they piled into Jack's truck and drove off, leaving the shop in darkness.

"Yeah, pull in over there." Donny pointed in front of Jack's face to park the truck in the alley. It was the back of some food joints and retail shops. "Alright, I'm gonna walk from here."

"Perfect. I'll expect you back at the shop in two and a half hours at most. I'll stay here for the next hour but call me if something goes wrong." Jack told him.

They gave a quick hug in the cab of the truck but when Donny got out, his black clothes blended into the night. Grabbing the wire cutters and walking off, the figure disappeared from Jack's view within feet.

Donny walked to the end of the alley, then down a sidewalk. The metal fence of the bakery was just across the street. He put on his black ski mask and mechanic gloves before jogging across the road. There was no traffic on the road but the bakery was in full motion. Trucks were picking up from the loading docks to take to early morning grocery store deliveries. There were about eight trucks just sitting inside the lot being unused.

Donny carefully made his way to the blind spot on the metal fence. It was in the back corner of the lot. The wire cutters tore through the metal fence effortlessly. Working in a square pattern, it was long before there was a hole big enough to squeeze through.

Grabbing the fence with his gloves, Donny peeled it back and slid under. His pants got caught sliding up and the metal dug into his skin. Scraped up, but still determined, he knelt looking for his time to make a move.

There was a good one hundred yards between his position and the sitting box trucks. Just by overlooking the yard, there were two guys on the loading dock, three trucks in the bays, and a single guard at the front gate guardhouse.

The three box truck drivers went in and out of the bakery, following the guys loading the trucks. There was a routine Donny saw. A flow to the pallets being loaded on the truck. If he wanted to get to an empty truck, then he needed to be in sync with the harmony of the loaders.

Donny waited. Off in the distance, lights were approaching on the road behind him. It was coming quicker and quicker by the second. He laid down, pressing his face into the parking lot, and spread out as flat as possible.

The headlights of the approaching car passed over him and kept going. The car was just feet outside the fence.

Looking up, with the car passed, all the guys were inside the bakery. Casually, Donny got up and walked across the lot, knowing a fast movement could draw attention. It felt like the longest walk being exposed but the night provided the much-needed cover.

His clothes pressed up against the shadows on the back of the box truck. The back of the shirt turned gray from rubbing the dirt and dust off the truck as he hugged it tight.

Slowly, Donny slid around to the side of the truck. The driver's side was opposite the loading dock as the unused trucks were parked horizontally to the docks. Peering through the driver's side window, there was a straight line view of the loading docks.

In rhythm, the dock workers came back out, put more on the three trucks, and went back inside. It was the opportunity Donny was waiting for. Using the screwdriver, he forced his way through the lock on the door and slid belly down onto the driver's seat. As quietly as possible, closing the door behind himself.

Prying the screwdriver into the ignition, Donny twisted it. Foot on the brake, it cranked over. The truck was on and idling. A silhouette appeared on the loading dock again, pushing a pallet into one of the trucks.

This is gonna be the end. Donny thought to himself as he sat nervously in the driver's seat. They are gonna hear this thing running.

To his surprise, the worker wheeled the dolly out of the truck and back inside the bakery. Donny couldn't see from afar that the loading dock employee had headphones in on his late-night shift.

Switching on the lights, Donny slowly drove the truck across the yard and approached the guard shack. He pulled off his black shirt and revealed a gray polo under it. The polo shirt's color matched the other delivery drivers that Donny had seen the night before. At the last second before pulling up to the shack, he took his mask off too.

The shack was illuminated and had glass windows on both sides. As the truck pulled up to the gate, it lifted automatically. The guard gave him a quick look and Donny gave a confident wave back using a few fingers on the steering wheel. It was effortless at the guard shack and the truck was through.

The roads were silent. Donny's truck was the only one on the roads. He put his mask back on and pulled up to a red light.

"Hell yea!" He smacked the steering wheel in excitement. All his blood was rushing as he had made it cleanly past the guard back there. The light turned and Donny stayed right on the speed limit to get on the highway. Even though it was early morning, his eyes were alert looking for police sitting on the side of the road.

Just two more exits baby. The mile markers decreased as Donny's excitement increased. The further away from the bakery, the safer it felt. He took his exit and only had less than a mile to his shop. Then there was suddenly a loud pop! The steering wheel started to shake violently between Donny's hands. Slowing his speed, the van kept rolling. With less than a quarter mile left, the rim started to rub the pavement. Little orange flickers lit up the left mirror from the back wheel.

The truck pulled into the front of the shop and out front sat the Ford Ranger. Jack was supposed to be ready and open up the bay door when Donny got back but there was no movement.

The box truck pulled right next to the Ranger and the grinding of the rim woke Jack up. He hopped out of the Ranger and went over to the driver's side of the box truck.

"Geez dude, you got it." He was surprised to see the box truck but at the same time knew they were going to get it.

"Man, just get the door. The wheel is fucked." Donny was livid that Jack wasn't prepared and the tire had blown out.

Quickly, Jack opened the roll-up door and the guys got the truck inside and onto a thick sheet of plastic. The hands on the clock pointed to ten minutes till three.

Closing the roll-up door behind them, Donny hung plastic from the ceiling around the whole truck.

"Let the real work begin." Donny joked with Jack while grabbing a respirator and spray gun. "Get the coffee on, would ya?"

Donny went to work putting on a coat of white paint. The bakery logo disappeared as the droplets of white paint covered it. His pants went from black to spotted with all the paint on them too.

"Here's what you need," Jack said while handing Donny a thermos of black coffee. They stepped back and appreciated the spray job on the now white truck. It wasn't recognizable from the one just a few hours ago except for the bent rim and the VIN.

"We just gotta fix that," Donny said, pointing to the rim. "And wipe the VIN clean."

Thankfully, the garage had a rim that fit the truck. There was also a set of four used tires so the brand didn't match the ones the bakery used. Finally, Donny took off the VIN from the dashboard and ground it out of the frame near the driver's door jamb.

Exhausted, the guy's adrenaline had run off. They tore down the plastic and threw it in the dumpster out back.

"Back to my place for some shut-eye?" Donny asked Jack as the sun was going to come up.

"Yeah, I can't head back to my house at this time of morning."

The two guys got back to Donny's apartment and Jack flopped onto the sofa.

"Hey, good work today," Jack said to Donny before he walked into his room.

"Thanks. Yesterday too." Donny laughed as they had been working for hours straight. He turned off the living room light, sending Jack into a world of darkness once again, and went to his room. The payday felt closer.

Chapter Ten

Checklist

The sound of bristles vigorously brushing across teeth echoed into the hall. It was the last Saturday before St. Patrick's Day, and a long one at that. The amount of things Jack needed to accomplish was a full day's worth ahead. The toothpaste splattered against the sink as he spit it out. It was a rare occasion to be dressed in jeans and a black tee shirt. Something other than a Presto Pest uniform for once.

"Hey babe. Do you need anything from the stores today once I'm done at Donny's place?" Jack asked as he walked into the kitchen.

"Nah, that's alright. I'll be stopping by the grocery store Monday once I take the little one to school," Jen replied.

The golden-brown toast popped up in the toaster behind her as she was pouring a glass of orange juice.

"Sit down for a few minutes and I'll bring breakfast over." Jen put bright red strawberry jam on the two pieces of toast and carried over a tall glass of orange juice.

Jack grabbed a pen lying on the table and an advert from the stack of papers.

- First aid kit

- Walkie talkies

- Sprayers

- Respirators

The list grew as he finished his first piece of toast.

"What do you have in store today?" Jen carried on a conversation from the kitchen.

"Just the usual with Donny. Work around the shop a bit, then run some errands."

Walking into the kitchen, Jack put the plate and glass into the sink.

"I'll see you later on today." He kissed Jen before grabbing his coat off the rack, taking his list, and heading out the door. As Donny and he discussed, Jack was to drive to three different towns to pick up all the items needed. Chemicals were going to be the trickiest part.

Fumbling through static-filled radio channels, country was the choice for the long ride. Jack got on Highway 57 and hauled it all the way south of Manteno. Tractor trailers shook the little Ranger as they flew by in the fast lane. The GPS had five more miles to the first destination and Jack couldn't wait to get off the highway.

He pulled into a family hardware shop and headed inside.

"Need any help, mister?" A young store clerk greeted him from behind the single register. The boy didn't look old enough to even be out of high school yet.

"No, I should be alright." Jack said before disappearing down into the highly stocked aisles. The first item that was able to be checked off was the respirators. He tossed four into a shopping cart after reading the labels. Rounding the corner of the aisle, the cart almost ran into another shopper.

"Excuse me!" Jack navigated by.

Turning the cart up his favorite aisle, Jack saw a plethora of insecticide sprays. His eyes scanned the shelving from top-to-bottom, stopping on the big bomb. The back label had all the ingredients he was familiar with but was unreadable to an average person. Adding eight one-gallon bottles to the cart, Jack paused. *"eight bottles could come back to bite me."* After just loading up all the bottles needed, he removed two.

Over in the home and garden section, stacked high were pallets of fertilizer. The different colored bags and sizes took up an entire aisle. Shoppers weaved past Jack as he fixated on reading the ingredients of a large green bag of grass fertilizer. He threw two to the bottom of the cart, a bag of soil, and some plastic pots.

"That ought to make the purchase more realistic."

"Did you find everything you were looking for?" The boy behind the register started scanning items. He twirled the scanner in his hand and fired long-range to get the bags of fertilizer at the bottom of the cart.

"Yep, all good." Jack started counting out twenty-dollar bills from his wallet. Donny had fronted him several hundred dollars to get the last items needed.

"That will be $157.93."

Jack gave him eight twenties and pocketed the change. Pushing the cart through the heavy doors, he threw the bags of fertilizer and soil into the truck bed. The rest was behind his seat. Firing up the GPS on his phone, he put in the next stop, Rockford.

"Two hours and fifteen to your destination." The lady's voice on the GPS calmly said. "Time of arrival 11:57 a.m."

One stop down and two to go, Jack was back on the road. As his truck rolled up to a red light, his mind drifted off.

What will the kids think if I get caught? There are genuine risks and consequences with everything I am doing.

His conscience kicked in. It battled with him for over the next hour. "Look at how these banks have treated you. The employer, society. This money will right all the wrongs." While Jack couldn't pick a side, he knew he had three other guys counting on him at this stage.

Road signs for exits to Schaumburg and ten miles to Rockford approached the second destination for the goods.

Chapter Eleven

Roundtable

"I've assembled you guys here tonight, for one reason. Not to rob a bank but to take what we deserve. To rise as the working man." Donny looked all the men in the eyes.

Then he looked at Jack. "To stick it to the banks that hold your mortgages."

"To live a better life!"

Donny raised his beer to a toast. Ray, Tommy, and Jack all sat around a round plastic table in the middle of Donny's shop.

Ray's hairy arms leaned on the table as Tommy slouched back in his seat. An ashtray made for a centerpiece like a bundle of roses to the workingmen. There was an energy in the air.

It was the closest feeling to retirement for a few guys who thought they would never retire. Ray felt the excitement, as if he was going to step into battle again. Donny, with his smug grin was exactly the glue they needed to hold them together.

"I can see myself now. After this, I'm flying out to Northern California and will live the rest of my days on the coast in the sun," Ray told the table. "What about you Donny?"

"Once stuff cools off a bit. I'll vacation some, pay off the apartment, and spend some on the shop."

"With us all gathered, I want to lay a few rules for the big day. We are not bringing guns to the robbery. Sprayers only. It will reduce our time if caught. Once we start spraying, no one will take their respirator off. Last, no man is to be left behind."

"Here, here!" Ray lifted his beer again.

Jack chimed in with the roles next. "Donny will be our driver. Ray, you are the muscle. Tommy on lookout."

"Well, what's your role then?" Tommy jutted in quickly.

"I'll do all the talking. To the guard and the bank manager. You three are way too hot-headed to handle that."

"That's a lie. I'm calm, cool, and collected. I'll get us past the loading dock guard." Donny cut in.

After the guys settled down, Donny wheeled over a whiteboard that was covered. Pulling off a sheet, it revealed a map of the bank. He clicked on a laser pointer and shot it around the room.

The red laser outlined the entrance area. The loading dock of the bank was just off a major street in the city and had a single guard shack at the entrance and a gate for leaving vehicles.

"The key here is trust. We're gonna get that guard on our side from the beginning to the end. We're coming in and coming out this entry point."

The laser moved to the bathroom, vault, and front doors. Donny made a circling motion around each.

"It's crucial we go in this order when we get inside. We'll start in the bathrooms, then the bank manager can open the vault for spraying and last we need to secure the front doors."

"How long will they be knocked out?" Ray asked while running his hand through his short beard.

"Ninety minutes based on my estimates." Jack stood up and held out his hand for the pointer.

Donny handed it across and sat down. "Like Donny mentioned, the critical choke point is the bathroom. We will immediately be up on man-power numbers if we take out one employee there."

Ray interjected with another question, and then Tommy. After the guys sorted out their plan to get into the bank, Donny got back up to introduce the second phase.

"Once into the vault, every man is loading his backpack. You'll get fifteen minutes each. Everyone is sticking to the time plan." Donny pulled out black digital watches and handed them to all the guys. Each one read the same time and had been synchronized.

"The next order of business," he said aloud, then disappeared into his office.

When Donny came back, he put a cardboard box on the floor. Opening it up, he held up fake Presto Pest uniforms and tossed them out to each guy.

"I even have one for you, string bean." He threw one at Tommy.

Once the uniforms were distributed, he passed out hats and sunglasses to match the uniforms.

"Now my backpack will have a signal jammer for the first camera near the rear entrance but keep your glasses on as we enter," Donny instructed.

He paused there and asked if anyone had questions. The men were quiet.

"So the key thought I know you are all sitting here with is how we will get away. There are two plans. One if everything goes to course and well, let's just say a backup plan."

Donny explained where they would take the truck after the heist and the plan for the four of them. It was clear. No communication after the heist for six months.

If anyone got in a jam after the heist, they were told to deal with it themselves. During the heist, the guys would be a team. Afterwards, they wouldn't know each other.

"I'm sure you are all familiar with these sprayers." Jack held one up. It was a large backpack cylinder. "This is your only weapon. You will each have one. Just pull the trigger to activate the wand sprayer."

"We're not all pest control experts like you," Tommy joked.

The last thing Donny wanted to show the guys was the truck. He had put two seats in the back of the box truck and made a rack to hold the sprayers. There was a first aid kit mounted to the wall as well.

"I'll paint it up the night before we head out," Donny said, referring to the blank white outside walls of the truck. "We're gonna be staging in an abandoned warehouse outside of the city. Bring a change of clothes on Wednesday as well. Lucky Irish colors, just in case."

Tommy and Ray stuck their heads in to look over the truck. Ray gave his silent nod of approval as he walked around the hood.

"If you guys have nothing else, I'll see you at nine sharp Wednesday and we'll head over to stage from here."

"Is staging and the rendezvous point afterward at the same warehouse?" Ray asked.

"No, separate ends of town." Donny gave him the last bits of his well-thought-out plan.

Chapter Twelve

The Full Plan

The week flew by faster than Donny could imagine. He couldn't believe it as Friday morning came around. During the week at night, he was losing sleep the closer they got to Saturday.

The sun was shining and blue skies were overhead as he unlocked the shop to start his day. His two mechanics came in minutes later and put two cars up on the lift. Donny had moved the white box truck to his back lot in the fenced-in lot.

"Got any weekend plans?" The younger of the two mechanics asked Donny while looking up at the undercarriage of the car.

"Nah, just going to take it easy. Maybe hit the gym. What about you?" Donny asked.

"I'm headed down to the parade with the wife and the little one," the mechanic said.

"Should be a fun weekend in downtown." Donny smiled.

Donny had a small wrench in his gut. Disappearing into his office, he put some dog food in two bowls and brought it back out onto the shop floor. It was part of his morning ritual.

The dogs got up from laying on the cool concrete floor and came over to eat breakfast. Donny stood by them, reading a clipboard with the customers that were lined up for the day. The phone rang on the counter behind him.

"Hello? Yeah, this is Superior Auto and Wheels ... No, we're full for the day but I can put you in for Tuesday."

As soon as he got off the phone, a lady was walking through the door to drop off her keys. Donny couldn't even get a five-minute breather during the morning.

He put the keys in his safe box behind the counter and the lady got a ride, leaving her tan Camry out front.

Donny looked at the clock on the wall and just wanted the day to go by. Stepping back into his office, he sat down on the tattered leather chair. The shop window in the office looked like it hadn't been cleaned in months but Donny could see the two mechanics hard at work through the grime. He spun around and dialed up Ray on his cell.

"What's up, man? Everything good?" Ray answered with the sound of a train car running by him in the background.

"Yeah man, for sure, but look, I gotta ask for a favor if you have time today." Said Donny.

"Yeah, I ain't got too much going on. What's up?" Ray repeated.

"So, I know I mentioned no guns on the job, but I was thinking you and I take a little protection. With just these sprayers, we could be bringing a knife to a gunfight tomorrow."

"I don't disagree. Do you want two pieces?" Ray asked.

"Exactly. I was hoping you could get some clean ones tonight."

"Let me call a few guys I know and I'll see what I can come up with."

"Alright, thanks, man. And hey, keep this between you and me. I don't plan to use them, so no need to mention it to Tommy or Jack. Not this close to the day. Might shake up the rookies." Donny said.

"Yep, no worries. I got you." Ray hung up.

It was unpredictable what could happen tomorrow but Donny knew it just wasn't realistic to rob a bank without a gun.

Back out on the shop floor, Donny put on his mechanic's gloves to relieve one mechanic for lunch.

The guy sat down next to the counter in an old office chair overlooking the floor. He opened up a brown paper bag and pulled out a peanut butter sandwich. The dogs picked up the scent through the garage and came over to sit. As the guy got to his last bite, he broke it in two and tossed a piece to each of the dogs.

Donny swapped back out and went to take care of billing in the office. The day dragged like a hot July day.

The shop usually stayed open till 5:30 but as it crept towards five, Donny made an announcement.

"Alright guys, I know you have been busting your butts all week. Feel free to wrap up, get out of here early, and enjoy your weekend."

The mechanics were surprised. While Donny was known to be a laid-back boss, he never let the guys go home early.

"What do you have, a hot date tonight?" The one mechanic asked and the two laughed together.

"Ha! Something of the sort. I gotta close up shop myself and get out of here."

"Fair enough, we'll take it." The second mechanic chimed in. "But whoever the lady is, see her more often."

The two mechanics gathered up their tools and put them back in the tool chests. They lowered the cars that were on the lifts and closed the shop doors. It was just before five thirty and Donny had the shop to himself.

Once the guys had pulled out of the parking lot, Donny opened up the back bay door. He took a Honda off the car lift and swapped it for the box truck that was sitting outside in the lot. The sun was still setting over the lot outside and he knew he had about one hour until it was down.

Back inside, Donny pulled together the items to put in the truck. He put the four sprayers from his office into the back of the truck. Then he put the chemicals for mixing and the uniforms. Along with the first aid kit and a duffel bag with his Irish green change of clothes. Just as he finished putting those items in the truck, there was a loud pounding at the front shop door.

Donny ignored it and it stopped briefly.

Then again, a loud pounding sounded at the front door.

This time, Donny couldn't ignore it. The dogs started to bark and get riled up. He walked over to the door and the two dogs followed closely behind. Opening it up, Jack was on the other side.

"Hey, I tried to call you three times to let you know I was going to drop by," Jack said.

Donny checked his pockets for his cell phone.

"Shit, you scared me at the door. I must've left my phone in the office," he replied while not being able to find it.

"Well, do you need any help to get ready?" Jack asked.

Jack came inside and shut the door behind him. As soon as the dogs saw it was him, they calmed down.

"I should have it all but just need to throw the painting stuff in the truck and some lights," Donny replied.

The two walked over towards the truck and Jack climbed up in the back to look around. He gave his formal approval of Donny's handiwork.

"Follow me over to the staging area, would ya?" Donny asked.

"Of course, here to help."

"Great, take the CRV in the front lot. It's clean." Donny tossed Jack the keys, referring to the VINs that had been wiped off.

Donny was in a hurry to get out of the shop and over to the abandoned building as night set in. The box truck led the way on a twenty-minute drive from the shop to the building. Turning down an eerie back alley in the industrial part of town, the street and buildings looked deserted.

The street lights flickered as Donny parked the box truck on the side of the road. He hopped out, opened a warehouse door, and pulled the truck inside.

"Man, this is scary. How'd you get this place?" Jack asked while getting out of the SUV.

"That's the whole reason we're here. I rented it for six months, cash, a fake name, the works. But not to worry, this place is so run down. There are no security cameras on the streets around here."

Donny instructed Jack to grab the lights out of the truck and set them up so he could start painting. Jack positioned the floodlights to illuminate the side of the box truck and Donny got to work.

He started spraying on the orange logo for Presto Pest. As the night drew on, Donny finished the first side and moved to the second. It crept into the wee hours of the morning as he put on the finishing touch. The signature Presto Pest roach.

"It looks like the real thing." Jack approved while Donny finished his last brush stroke.

"Thanks. That's all the years of practice." Donny replied. "I think that's it for tonight here. Let's lock it up and we can come back later today." Looking at his watch, it was already 12:37 a.m. on Saturday.

The guys put the lights and painting supplies back into the CRV, locked up the warehouse, and drove back to Donny's shop.

"Thanks for your help tonight."

"No problem," Jack replied. I'll see you in a few hours, around ten am.

"Cool. Sounds like a plan and time to grab some shut-eye." Donny gave Jack a wave as he got back into his Ranger and headed off for the last night.

Donny unlocked his shop and pulled the CRV back inside. He took out the floodlights and painting supplies. The dogs watched with their eyes half open but not even moving to get up from the floor. Just before Donny went to leave, he saw the phone receiver on the wall blinking with missed calls.

It's strange for the shop to get calls on a Friday, after hours.

Scrolling through the missed calls, there were two, both from Ray. One call early in the evening and a call just past eleven.

Donny dialed him up on the cell and called him back.

"Hey is everything alright? Hope I didn't wake you."

"Yeah, it's better than alright. I was just calling to let you know I sorted it out. I got my hands on two clean Glocks. It was a struggle, but I got them." Ray replied.

"Well done. I'm not even going to ask where ... I just finished up at the staging site for tomorrow as a matter of fact but I'll see you at my shop at ten."

"Sounds good. See you soon."

Chapter Thirteen

The Roaches Enter

There was little sleep for everyone except Tommy. Almost everyone awoke to the sounds of alarms on Saturday morning. Donny was the first to roll out of bed, wipe his eyes, and look at the clock that was a few minutes past eight.

He knew he ought to be back to the shop before the rest of the crew arrived. Finally, all the preparations have come to a head, he thought while pouring his cup of coffee. A light breakfast of scrambled eggs calmed his growling stomach before going to shave.

Donny put his fingers up to his scratchy hair on his cheeks and inspected a few gray hairs before cleanly shaving. He wasn't getting any younger day by day.

This retirement is going to do me well.

Getting dressed, he threw on his classic black hoodie, jeans, and Converse shoes. There was nothing else to wait for. Donny locked up the house and fired up the Mustang. He sipped on his black coffee while he drove in, with heavy metal music accompanying his drive.

Across town, Ray woke up around the same time. The stress was more prevalent as dark bags sagged under his eyes when looking in the bathroom mirror. His hand splashed cold water on his face to jolt himself awake. Who is this guy anymore? He stared at his reflection.

Ray slicked back his dark hair and put on a white tee shirt with his pair of jeans. His wife already had bacon and eggs on the table before he could even ask.

"Thanks, hon. This is wonderful." He praised her food while he crunched on a crisp piece of bacon.

Five minutes later, the plate was spotless. He brought it back to the kitchen and kissed her before heading downstairs.

In the basement, Ray started spinning the padlock on his large safe. The tumblers clicked into place and the door opened up. The black Glocks sat on the shelf staring Ray in the face. With no hesitation, he holstered one on the right side of his hip and one on his left.

The heavy safe door slammed shut and Ray went to the garage. A large rumble came from the garage. Before the garage door was even up, the sound traveled outside. Ray pulled in the clutch with his left hand and pushed his motorcycle down into first gear to exit the garage. His matte black half-shell helmet soaked in the sun while the shiny paint on the bike reflected it off. It looked sinister and nothing short of mean.

No alarm clock was needed to get Tommy out of bed. With the least amount of work to get ready for the heist, he got a full night's sleep and woke up at seven. His bed head blond hair was a mess, but he was feeling fresh. The youngest of the group, what he lacked in experience, he brought in energy.

Tommy threw a gray button-down mechanic shirt over his shoulders and tightened the belt to the last loop to keep his jeans on. Even though he was the skinniest of the group, his breakfast was the largest. While he could always pack in the food, it just burned right off while he did construction.

Every day Tommy brought energy but today was different. Rap music played in his kitchen as he quickly flipped through the newspaper during breakfast. After finishing his orange, 4 eggs, toast, and sausage, Tommy had a war-ready mindset.

Getting into his service truck, he got on the road to head over to the shop, just after nine thirty.

Beep, beep, beep! Beep, beep, beep! The alarm went off and Jack shifted his feet out of bed. Jen was already up and had started her day. He yawned, saw the clock, and knew time was of the essence.

"Babe, can you put something to go together for breakfast" Jack shouted while getting tripped up putting on one leg of his blue jeans.

"Yea! It will be ready by the time you get out here," she replied.

Jack quickly finished up in the bedroom and walked down the hall. Jen laid a breakfast burrito wrapped in tinfoil on the end of the table. She was still walking around in a bathrobe with her glasses on. To Jack, she looked pretty in anything she wore.

"Give me a kiss before you get on your way." She propositioned him. Always making an effort.

He pecked her on the lips.

"Do you have coffee too?" Jack said just before getting out the door.

"Let me grab it and I'll bring it out to the truck."

"You're the best babe."

Jack took his burrito, laced up his boots, and went out to start up his truck. Seconds later, Jen ran out with a to-go cup of coffee.

"Alright, have a great day." She watched him drive off.

Ray pulled into Superior Auto and Wheels, quarter to ten. Donny heard the bike coming two blocks away and opened up the bay door. Ray hardly slowed down all the way into the shop. The idle of the motorcycle rattled the inside of the shop.

"Turn that thing off!" Donny shouted at Ray over the exhaust. Ray killed the bike with a smile on his face.

"Ha. Yeah, good to see you too!" Ray took his helmet off and greeted Donny with a firm shake of hands. "I got your present right here for you."

Pulling out the Glock from his waistband, Ray cocked it and handed it to Donny.

"This right here is your get-out-of-jail-free card," Ray said.

Donny looked it over.

"She's perfect," he said, speaking of the gun. "The other boys should be here any minute." Donny put the gun in his waistband as well.

"The bike is good here?" Ray asked while setting it on the kickstand near the lift and putting his helmet on the hand bars.

"Yeah, that will do," Donny replied.

With the bay door still open, a white work truck pulled in front. Tommy hit the horn twice, just in front of the bay door. Startled, Ray and Donny turned around and gave him a frustrated look.

Tommy got out and walked into the shop.

"What's happening, guys!" The nervous energy came through his voice.

"Relax man. Just waiting for Jack to get here and we'll get moving to the staging area," said Donny.

"I can't wait for this payday," Tommy said with a grin on his face.

Donny looked at the shop clock on the wall and it was already a quarter past ten. Come on Jack. Where are you, boy?

"I'll give Jack five more minutes, then give him a ring," Donny said.

The guys were getting antsy standing around the shop, except for Tommy, who made new best friends with the dogs. He squatted down and rubbed the belly of the one laying dog.

Making a left into the shop parking lot, Jack's Ford Ranger pulled in.

"Finally, this guy." Ray saw him first.

Jack came inside to meet the circle of guys, giving each one a handshake.

"Good to see you, good to see you," he said, greeting Donny, Ray, and Tommy.

"About time you showed up," Donny said. "Almost thought you would not come, and you need this cash the most."

The energy was high with all four guys finally together. Donny closed the front bay doors, getting ready to lock up the shop.

"Everyone has everything they need?" he asked.

There were no objections from the other three men.

"Before we head out, I'm going to put three keys inside the planter by the front door for you guys. If anything happens and when we split up at the end, feel free to get your trucks or anything you need inside the shop. Ray, your bike is fine to stay inside as long as you want."

Out front, along with the other cars littered in the shop's front, was the CRV. The guys piled into the SUV and drove out from the shop, leaving the Superior Auto and Tires sign in the rearview mirror. It was cramped quarters on the ride over to the staging area.

Tommy's long legs had his knees pressing into the back of Ray's seat, who was sitting in the front passenger side. Jack lit up a cigarette in the back seat next to Tommy and the SUV smelled like an ashtray.

"After this, you'll have enough money to buy a nicotine patch." Tommy poked at Jack.

He shook the ash off his cigarette out the window, ignoring Tommy's remarks. Spray the perimeters, secure the bank, and fifteen minutes in the vault. Jack looked out the window and repeated his steps inside his head.

Donny drove down the slow lane on the highway, staying cool. Jack watched the families in minivans, SUVs and trucks pass them by.

Taking the off-ramp, they were just minutes from the staging area. Donny tapped the steering wheel impatiently, waiting for the light to switch over. *Well, we couldn't have better weather.* He thought while looking up into the clear blue sky.

He took a few side streets, which were littered with bottles, trash, and garbage cans. A few broken-down cars lined the side of the alley too. Donny pulled up to the brick warehouse. The roof itself was missing shingles. Chipped paint was falling off the outside of the wooden black sliding door.

"Get out and open the door, would ya?" Donny tossed Tommy a key ring. He got out of the SUV navigated past the standing mucky water on the side of the alley and put the key in the side door. Seconds later from the inside, Tommy rolled back the warehouse bay door. The CRV pulled in and Tommy was quick to shut the door behind it. He took a quick look down either side of the alley and still no one.

"We've made it, gentlemen!" Donny popped open the doors to get out of the CRV.

"Wow ..." Ray saw the painted-on Presto Pest logo.

"Wow, is right." Tommy chimed in. "It looks like you stole a truck directly from their lot."

"We have two hours before we need to be at the bank and I expect with the St. Pats parade, the traffic will be thirty to forty minutes. Any last-minute checks, do them now." Donny instructed the group.

"Get changed as well."

"Hey, should I mix up the chemicals here?" Jack asked Donny.

"No! What happens if we spill or get in an accident on the way there? Mix them up when we get past the first guard."

Ray and Donny went to change around the front of the box truck, concealing their pistols. They re-emerged in their tan pants and working shirts with their caps on.

Tommy stood off in a corner of the warehouse by himself. In his right hand, he gripped the wooden beads of a rosary tightly. His back was turned to the other guys as he was dedicated in a moment of prayer.

Lord, whatever happens today, protect us. He ended his prayers and returned to the crew to get dressed.

"Are we about ready?" Donny asked the guys.

"I'm ready. Let's get this show on the road," said Ray.

"Me too." Tommy seconded Ray.

"Jack, you good?" Donny asked, as Jack didn't immediately respond.

"Yeah, let's do it," he responded, dressed in his tan pants and gray matching shirt.

"One last thing before we kick out. Here you go." Donny handed each of the guys a fake name tag to pin on their shirts.

"I want you to have this Jackie boy." Tommy took off a silver and emerald necklace in the shape of a three-leaf clover. "Let the luck of the Irish be on your side."

The guys got into the box truck with Donny and Ray upfront. Tommy and Jack sat in the back of the truck. Jack put his feet up on the bags of fertilizer for the ride.

Ray opened up the sliding door of the warehouse to let out the truck. He closed it up and then got back in the passenger seat.

"Tune something in," Donny said to Ray while pointing at the stereo.

Ray slipped past the music and switched it to AM band. A Chicago news announcer was covering the pre-parade festivities.

"The crowds have been steadily increasing in the streets and the river walk throughout the morning. Chicago police department reminds residents of road closures throughout the day. CPD will have bag checks at all the major entrances to the river walk."

The station went to a commercial break and Ray flipped it back over to 95.5 where they were playing hard rock.

Jack and Tommy sat in the back without windows as the truck headed towards the city. There were no windows for them to look out of and the only light came from the front between the seats. A pothole sent Jack and Tommy up out of their seats. They bounced quickly in the air and slammed back down.

"Geez Donny! Watch it, would ya?" Jack shouted as the two seats in the back didn't have seat belts.

"You ready Tommy?" he asked.

"Excited," Tommy replied, but looked nervous.

As the guys got closer to the city, Donny and Ray could see the peaks of the architecture out of the windshield. The traffic was backed up as far as they could see.

"Man, what the hell is this? I knew the parade traffic was going to be shit, but this is ridiculous." Donny said to Ray.

Ray checked his phone, which showed a red line for the next several miles on the GPS.

"Must be a fender bender ahead with a bunch of lookie loos but that's what happens when you pick taking the Ike into the city," Ray replied.

The truck inched along as they were caught up in the standstill. A police cruiser came flying down the shoulder of the road and disappeared along with the sea of taillights in front of them.

An hour later and shut down to a single lane, the guys finally got past the small wreck. A lady stood outside her white sedan with the hood crumpled up, talking to a police officer. She had a green dress on, clearly headed to the parade. The other car, a red Mustang, was already on the back of a tow truck.

"Take the Mustang to my shop, and I'll fix her up." Donny joked.

Another fifteen minutes and the guys were into the city. It was packed with traffic at all the lights. There were swarms of people dressed in green, walking about the sidewalks. The glass and steel of skyscrapers towered over the people below.

"Turn left onto Wells St." Ray's GPS said aloud while trying to find the best route.

"Your girl there clearly can't see Wells is blocked off today. May as well shut her off. We'll just go up to Michigan and loop back around." Donny said.

Every red light seemed to catch the guys as the clock hit twelve-forty.

"You better be ready to mix up the chemicals!" Donny yelled back to Jack, stressing the time.

Out the right window was the Bean and Millennium Park. The truck made a left onto Washington St.

"Ok. Slow down up here," Ray said while pointing. Donny and Ray kept their eyes peeled for the truck entrance to the bank.

"Right here, right here!" Ray shouted at Donny as the entrance was being hidden by two parked SUVs on the street. "Don't miss it!"

The white Presto Pest truck pulled into the guard shack just off the road. Both the entrance and exit were blocked by security lift gates. A short Mexican guard with a dark mustache came out of the guard shack and walked up to Donny's window.

"Bank's closed." The guard looked down at his clipboard for a moment. He looked some more. "But you are in luck. I see you as the last on the list for today. Let me get you to sign here." He handed the clipboard to Donny.

"And here."

"OK, you are all set. You are going to park at the bottom of this ramp in the visitor spot. My partner will be down there momentarily to let you into the bank and see that you get settled."

"Great, thank you, sir!" Donny said with a friendly smile, with his face hidden by the tan ball cap and sunglasses.

The look-a-like Presto Pest truck went under the lifted yellow security gate and started to make its way down to the parking.

"Be ready to mix everything up Jack, the three of us will get out and greet the additional guard but you are going to have to hurry with the sprayers," Donny yelled to the back of the truck.

The underground parking veered off to the left and deeper for employee parking but visitors were the first level on the right side. A white uniformed guard was already standing near the spot, pointing to Donny where to park.

"Greet him with a smile, boys!" Donny said with a cheeky grin on his face.

Parking the truck, Donny was the first to get out and chat up the guard.

"Hello, sir! How's your day going?" he asked.

The short Filipino guard started to walk a circle around the truck.

"Good, good mister. Waiting for the day to end. You are the last people for the day," the guard replied.

"Wonderful, well we hope to not be here too long," Donny said.

Ray and Tommy got out of the truck with their sunglasses and hats on and stood next to Donny.

Jack was still in the back of the truck and was quickly taking the caps off the sprayers. He threw the caps on the bed of the truck as the sprayers hung on the wall. His hands were shaking as he opened a one-gallon jug of bug spray and dumped it into the first backpack sprayer.

He sped up, moving to the second and third sprayer. Again, reaching for another one-gallon jug of the spray he knocked it. It wobbled around on its edges, splashing out a bit. The jug almost tipped over and Jack's reflexes caught it.

"Hey, Jack!" There was a brief pause.

"We are going on inside. Come on, man," Donny yelled while walking around to the back of the truck. Donny put his hand on the back door of the truck.

Just before Donny opened the door, with the guard behind him, Jack popped out of the front passenger side.

Donny looked at Jack.

Jack stared back at Donny.

A mental connection in the brain sent across the same signal.

Donny used his index finger and pushed his sunglasses higher on the bridge of his nose.

Jack wasn't wearing his at all. Only his hat. In all the rush, he had forgotten.

In response to Donny, he turned his back on the guard.

"I gotta get one more thing from the truck, guys." Jack hollered as he unlocked the truck and climbed inside, re-emerging with his sunglasses on.

"Let me show you guys inside." The guard led them over to a steel door.

"The glasses have to come off before I let you in," he said, pointing up to a camera next to the door.

Donny squeezed his way from behind the other three guys to the front.

"Unfortunately, we can't do that, sir. It's company policy of Presto Pest so we don't get any spraying in our eyes."

Reluctantly, the guard took the response and swiped his ID badge on the electronic card reader.

Beeeeeeeeep!

The guard pulled open the large metal door which opened to a long back hallway in the bank. Brightly lit, white painted walls and polished porcelain floors stretched along the hallway. The guys followed the guard past multiple doors, all with wooden name plates next to the doors and the doors locked by card readers.

"I'll be accompanying you guys while you spray today. Let me show you around quickly," the guard said to the guys while walking forward.

"What'd you say?" Ray shouted from the back of the guys. Hardly able to understand the guard's accent.

Donny repeated the guard's comments to Ray.

"And here is our main floor to the left, tellers over here, and restrooms."

The main lobby had high ceilings with marble floors. Light poured in from the front spinning door and windows near the ceiling. It reflected off the polished stanchion posts in the lines before the tellers.

Exactly like the blueprints. Donny thought.

Seeing a bank this empty was never a sight any of the guys had seen before. Jack counted exactly three tellers behind the counter, finishing up their drawer counts for the day.

Behind the two ladies and a gentleman was an office with frosted windows but an open door. Tommy could see an older man in glasses typing away on his computer.

"Let me introduce you to Mr. Phillips while we are out here on the floor." The guard led the guys over to his office behind the tellers and knocked on the open wood door.

"Come in!" A loud voice from the man behind the desk.

"Sir, the gentlemen from Presto Pest are here to see you."

"Thanks, Dan. Hi guys." Mr. Phillips stuck out his hand and shook Jack's hand. "Nice to meet you Bill", Mr. Phillips said, looking at Jack's name tag.

"Pleasure is mine."

"Well, you've got a good guy here to show you around for the next few hours. If you need anything and when you need to spray in the vault, just come grab me."

"Perfect. We'll be out getting our gear, get started, and will be gone before you know it," Donny said with a smile.

The security guard led them back through the halls, out the metal door and to the underground visitor parking.

"We're just going to finish mixing up our sprayers and then we can head inside to get started," Donny said to the guard.

Jack climbed through the passenger side door and went into the back of the truck, keeping it closed as long as possible.

"Can I smoke in here while we wait?" Ray pulled out a pack, offered the guard a cigarette and asked.

"No, no, sir. That is not allowed in here," the security guard replied.

Jack grabbed the jug he had left of bug spray and poured it into the fourth sprayer on the wall. Behind him was a stack of the pellet fertilizer. He put the three respirators aside from his own on the front seat, then strapped his on.

"So, how long have you been working here?" Tommy asked the security guard as they were waiting.

"Ohhh long time. Been here fourteen years."

"Damn, that's a long time at this bank."

"You mean the bank? Five years! Been in the U.S. for fourteen. Chicago all that time," the guard replied.

Grabbing a bag of fertilizer, Jack stabbed it with a pocketknife. The bag ripped open just over the poisonous warning logo. The pellets bounced off the wood floor inside the back of the truck and sounded like hundreds of tiny pebbles.

Jack poured half of the bag into the first backpack sprayer and the other half into the second. The liquid started fizzing and hissing as he tightened down the lids. Repeating the same, he filled up the other two sprayers.

Opening the front passenger door, Jack jumped down from the truck and took off his respirator.

"One for you, one for you, and one for you!" Jack tossed a respirator to each of the three men.

"Are your fumes toxic?" the security guard asked as the fake Presto Pest crew put on their masks.

"No! It's just company policy!" Donny's muted voice shouted through his as he fixed the straps on the back of his head.

Ray was the first to go to the back of the truck and roll up the door. He climbed inside and tossed the three guys a pair of gloves. Then passing out a sprayer to each. They were heavy on the shoulders, even with the sturdy straps.

Tommy put his gloves on and walked up the parking incline a bit to test his sprayer. He pressed the trigger on the sprayer soaking the concrete from a light gray to dark gray.

Hopping out of the truck, Ray pulled down the door and locked it up.

"Ready to go to work?" Donny asked.

The crew nodded, and the guard led them back inside the bank.

Chapter Fourteen

Nap Time

"Hello! Is anyone in here?" Jack knocked hard on the door and there was no answer.

He went inside the ladies' restroom with Ray. Tommy and Donny split up from the two and went into the men's restroom. The guard stood out front in between both by the water fountains.

Tommy ripped the mask off his head.

"Fuck, man. This thing is fucking hot. I'm sweating like crazy under this." He complained to Donny.

"Put it back on," Donny said sternly.

"No, there are no cameras in here anyway, man."

Donny pushed Tommy into the wall.

"What if the guard walks in? Be smart man. Come on." Donny tried to reason.

"If he walks in we spray his ass. Pa pow!" Tommy motioned around with his sprayer.

"Yeah, sure. I'll start spraying him while you have your mask off and you'll both pass out." Donny said.

"Good point." Tommy put his respirator back on.

***

Minutes earlier, walking down the hallway, the guard led the way.

"Where do you want to get started?" the security guard asked Donny.

"Let's knock out the bathrooms first. It's going to be a busy day." Donny replied.

Dan led the four guys down the hall and to the bathrooms off the main lobby.

"Just let me know when you finish."

Inside the bathrooms, the men were still standing around. Ray knew the phrase Donny used. They weren't going to spray the bathroom. The risk was too high that someone would pass out before they got into the vault. They'd just wait it out for five to ten minutes and come out. Plus, no one would ever know if they sprayed anyway.

Tommy sat on the sink countertop, waiting for Donny to give them the go signal so they could walk back out into the hall.

"Get up man" Donny had enough with Tommy and the heist just started. "Two minutes and we're out of here," he said while checking his watch.

The time passed and Donny led Tommy back out into the hall. Shortly followed by Ray and Jack from the women's restroom.

"Perfect, that's all set," Donny yelled to the guard. "Go get Mr. Phillips to open the vault next, please."

The group walked back across to the main marble floors towards Mr. Phillips's office. One teller, a short older lady wearing a green festive dress with a pearl necklace and curly gray hair, was in his office striking up a conversation.

The security guard stuck his head through the doorway. "Sir, can you open up the vault for the gentlemen to spray?"

"Just give me a minute and I'll be over."

Behind Mr. Phillips's desk were two small solid metal safes. He put his fingerprint on the scanner of the first one, opened it up, and took out a ring of keys. Next, typing in a digital passcode on the second safe, the door popped open and he grabbed another set of keys.

Mr. Phillips locked his office door and followed the security guard back behind the tellers' desks.

An oversized metal door kept the vault shut like a fortress. Fumbling for his set of keys, Mr. Phillips put a massive key into the lock. There was a loud click as the lock's pins shifted into place. He opened the door and revealed a black metal gate behind the vault door.

Standing behind Mr. Phillips and looking over his shoulder, Donny could see metal tables stacked tall with banded cash. The stacks of cash formed a sea of green.

Switching his set of keys, Mr. Phillips unlocked the black metal gate, pulling it to the side. The security guard led the men inside to the vault but to the crew's surprise, Mr. Phillips stood by the door. They couldn't start spraying with him outside.

There was an awkward moment as the guys all had the same thought until Donny spoke up.

"Excuse me." He waved his arm high in the air, in the room's corner. "Come have a look at this." Donny got down on a knee and pointed into the corner. The guard turned to look at Donny and came over. Mr. Phillips followed suit and came to see the issue Donny was pointing out. Tommy and Jack both went closer to the entrance of the vault to close it off with their bodies.

Holding his respirator tightly to his face with his left hand, Donny used his right hand to make a commotion. Ray excessively sprayed the floor all around the guard and Mr. Phillips until it was saturated.

Mr. Phillips let out some coughs and tried to push Ray, who kept spraying. His words cut off as he choked. Donny stood up and covered Mr. Phillips's mouth till he passed out.

Loud choking and coughing ensued from the guard as well. He wobbled while Ray kept spraying and Donny sat down Mr. Phillips against the wall of lock boxes.

"Watch him!" Jack tried to get around the table of money but the guard fell back. His head bounced violently off the stainless-steel table holding the money as he fell to the white tile floor.

"Oh fuck! Fuck, man!" Jack slid onto his knees next to the guard and put a hand under his head. "Tommy, give me some of that money to prop his head up, quick!"

Tommy started tossing the banded stacks over to Jack until he had enough for a small pile. Forming a small square with the bills, Jack laid the guard's head onto them as a makeshift pillow. The bills and Jack's gloves were stained with blood. It dripped down onto the floor, filling up the crack of the tiles.

"Is it a big one?" Donny asked, looking down at Jack's hands.

"No, just a small laceration but he will surely need a few stitches. We gotta stop his bleeding." Jack replied frantically. It wasn't a lot of blood but it was some of the most blood Jack had seen in his life.

"Now's not the time to be playing medic," Donny said. "Ray, go take care of those tellers out front. Take Tommy with you. Jack, go get the zip ties and backpacks out of the truck."

The bodies were strewn across the vault floor. Mr. Phillips laid half against the lock boxes on the wall and his legs on the floor passed out. The bills got redder as Dan continued to bleed with the paper soaking it up like a sponge.

"We gotta help this guy," Jack said again as he got up from next to the guard.

"Well then, get the backpacks and the med kit. Hurry up!"

Jack grabbed the employee badge off the guard, put it in his pocket, and handed Donny the staff radio before leaving the vault.

Ray and Tommy saw the one female teller talking to the male tellers but the lady that was seen earlier was nowhere to be found.

"Hello." Ray broke up their conversation. "We found the employee badge for the lady that was in the green dress earlier. Is she still around?"

"Do you mean Maria?" the gentleman asked.

"Yep, that's the one," Ray said. "Our boss has it in the vault."

"No, she left for the parade. Can you just put it on her teller's desk over there? Put it on the lower shelf and she will see it come Monday."

"We can do that!" Ray replied in his muffled voice behind his respirator.

Knowing there were just the two employees left in the bank, Ray gave Tommy a nod. The sprayer hissed as the liquid shot around the feet of the two employees. Tommy lifted the spraying wand, spraying the pants and dress shirt of the man and woman.

"What are you doing?" The guy didn't have enough time to even get the full words around his mouth. Instantly crippled onto one knee, he grabbed his throat and collapsed. The woman coughing loudly, dropping the papers she was holding to the floor. They flew behind the teller's desk and she fell to the floor too.

"That oughta take care of them for a bit," Ray said with a dark chuckle. Proceeding to grab the incapacitated male teller under the armpits, he dragged the guy back across the floor and into the vault. Tommy reached down and put the woman into a fireman's carry, taking her limp body to join the others in the vault.

"Good work, men!" Donny said while standing over the four passed-out employees. "Jack should be back any second now with those bags."

In the back of the truck, Jack was fumbling around. He grabbed the backpacks, zip ties, duffel bags, change of clothes, and med kit. Seemingly, he just couldn't find the duct tape. Putting his sprayer back on the wall, he continued to rummage around. Finally, opening the glove box, revealed the tape.

"Where's he at?" Ray asked, growing impatient in the vault.

"Give him another minute." Donny paced back and forth.

Jack closed up the truck and looked like a mule carrying everything back inside. Taking the duffel bags and backpacks off his shoulder, he threw them to the floor in the vault. Reaching into a bag, Jack tossed Ray the duct tape and threw the zip ties to Donny.

Ripping off four long rectangle sections of tape, Ray pressed them tightly to the employee's lips. Donny flipped over Mr. Phillips on his stomach and zip-tied his hands behind his back. He did the same with the other three individuals and put them sitting back-to-back. The slumped-forward head of the security guard had dried blood on the back.

"Tommy, go stand guard at the front door. Ray to the back hall. I'm thinking we just get Jack to fill these backpacks since he decided to leave his sprayer in the truck. That work for you boys?"

"Yea, let's do it," Tommy said. "Those bags better not be a dollar short."

"Forty-five minutes and we're outta here or that other guard is going to come knocking at three."

Tommy went out to the revolving door in the main lobby and watched the push door next to it as well. Through the glass, Tommy could see families walking by in their green outfits to catch the festivities down at the river walk. From orange beards to oversized green hats, people had it all. Tommy paced back and forth, constantly looking up at the clock.

Man, they better hurry up in there and fill up those bags. His anxiety ran high.

"I just gotta wrap up his head but you can start loading the book bags," Jack said to Donny.

Grabbing a bag from the floor, Donny threw it onto the stainless-steel table. With no regard to counting the money, he started throwing the stacks of hundred-dollar bills into the book bag.

Jack popped open the red medical kit and grabbed a roll of gauze. Kneeling next to the guard, he circled his head four times. The blood was already seeping through.

"Ok. I can fill the rest of these." Jack offered to relieve Donny from filling the rest of the backpacks as he finished up attending to the guard. The first backpack had every zipper filled with cash to the brim. The side pockets and pouches couldn't possibly fit another crisp bill.

"Sounds good. I'll head out and check on our other guys."

Opening the next black book bag, Jack grabbed a brick-sized stack of hundred-dollar bills and shoved it deep down in the opening. It shook him for a moment, seeing the sheer amount of money he could grab. *This is a car.* He thought to himself, putting in more and more bills. *Now I have a paid-off house. Let me get the college fund.* Looking to see if he could fit any more money inside, he couldn't. Jack opened a stack of bills from the table and folded them in half so they would fit in his front and rear pockets.

"How are you doing out here? Holding down the fort?" Donny asked Tommy, who was fixated on the front glass windows. "You're doing great for a first-timer."

"Yeah, I seem to have it all under control. Just waiting to get out of here and get paid." Tommy replied.

"Soon enough."

Leaving Tommy, Donny walked back across the main lobby, looking up and taking in the majestic height of the ceiling, marble and light coming inside. There was a feeling of power, being in such a large empty building and having control. Donny navigated behind the teller's desk and down the back hallway.

"How you doing, man?" Donny gave Ray a shout while approaching him. Ray, at the far end of the hall, turned around. He was pulling security.

"Ha!" He laughed. "I can't believe we're doing it. So far, so good. Should be wrapping up in the next thirty minutes or so I'd imagine."

"That seems about right," Donny replied. "Alright, I'll check on you here in a little but Jack should be finishing up with the money and we will start getting it to the truck."

Donny walked back to the vault, feeling untouchable. Everything was playing out as if he was a musical conductor to a well-orchestrated symphony. He was humming a tune in happiness until he walked back into the vault. There were two bags full of money but the last two still weren't filled. Instead, Jack was wrapping more gauze around Dan's head.

"What's taking so long?" Donny asked, surprised that the money wasn't loaded up.

"He's going to die if I don't stop this bleeding. It went through all that other gauze I put on earlier."

"Well, we have a little less than thirty minutes before they all wake up, realize they are tied together and the bank is being robbed. Don't you think it would be a good idea to get the money we came for in the first place?"

Jack finished with his last wrap around Dan's head and then grabbed a backpack. Next to him, Donny had already grabbed the other backpack and started filling it up. Donny reached into his pocket and pulled out his pocketknife. The blade sliced through another plastic band, holding together stacks of money. Bright green stacks fell and spread out all across the stainless-steel table. The pace was rapid as the guys' hands moved like machines, putting money into the backpacks.

Putting in the last few bills that could fit without breaking the zipper, Jack held up the backpack.

"Feels like a small child in here. Must be at least twenty-five pounds." He tossed it over by the vault door with the other two black book bags. The mountain of cash that was on the tables was still large but the packed book bags stacked up tall themselves.

"Can you take those out to the truck while I finish up this last one?" Donny asked.

Weighted down like a mule again, Jack put the backpack on his back and picked up one in each hand.

"Good lad, Jack!" Tommy shouted from across the lobby when he caught Jack in his peripherals. Struggling to carry both, Jack set down the two in each hand, then picked them up and resumed walking. Ray saw Jack coming down the hall and headed in his direction.

"Let me smell the money baby! Get over here and let me see that stuff."

Jack handed Ray a backpack to help carry out to the truck.

"Sheesh this thing has some weight to it," Ray said while grabbing it. He unzipped the top and peered inside. It is not like he could ask Jack to have put any more money inside because it physically wasn't possible. Hitting the red exit button on the wall, Jack used his back to open up the door and hold it for Ray. Jack opened up the back of the truck and threw in his two bags. Ray unzipped his and started dumping it in the back.

"What are you doing?" asked Jack.

"You're gonna fill it back up Jackie!" Ray insisted by giving him the backpack.

"No, Donny wants to get out of here."

"Well, tell him to fill it up and we can get going."

The guys went back inside and Ray leaned against the wall in the hall, out of boredom. Walking back into the vault with his empty backpack, Jack saw Donny had filled up the fourth backpack.

"Ready to get out of here?" Donny asked as Jack came back in. He saw the empty backpack and paused. "No, we don't have time for that. It's ten minutes till three." Jack wasn't even able to get a word out of his mouth.

"Ray wants it filled," Jack replied.

"Ray's not going to get what Ray wants because we need to pack up and get out of here."

In the front lobby, Tommy looked up at the clock eagerly. The amount of people that had walked past the front door in the past hour in a half could have filled a small stadium. Suddenly, something wasn't right. Outside and in front of the glass door was a lady standing. She was digging deep into her purse, looking. Tommy had just seen her before they went into the vault. The older teller with her green dress.

There wasn't time. Tommy couldn't even get on his walkie-talkie to Donny. She found her employee badge in her purse and swiped it. *I'm going to have to spray her. I'll surely have to.*

The card reader beeped and she pushed open the door.

Letting her get just inside and the door shut behind her, Tommy turned around and rushed her. The scream was muffled by the immediate hand over her mouth. Tommy could feel her shaking in terror between his fingers.

"We going to the vault. Do what I say and you'll be fine."

Short of breath and with Tommy still covering her mouth, he dragged her to the vault.

"Boss, we have a serious problem," Tommy said, showing the older woman whom he was dragging with his arms under her under arms.

"That's fine. Just get some duct tape on her, zip ties and put her with her friends," Donny said.

Sitting her down next to the other four, Tommy tightened the zip ties around her wrist and pressed the silver duct tape over her mouth. Mr.

Phillips's eyes started to flicker open and his head swayed from side to side, dazed.

"Wakie Wakie!" Tommy stuck his face in front of Mr. Phillips and gave him a few gentle slaps to the cheek.

"Grab the hoods from the duffel bag." Donny directed Jack.

Unzipping the long duffel bags with their change of clothes, Jack pulled out four black hoods and draped them over his arm. With Mr. Phillip waking up, he put one over his head, taking away all his vision and sending him into darkness. The guys stood there waiting for the next of the three to wake up safely but the clock was already ticking past three. They wanted to commit a robbery, not a murder. Tommy had a sense of relief with all the hostages awake.

"Put them on the two not facing the walls and let's get going."

Jack pulled the hoods down quickly over Dan and the female teller who wasn't facing the wall. Then the walkie talkie on the table had the outside guard on it.

"Dan, checking in for security rounds. Please confirm." The voice on the other end of the walkie came through.

"What do you want to do about that?" Tommy asked Donny.

"We're going to ignore it and get out of here," he replied.

"Dan, you copy?" The radio chattered again.

The three guys started walking to the hall toward Ray with bags in hand. Rounding the corner, they saw Ray at the other end, standing about fifty feet back from the exit door. Just as Ray turned around to look at Donny and the guys, the metal door at the end of the hall opened. In a bright white collared shirt with no wrinkles, the outside security guard walked in. Ray quickly turned around. He was too far to spray the guard. All four men started walking towards the guard but there was no Dan over the radio.

"Hey, stop where you are!" the guard yelled with his back against the outside metal door. The guys didn't stop walking. "Stop!" he yelled again. Motioning his hand onto his holster, he pulled out his gun and pointed it at Ray who was less than forty feet away.

Ray turned his back toward the guard and faced his crew. He lifted one hand and put it up in the air, as to comply. The other hand reached into his waistband. Spinning around, Ray pointed his gun at the guard and unloaded. *Pop. Clink! Pop. Clink! Pop. Clink!* The metal shell casings bounced off the metal door and thick walls.

A bullet whizzed over the guard and smashed into the metal door behind him. The second sent a sea of red flying into the air. Hitting him in the right shoulder, he grabbed it with his left arm while the last shot missed him.

Pushing open the door behind him, the guard fired back a few rounds.

"What the fuck!" Jack yelled as Ray put his gun back in his waistband.

"Hey man, we weren't getting out of here unless it was for me. Now follow me." Ray directed. Donny knew this was where Ray would shine.

The guys lined up in a single file line just before opening the metal door. Ray was in the front with Donny right on his hip, guns drawn. They slammed through the door, looking for an immediate threat but the blood spots were leading back to the guard shack. Looking up, the guys saw the guard was halfway to his guard shack near the street of the parking garage.

"Leave him, get in the truck!" Donny yelled.

"He's going to call the cops once he gets up there." Ray replied.

"That's alright we're getting out of here."

The four guys rushed into the box truck with Donny behind the wheel.

"Give me the card key!" Tommy reasoned. "I'm going on foot. The truck is going to be too hot with police!"

Grabbing one of the backpacks, he caught the key from Donny and opened up the back door. Just before he jumped out, he grabbed his change of clothes.

"Good luck, lads!" He shut the truck door behind him.

Tommy swiped the ID badge and hurried back into the bank. Meanwhile, the truck started up the parking structure at a fast clip. Just as they were passing the guard on the incline, more shots rang out.

"Duck!" Donny yelled just before the guard pointed his weapon at the truck and more shots went off.

Chapter Fifteen

Sprayed

The bullets peppered the side of the truck. Plinking metallic noises filled the air as four bullet rounds cut through the side of the box truck like Swiss cheese.

"Drive!" Jack yelled from the back of the truck with the metal rounds coming in around his body. There was a fast crack as a bullet ripped through the driver's side window. Donny was hunched down as it thudded up into the above headliner.

The second bullet to make it through the cabin wasn't so lucky. The warm round connected straight into Ray's collarbone from his left shoulder and ripped out his back.

"Fuck!" Ray cried out. "I'm hit." He applied pressure to his left shoulder, but his hand was covered in blood. The box truck got up to the gate, which slowly started to rise. In the left rear-view mirror, the security guard was approaching quicker than the gate seemed to open but he was still fifty yards back as they passed him driving up.

Jack scrambled for the med kit in the back of the truck. Once he found it, he threw Ray a pouch of quick clot to pour onto the wound, followed by a roll of gauze.

The yellow gate lifted and Donny turned onto the street but he knew it wouldn't be long before the guard called them in.

***

Back inside the bank, Tommy rushed to the men's room. Throwing his backpack on the floor, he put his change of clothes onto the counter and stripped out of his fake Presto Pest uniform. Looking in the mirror, Tommy adjusted a green baseball cap to sit low on his head and cover his eyes. A green shirt that said "Luck of the Irish" went with his blue jeans. Finally, he switched out of his boots into a pair of green running shoes.

Tommy threw the backpack over his shoulder and clothes in a plastic bag he had. Just don't look at the cameras. No eye contact! He repeated to himself. Pushing through the large wooden bathroom door, Tommy walked across the main lobby marble floor with pace. The extra twenty pounds on his back felt like a feather with his adrenaline still pumping.

The footsteps were like music to Mr. Phillips's ears in the vault.

"Help!" he shouted with a hood over his head. The words were severely muffled by the duct tape over his mouth and quite inaudible. Tommy kept walking, unfazed. Pushing through the door to the outside, he felt freedom. Freedom mixed with anxiety. He felt as if everyone was staring at him and looking for him. His eyes scanned the sidewalk till he found a trashcan he could shove his clothes in from the heist.

The crowd of people on the sidewalk was all headed in one direction. To the river walk.

Tommy didn't fight it and joined the crowd. He blended in, just another shade of green among the masses. Looking for a taxi, there were none. Before he knew it, the roads were closed. Crowds were in the street and police officers seemed to be everywhere.

Two officers stood on the sidewalk with their shifty eyes moving back and forth. They locked onto Tommy. Only to shift off momentarily later to a mother and her two young children. I just need to make it to the other side of these crowds to find a lift. Navigating the crowds and streets reminded Tommy of getting lost in corn mazes as a child. Everywhere he looked, it seemed like four boxed-in sides.

***

Bloodied, feeling defeated, and wanting to be off work, the guard picked up his phone inside his guard shack.

"Please send help... Yes, we have been robbed!" the guard started answering questions to the 911 operator. "Yes, I was shot and am still bleeding. An ambulance is needed."

"Ok, the police are on their immediate way, as well as an ambulance," the operator replied.

It wasn't over three to four minutes that two officers were pounding on the front door of the bank. Two additional officers showed up around the back of the guard shack at the parking structure. The guard was sitting on an office chair, slumped, pressing his gunshot. The officer took away the gun that was covered in the guard's blood from the desktop.

"Hi, I'm Captain Patterson and this is my partner, Lieutenant O'Malley, from the Chicago PD."

Mr. Patterson was exceptionally tall, even for a police officer. He stood above Officer O'Malley who was six feet tall and had a thick muscular build. Officer Patterson was skinny, a runner. He hadn't missed the city marathon in October for the past five years, which he started running when he was thirty.

The blue short-sleeved uniforms were crisp, covered in dark bulletproof vests. Officer Patterson's black shoes were shinier than O'Malley's. They both donned formal blue hats with white checkered fabric running around the rim. Their silver insignias didn't just represent justice, they vowed to find it as they told the guard. Patterson always walked around with his badge out and hanging around his neck. Standing over the guard, he stroked his thick dark mustache, wondering. *Who did this? How far gone are they?*

The sirens wailed down the street as cop cars started to pull in and block the street. A wailing ambulance could be heard not far behind. It pulled right up onto the curb with the red and white lights flashing. More officers came and redirected the crowds of foot traffic that were walking down the street shortly before.

A medic hopped out of the back of the ambulance and pulled out a stretcher. Yellow tape was strung like Christmas lights around the street.

The stretcher rattled across the concrete as the medic wheeled it quickly to the guard shack.

"Is this our guy?" the medic in his light blue uniform asked Officer Patterson.

"Yeah, he's the one. Stable but took a tough one."

The medic helped get the guard onto the stretcher with his partner. Wincing in pain, the guard put his head onto the pillow and looked up into the sky. Opening his shirt, the medic had a look at the bullet hole.

"We gotta get him into the hospital ASAP," the one medic said to the other.

"Wait a minute." Officer Patterson put his bony hand on the side of the stretcher, stopping it immediately. "Is he stable? We haven't even questioned him yet."

"Well, that's going to have to wait. You can come on down to the hospital once we get there." The medic pushed Patterson's hand off from the stretcher and loaded the guard up into the ambulance.

"Clear the road!" an officer yelled in the middle of the street while stopping pedestrians with his hand signals.

The last words the guard told Patterson before being wheeled off were game-changing, "check the inside tapes."

With the computer still logged on in the guard shack, Patterson rewound the available footage. The issue though, it only recorded cameras outside the bank. He watched the segment of the guard unloading his clip into the side and cab of the box truck. His face peered close to the monitor as he pressed rewind. Then play. Then rewind. Then play. Zooming in, there was something useful at least. Grabbing his radio, he pressed down to call into dispatch.

"Put out an alert for license plate UT718C3. It is a white box truck with a large roach on the side."

Walking down the decline from the guard shack into the garage, Patterson's partner followed footsteps behind.

"Get some marker cones and tape this area off," Patterson said while kneeling and inspecting spent bullet casings. Standard nine millimeter caliper from the guard's Glock.

Patterson continued to look around. No signs of skid marks or anything else out of the usual. He put his hand on the metal door handle to the back of the bank but couldn't open it without the key. Rasping on it three times with his baton, there was still no answer.

Over the radio, he asked officers at the front of the bank if they were inside yet. They were locked out too but Chicago Fire was just showing up. The large engine and roaring sirens pulled up in front of the main entrance.

The two waited in the back while the fire department worked to get the guys inside the front door. Firefighters, dressed in their full turn-out gear, stuck a Halligan bar into the door to open the lock. Prying back and forth, the lock finally popped, immediately setting off the alarm to the bank.

The two cops radioed to Patterson they were in the main lobby. Behind them, more officers filled into the bank.

"In here!" the lead officer called out. "Requesting more buses."

Running inside the vault, he took the black hoods off the three individuals and then the duct tape. All the hostages were awake except for Dan.

"Go open the back door for Patterson." The officer told his partner.

"You ok sir?" the officer asked Mr. Phillips, whose face was pale. He reached around and cut the plastic ties off his hand.

"Just distraught. Let me get this alarm turned off for you guys." Mr. Phillips said while standing up and getting his bearings. "Can you see Dan gets to an ambulance as soon as possible?"

"Yes, the medics are on their way."

To the back of the bank, the other officer pushed open the metal door, letting in Patterson.

"About time," he said to the younger officer while swiftly walking past him.

Patterson walked down the long hall, taking notice of all the security cameras he could see. He walked into the vault and greeted the other officers on the scene. Standing with his hands on his hips, he saw money strewn across the tables and floors. Dried blood from Dan's head injury and Mr. Phillips was left talking to another officer. The rest of the hostages congregated in the lobby and were talking with officers and detectives.

"Hey Captain?" a young officer talking to Mr. Phillips called him over.

"I know you are taking everything in but Mr. Phillips here, the bank manager, is more than happy to help."

"That's great. Thank you." Patterson replied while looking at all the money left behind on the tables. *If they used a truck, why didn't they take more money?*

He passed some of the money through his hands.

"Let's get two guys on guard of the vault, please." Patterson directed the young officer.

"Mr. Phillips, what happened here in your own words?" Patterson gave his full focus to him.

Mr. Phillips described the events of the day. "And my employees were just getting ready to leave for the day."

Patterson nodded in agreement. Stroking his mustache and listening.

Phillips told Patterson how he had worked with Presto Pest for the past five years and thought nothing of it as they were always professional.

"It was in the sprayer though. Whatever they used knocked us out."

"Ok. Let's get you checked out then too." Patterson walked with Mr. Phillips to see that he had been checked out by a medic. "Do you have a camera room inside here?" asked Patterson.

"Of course! Let me show you to that first." The little old man went back into his office and grabbed a separate key from his desk drawer. Phillips went to another door behind the teller counter and opened it to the server room. "I'm one of the few people with access to this room." Phillips chimed in. "Let me log you in."

There was a bay of hard drives just inside the room, as well as four monitors hooked up that were used for video. Patterson sat down after Phillips logged him in and started clicking around. Putting the speed of the video to two times speed, Patterson sat there for the next fifty minutes to watch the entire heist. Rewinding the beginning, he saw no struggle when the guys initially came in. Looking out for markings, or just anything that could identify them, he zoomed in and out of the film.

Lieutenant O'Malley stuck his head in the security room.

"Hey! Chief wants to know if you have any leads. Gotta press conference for the city in thirty minutes."

"Four persons of interest. Three with no details at this time. Be on the lookout for a white Presto Pest truck. Our one man is out there in the crowds." Patterson replied. He showed O'Malley a screen grab of Tommy in his ball cap and green shirt.

"Let's send it out to the officers on the street." O'Malley replied. Nodding his head, Patterson agreed.

He couldn't wrap his head around the sprayers and the liquid. A gas of sorts. Also, only taking a certain amount of money. Emailing himself the recordings, Patterson told himself, he had to be missing something.

Walking out front of the bank, he could see the crowds of reporters gathering for the press conference. It was chaotic as News Five and Channel Nine were both down on the scene, with cameras shooting at the bank. Patterson went and stood behind the police chief, who tapped on the podium microphone. The chief tilted it down closer to his mouth. Average height, average build, and the people of Chicago thought of him as an exceptional police chief. With everyone watching, he gave a briefing.

"And at this time, we have no clear motive and no suspects," said the chief. The reporters all blared out at once and no one could get a question in with them talking over each other. It was like a pack of dogs in a kennel waiting to pounce on the chief.

Calmly, the chief waved his arm and took control of the situation, putting the reporters at bay. Starting with a younger red haired reporter's question. The chief took on question after question. Until he turned and gave the microphone to Patterson.

"That will be all. Thank you for your time and we will keep the public updated as the investigation progresses." Patterson shut down the press conference as the chief left the podium.

"Sir, sir!" the reporters screamed in unison. "One more question here on your right."

"Thank you again," repeated Patterson, as he pushed the microphone down and walked away as well to find O'Malley. Two coffees in hand, O'Malley was standing off to the side in a sea of blue. He left the other officers and gave a cup to Patterson.

"It's going to be a long night." O'Malley took the lid off his coffee and blew on the shiny black surface. The steam came up, making a cloud in front of his face.

"Yea. Thanks man." Patterson took a sip. "Did you get the photo sent out of that one guy during the conference?"

"Of course, over 11,000 of our men are getting a nice glimpse of that grainy black-and-white picture." O'Malley laughed. "At least we could see a ball cap and backpack. The boys are on the lookout for anything suspicious across the city."

Patterson and O'Malley passed two officers standing by the bank doors when going back inside and left the reporters in their hindsight. They caught up with a detective who was dusting for fingerprints in the vault.

"Anything?" asked Patterson.

"Not yet," replied the detective.

Patterson's pants pocket vibrated. Reaching in, he pulled out his phone and answered the call.

"Yeah."

"Uh huh."

"Yep."

"Perfect. We'll be there in twenty."

He put his phone back in his pocket.

"What was that all about?" O'Malley asked.

"Possible suspicious male spotted by one of the officers on the bridge. The guy matches our description."

Patterson and O'Malley jogged out of the vault and down the back hall. Patterson hit the exit button and pushed through the back door like it wasn't there. They ran to the street level and hopped into the squad car they had parked earlier.

Flipping on the light, Patterson buzzed the sirens a few times to clear the pedestrians and traffic. The officer on the call told him he was just three blocks up and had an eye on the guy.

"Turn on the sirens." O'Malley directed Patterson.

"We can't roll in that hot. These lights are bad enough." Patterson replied.

The cop car parted traffic like it was the Red Sea. Cars left and right pulled to the side of the street as Patterson almost doubled the speed limit. It felt like the longest amount of time to drive two blocks in the city due to the masses of traffic.

Pulling up to a police barricade with two sawhorses blocking the road, they parked the car in the street and threw their hats on the seats. Patterson asked the standing officer to keep an eye on the squad car but the officer barely had time to say, yes. O'Malley and Patterson were already booking it up the street to find the officer who called in the tip.

"Move out of the way!" Patterson yelled with his badge bouncing off his chest as he ran.

"Excuse me, excuse me." O'Malley followed behind. Dodging in and out of sightseers dressed in their festival greens.

The officer who called Patterson was standing on the corner, gave the guys a whistle, and waved to flag them down.

"Where's our guy?" Patterson quickly asked the officer while trying to catch his breath.

"Just over here across the street. He's been standing with that group of guys since you two sent out the picture."

The man in question was almost identical to the bank photo. His height could roughly be said to be the same, judging by a picture on a cell phone. He was sporting a dark green ball cap, a light green shirt with jeans, and a black backpack.

"How long have you had eyes on him?" Patterson asked the officer.

"About fifty minutes or so. It's hard to say if that's the other three robbers since we don't have a picture," the officer replied.

Patterson was cutting through the crowd across the street as O'Malley fanned out to his right.

The group of guys, all looking to be in their late thirties, turned their heads and saw the sun kissing Patterson's badge as he moved in closer through the crowd.

When the suspect turned around, his eyes, hidden under his dark sunglasses, locked with Patterson. The guy jolted. As did the other three men. They dispersed in all directions but Patterson was locked in on the man with the backpack.

"Move! Move! Move!" he shouted, but was stuck. A woman and her stroller blocked Patterson and the man quickly moved further away.

Turning his head away from Patterson, the suspect ran right into O'Malley who grabbed him as hard as he could. The collision of men was like two trains colliding.

"Where you going, man!" O'Malley yelled at the guy as his Irish accent thickened. "Sit down!" He pushed the guy to the curb. "You're not going anywhere."

Yanking off his hat and sunglasses, O'Malley tossed them to the curb.

"What are you doing, man!" the suspect asked aggressively.

Patterson caught up and used his presence to block off the scene, followed by the third officer.

A small crowd started to gather as other people just walked by. One after another, a few people started recording the whole scene on their phones.

"We have reason to believe you were involved in a crime today. You currently match our description and it didn't help that you ran." Patterson explained.

"I don't know what you're talking about but I ain't talking to you cops," the guy in his early 30s replied.

"Do you have an ID on you?" O'Malley stepped in and asked nicely.

"Nope." replied the suspect.

"How about a name?

"You don't need that."

Rolling his eyes, O'Malley stepped back as the guy wasn't answering anything. Patterson looked at him and was a bit more verbally forceful.

"We need to search your bag. Is there anything illegal in there or items that could hurt us?"

"It's not your business what's in my bag man."

"Are we free to search it?" Patterson insisted.

The suspect looked around. Back and forth, his eyes shifted around rapidly. All eyes from the crowd shifted from O'Malley and Patterson back to him as he was the one causing a scene.

"No, you can't search it! It's my property. Am I free to go?"

"We're going to have to ask you a few more questions and take you downtown to the station if you don't comply." Patterson threatened, "The bag will eventually be searched."

Patterson played his last card. He didn't have anything to connect the guy to the bank. O'Malley huddled with the other officer.

"You sure this is our guy?" He asked.

"I mean, it's almost a direct match to the photo the department sent out," the officer said to O'Malley.

"Whatever man. Go for it. You already know what you are going to find." Finally, giving permission.

Giving the nod to Patterson, O'Malley put on a pair of white rubber gloves to get into the backpack.

Patterson motioned to the other officer on the scene to get the backpack off the man's back. It was visibly heavy. The backpack sagged down from the straps as the officer passed it to O'Malley who took it to the curb. Peeling back the main zipper of the stuffed backpack, O'Malley's eyebrows raised high.

He turned his head and made eye contact with Patterson, waving him over immediately.

Chapter Sixteen

Bloodloss

With the zippers spread wide apart, O'Malley moved the stuff around inside for Patterson to see. Drugs.

O'Malley handled a plastic baggie with, what it felt like, a quarter pound of marijuana. Below it were white tablets.

"Ecstasy," Patterson muttered. "Alright, take him in and book him. Clearly, not our guy though."

Checking his watch, it was 4:45 and Patterson knew since they hadn't caught any of the four men now, it was only going to get tougher by the hour.

O'Malley cuffed the guy, helped him to his feet, and loaded him into the back of a squad car that was just arriving. Onlookers disbursed in all directions as the busy streets just kept moving. A normal scene of chaos many people were accustomed to seeing in Chicago.

Across town, Tommy wasn't shy to be celebrating his victory. He walked into a small bar, The Mighty Fox. It was dingy from the outside and in. Tommy took off his sunglasses and grabbed a seat at the bar. The finish of the wood bar was worn away from countless late nights, customers, and spilled pint glasses of thick liquid. There was a sticky layer when Tommy rested his arms down on the bar.

"What are ya having?" A younger girl was flying around behind the bar and slid a coaster his way.

"Let me do a pint of Guinness," Tommy replied.

He stared up at the college basketball that was playing on the three TVs above the long wooden bar. A few minutes later, after most of the foam settled, the girl slammed the glass of Guinness down on the coaster. The foam spilled over and ran onto the bar itself.

For a moment, Tommy relaxed. He took his backpack off and barely fit it under his bar stool.

"Say, turn one of these over to the news, would ya?" an old man grumbled a few stools down to the bartender. It wasn't like the ballgame was close anyway.

She turned her back towards the older man, faced the TV, and flipped through the channels until she got to the local stations.

"And you are getting the latest breaking news straight outside the bank... reporting live, Wendy Johnson, Nine News Now." The TV changed to commercials. Tommy was about halfway through his beer and he turned his ball cap around backwards.

"Never seen anything like it in my life," the old man went on. This time turning to Tommy, who had two empty seats between him and the man. "Can you believe these scum? Doing that to Chicago and these folks on St. Pats. It's terrorizing."

"Unbelievable!" Tommy replied. Finishing the rest of his beer.

"Good for another?" the bartender asked him.

"No, I think I'm alright. Just the bill."

The news cut back from commercials with more scenes of the reporter live at the bank. Cops were everywhere.

"And let's go to our live look from Chopper Nine in the sky. Chris, up to you."

"Thanks, Wendy. We have been following our internal leads. You can mainly see the amount of police presence around the Bank of Chicago. There must be over twenty squad cars."

The whirling of the chopper blades could be heard in the background of the interview as the newscaster showed clips of the streets below. The broadcast then cut back to Wendy Johnson.

"If you see a man matching this description, then be sure to call Chicago crime stoppers at the hotline below." The grayscale image of Tommy in his respirator was put up on the screen.

Bar patrons looked around, including Tommy himself. His stomach turned upside down and the check couldn't get to him fast enough. It was the first he saw himself on TV. Thankfully the bartender brought the check over without looking at the TV. Tommy laid cash on the bar after checking the check, grabbed his backpack, and walked out. A few people did a double-take as he left.

On the sidewalk, it felt as if every person was staring at Tommy. He feared everyone had seen the TV. Dodging between the crowds swiftly he looked for the quickest way out of downtown. Debating on taking the Chicago L, Tommy axed the idea fearing it would be filled with blue uniforms. Standing on the side of the street, he looked to waive down a taxi for a second time.

"Excuse me, sir!" Tommy turned around and saw an officer a few feet behind him on the street corner.

***

"How are you holding up Ray?" Donny looked over to the passenger seat and saw Ray's red-stained shirt.

"Barely," he replied while trying to stay conscious.

"We gotta get him to a hospital." Jack chimed in from the back of the truck.

Pressing the pedal to the floor, Donny merged onto the expressway.

"No way. I'll sew it up when we dump the truck." Donny replied to Jack. "We're about thirty minutes out until we get rid of this truck. Just keep talking to us for now, Ray."

Ray grumbled. His eyes opened and shut slower and slower while they went down the highway. They passed exit after exit, but reality started to be a daze to Ray.

"The money ... wasn't worth it." His eyes shut as he fell asleep.

Jack climbed up to the front to check on him. Putting his hand on Ray's wrist, he still had a slight pulse.

"Come on, Donny!"

Up ahead, Donny knew the cops usually sat in the median taking radar. It was the last thing he needed to see but as he got into eyesight, it was empty. They passed the exit for Addison, drove further north, and took an off-ramp. They drove through the small town to get to its outskirts. The houses and buildings, older in age, were spread out.

"It's just up here," Donny said, pointing through the windshield for Jack. "Get ready to get out and open up the door." The white Presto Pest truck pulled up quickly to a brick warehouse. Jack jumped out. He unlocked a white side door, switched on the warehouse lights, and then opened up the main door to pull the truck in.

"Come on, come on!" He waved Donny in.

"We're gonna put fresh clothes on him and then I'm driving him to the hospital in the minivan."

Donny had stashed an old maroon minivan, days in advance at the getaway warehouse. He opened the back door and put the seats down. Then opened the passenger door to the Presto truck.

"Help me out here!" Donny yelled at Jack, who was just standing around. Jack grabbed Ray's legs and Donny grabbed under the shoulders. The guys carried Ray to the back of the minivan.

Out of the minivan, Donny grabbed a pair of blue jeans, a black shirt, and white Converse shoes. They worked together to get Ray stripped down and changed into cleaner clothes. Donny put on a clean black tee as well.

"Ughh!!!" Ray grimaced as the pain woke him back up.

"Hold tight man. We're gonna get you fixed up," Donny reassured him again. He shut the back door of the van. The back of the minivan felt like a coffin.

"Alright, I'll be back in an hour," Donny told Jack.

"It's fine, I'm coming," Jack replied.

"No, you are not. You are staying here. It's bad enough one of us has to drive to the hospital."

Donny got into the driver's seat and slammed the door.

"Grab the warehouse door for me," Donny shouted through the window to Jack. He was frozen, for just a moment but then moved into action. "Get the money ready to go for when I'm back."

Donny sped out of the warehouse and jumped back on the expressway. With no evidence of him from the crime, aside from phony plates, he sped past all the traffic.

"We're gonna get you down to Kindred," he said aloud to Ray. It wasn't clear if Ray would make it into the hospital in Donny's mind but he had to try. For himself, for Jack, for Ray's family. Calling ahead, he let 911 know he had an emergency patient on the way and would be there in less than ten minutes. After ending the call, Donny tossed the burner phone out the window.

The maroon minivan pulled into the C-shaped entrance, stopping just behind a parked ambulance. The bright red emergency sign couldn't be missed above. Before Donny could even get out, three nurses came out of the hospital. Two of them were wheeling a stretcher. Popping the trunk, Donny looked up into the rearview mirror to watch Ray get moved onto the gurney by the nurses.

Ray was rushed in so quickly that none of the nurses closed the trunk of the van. Donny got out to shut it, looked through the hospital windows to see Ray disappear on the gurney into the back doors of the lobby, and then drove off.

Half an hour later, he was back in front of the warehouse. He parked the van in front of the roll-up door and banged on the white side door. Jack opened it up.

"How was he doing?" Jack asked.

Donny shook his head in dismay. "He's a tough guy. Hoping he makes it but even if he makes it then I don't know how he will explain his way out of this one."

"He should have never brought a gun in the first place. It put us all at risk," Jack argued.

"And what? You were going to take care of the armed security guard?" Donny asked Jack. "You have no idea what you are even talking about. That guard could have killed us all."

The guys brought the van back inside and loaded the backpacks of money. Looking through the box truck, Donny looked for anything else identifiable.

"How'd you get this warehouse anyway?" Jack asked.

"Been paying cash rent for six months now. A guy from the industry. Grab the bleach." Donny ordered Jack.

The guys moved the box truck into the corner of the warehouse and started pouring bleach into it. They bleached down everything and scrubbed it for fingerprints.

"Looks good," Donny said while walking around the perimeter of the box truck. "Let's throw a tarp on it and call it a day."

Out of the minivan, Donny grabbed a few blue tarps. Jack took one side and Donny took the other as they pulled it up over the hood of the truck. They used tarp after tarp until the entire truck was covered. Covered, but not hidden.

Donny stuck his head outside the side door and looked down the main alley. It was still quiet. They turned off the bay lights and pulled out the minivan, locking up the warehouse behind them. Only about forty-five minutes to Donny's shop, the adrenaline was wearing off a bit, and worry setting in, at least for Jack.

The two stared through the front window in a state of melancholy going down the highway. Down to just two, it didn't feel like a crew anymore. The hype was lost, even with having all the money they could want.

"When we get back, I need a favor," Donny said.

"I need you to take my money and Ray's."

Jack broke his stare and looked over.

"Of course, I can do that. What's up though? You alright?" he asked.

"It doesn't feel good in my gut. Tommy running on his own and Ray is in the hospital. It's only time the feds come knocking at my door."

"You can't think like that," Jack replied.

"I can't be blind to the fact," said Donny.

Just blocks from the auto shop, Donny slowed down and looked at every car on the street. With the sun falling, it was hard to tell if any could be undercover cops but it was unlikely they had him staked out in just a few hours.

"Alright, it looks clear. Hop out and grab the door." Donny told Jack. Grabbing the key from inside the planter, Jack opened the doors to Superior Auto. Flipping on the shop lights from the tall ceilings, he illuminated the bays. The maroon van pulled into the bay where just earlier in the day the box truck had been.

Donny put his hands up to his face and massaged the stress and tiredness.

"You going to take care of the van tonight?" Jack asked.

"Nah, I'll run it out to the crusher tomorrow along with a few other vehicles that need to go to the junkyard." The guys pulled out the three black backpacks from the back of the minivan. Unzipping the bag, Donny poured the crisp banded stacks of bills onto a shop table.

"Just look at that. A little over a million dollars. All for one day's work!" He grabbed a stack and smacked it into his other hand, playing with the paper. His face was concentrated on the money. He loved the money and it showed.

"I'm going to pack up and get out of here unless you need anything else," Jack said, overlooking Donny.

Turning around, Donny hugged Jack. "No, all good on my end." He paused, "Thanks for today. We did it." They both grabbed a backpack and put it into the Ranger. Donny took four stacks off the table and stuck them in his pockets, then put the rest back into the backpack and Jack's truck.

"A little spending money never hurt anybody," Donny said and smiled.

"You think they will be tracking the serial numbers on these bills?" Jack asked.

"Yeah, but just be smart about it and we'll be fine. Once they are out of your hands, it doesn't matter."

Jack climbed in his Ranger and Donny shut the door behind him.

"See you soon." Donny gave him a fist bump.

"See you soon." Jack echoed back through the truck window. "Do you think we will see Tommy soon?"

"Tough to say, but hopefully he made it out of the city alright. I'm sure he's enjoying his spoils by now. Take care of that cash," laughed Donny.

"I will."

The Ford Ranger left down the street with the auto shop painting a backdrop to the night. To be fair, it wasn't even that late past dinner for a Saturday so Jen was unlikely to even get annoyed. Thanks for today. *Shouldn't I be the one thanking Donny?* Jack reflected while gripping the steering wheel, almost blinded by the oncoming traffic.

A left turn, then a right, and Jack was back in the driveway. Looking over at the black backpacks, he knew it had to be easiest to just leave them in the truck for the night instead of facing a barrage of questions from Jen and the girls.

Outside of the truck, Jack pulled on the driver-side door handle to make sure it was locked. Next, he walked around to make sure the passenger side was locked up as well.

Taking one last look at the dark street in both directions, he cautiously went inside.

"Daddy's home!" Jen shouted to the girls. "Late as always."

Taking off his boots, he walked upstairs and saw the girls sitting on the living room floor playing with their dolls in their nightly routine.

Jen had the TV on in the background and was drinking a glass of wine.

"Have you seen the news today? I'm glad you are alright," she said.

"No, I haven't got to see it yet." Jack stood behind the sofa to watch the red breaking news banners flashing across the screen. "Something happen at the parade?"

"Quiet, quiet, watch," she said, shushing him.

The newscaster came on the TV reporting live from the Bank of Chicago downtown. Her high-pitched voice and wild hand movements described the day's robbery as she ducked in and out of the yellow crime scene tape. Walking around to the back of the bank, she showed the entrance to the parking garage, where the guys made their escape.

"It's getting crazy out there in downtown. What a bold move on St. Patty's Day." Jen said aloud.

"There have been no reports of how much was stolen at this time or the motive." The reporter noted.

"Do they have any suspects at this time?" Jack asked Jen.

"No, they haven't mentioned any. They just show this" She was fixated on the screen. The image of Tommy appeared. Luckily, Jen had never met Tommy.

"Hopefully, they will get them soon. I'm going to clean up." Jack said and walked away. It was clear enough that he could see Tommy on the TV screen but he wondered if others could make out the vague shape in its graininess.

The steam rose above the shower curtains as Jack waited for the water to get hotter and hotter. Inside the shower, he took a bar of soap to his hands, dirty from the clean money. If not Ray, then Tommy. The feeling of being safe was met with the vulnerable loose ends. All it takes is for one to tell or get caught.

Between the loose ends and the money left in the truck, the sleep that night was restless. Jack heard gunshots and woke suddenly, only to find himself still lying next to Jen. His mind replayed Ray in the hallway but Jack could see the bullets in slow motion. Ripping into the skin of the security guard and blood splattering on the wall.

An hour past midnight, Jack climbed out of bed and tiptoed to the living room in his boxers. Drawing back the curtains, he peered out the window. The street was quiet. The Ranger looked untouched.

His mind couldn't get to sleep as it felt like the world's eyes were on him and with that, he turned on the TV. The light flickered off the walls in the living room in the darkness. Jack turned the volume down low and put on the subtitles. Every local channel still had special programming on the robbery when the news never continued into the early morning.

Flipping through the channels, they all looked the same. The only exception was Nine News. They were still on the scene with the bright police floodlights in the background. The red banner across the bottom had words that would keep Jack up the rest of the early morning.

"Police potentially have the first suspect in custody."

It repeated across the bottom of the screen while the female African American newscaster presented above. The information Jack didn't know was the one that haunted him. *Was it Ray or Tommy?* Jack was puzzled.

***

Fear was all Patterson wanted. Running on low sleep, his tactics changed to flush out the robbers.

"It feels like we don't have any leads," an officer said to Patterson. They were sitting inside the mobile command center outside the bank, fixated on more security camera footage.

"Something will come. Plus, that news segment could cause one of them to slip up."

"We're getting nothing from these tapes." The officer pressed the power button on the monitor and leaned back in his chair.

"Get us more coffee," Patterson instructed an officer standing near the door.

Patterson leaned back in his chair as well, thinking. The desk vibrated next to him.

"You going to get that?" the officer sitting next to Patterson asked.

"Hello?" Patterson answered the phone for what seemed the tenth time in the past hour.

"OK, at Kindred?"

"We'll be right over."

Springing out of his command chair, there was a renewed energy in Patterson. It masked the eleventh hour of work he was on.

"What is the word?" the officer sitting next to Patterson asked.

"They have a guy with a gunshot wound and want us to come down. The nurses think it could be a possible lead."

"You want me to join?" asked the officer.

"Nah, it is fine. I need you on the tapes. I'll call O'Malley on the way over."

Patterson opened the command center door, greeting the dark early hours of the morning. He yawned while walking to his squad car. Outside of the bright fluorescent lights of the command center, his exhaustion hit him. Ducking under the yellow tape, the crime scene had thinned out into a rather desolate scene outside. A misting rain spit down and reflected off the streetlights. Two officers stood just inside the bank doors, taking cover from the nipping chill.

Inside his car, Patterson grabbed his thermos from the cup holder and took a sip. The bitter, cold coffee made his tongue curl inside his mouth. Opening his door, he poured it onto the street, set it back inside the car, and pressed his speed dial.

"Where you at?"

"Down at the station," replied O'Malley on the other end of the phone. "Going to go home here soon. What do you need?"

"We are going out to Kindred Hospital, Northlake. There's a possible lead on the shooter."

"Man, this day is never going to end," O'Malley replied. "I'll be outside in ten."

Patterson's stomach rumbled in the car for going hours without food. He hung a left into a parking lot and went through the drive-through. Paying, Patterson tossed the bag on his passenger seat.

Sticking his hands into a bag of fries, Patterson shoved them into his mouth. O'Malley was just ahead, standing on the sidewalk in a large puffy blue police coat. The hood was lined with fur.

Patterson picked up his bag of food and O'Malley got inside.

"Smells like shit in here. Grease and all." O'Malley said.

"Nice to see you too. I see you are dressed for this past winter." Patterson replied.

O'Malley looked around in the car and turned his head to the back seat. "Where's my food?"

"I didn't know you were hungry." Patterson stuffed more fries into his mouth. "Fries?" he asked while opening the bag to share the few that were left.

Shaking his head, O'Malley wiped his groggy eyes and refused. The dark police car sped up the highway between sparse cars. It wasn't long before the guys were pulling in at the hospital. The neon red emergency sign lit up the night. Patterson pulled into the semi-circle and took the prime parking in front of the door. He killed the engine right under the sign that read, "Ambulances only".

Walking with intent to the front desk, Patterson greeted the sole lady holding down the night shift. O'Malley was slow to open the passenger door and follow behind. He could see the lady pointing to the clock and talking frantically to Patterson when walking through the sliding front doors to the hospital. Looking around the waiting room, it was nearly empty except for a scruffy older male and a weathered-looking female in her forties.

"Feel free to have a seat, guys. The nurse should be out shortly," the lady at the front desk said and then picked up the phone.

O'Malley and Patterson sat down in the chairs closest to the front desk with a view of the whole room. Patterson picked up the newspaper off the coffee table in front of him and started to flip to the sports section.

"You are going to read yesterday's news?" O'Malley asked, as it was almost two a.m.

"Officers!" A blond girl in her late twenties came through the double doors and into the lobby. "Right this way."

Patterson threw the newspaper back onto the table. There was no time to even get into it. The guys followed quickly behind as the nurse led them down a maze of halls. Bright lights and white floors were a disguise for the time of day.

The nurse brought the guys over to the nurse station where a doctor in scrubs was seated and reading a clipboard.

"I'll take you to his room but he's just recovering from surgery, so fifteen minutes max, ok?"

"He's hardly in a condition to talk but you might get some answers out of him."

Taking them down to room 347, the nurse opened the wooden door and let the officers into the faint beeping of the vital sign monitor.

Beep ... Beep ... Beep ...

Chapter Seventeen

Headlines

Patterson slammed the door loudly as he entered the room. Ray's head slowly drifted over to the direction of the door.

"Good morning," Patterson said. "Hope we didn't wake you."

"Mmm yeah," Ray replied in a low tone.

"So why are you in here? What happened?"

Ray ignored the question but pointed to his upper chest.

"That looks horrible. We're surely concerned about you but actually, we're concerned as there was a robbery in Downtown Chicago late yesterday," Patterson explained.

"I'm officer Patterson and this is officer O'Malley. We just want to ask a few questions."

Ray nodded his head.

"What was your name again?" O'Malley chimed in, looking for answers.

Closing his eyes, Ray tuned out the next few questions on O'Malley's notepad.

"How about you tell us where you were yesterday or how you got that gunshot wound?"

"Oh, this? My gun went off by accident," Ray mumbled.

"I see," Patterson said. "Well, hey, we don't have many more questions, but would you mind if we take a quick picture for our investigation and we will be on our way?"

"Ha. Not with me looking like this. Why don't you come back when I'm cleaned up in a day or two," Ray said.

"Fair enough, have a good recovery," Patterson and O'Malley exited to the hall.

"What are you doing? No picture? That's got to be our shooter," O'Malley said while getting worked up.

Patterson walked down the hall and pulled out his cell. He dialed back to headquarters.

"Do you have the location of the guard who was shot?"

"Mhmm. Yes. Put me through."

Weaving his way through phone lines, Patterson was connected.

"Hi sir, hope the recovery is coming along well, and on behalf of the Chicago police department, we all send our regards. I have a guy in question and think he could be one of the robbers. What can you tell me about him?"

"Thanks. Yes, trying to recover. I can't tell you much aside from that he is about six feet tall," the guard replied.

"How about some facial features or distinctive markings?" Patterson asked.

"He was all covered up."

"But ..."

"The one thing is, my bullet hit him in the upper left chest. That's the first place to start for a match."

"Thanks for your time." Patterson was cordial and hung up the phone.

Taking a beeline, he went straight back to O'Malley.

"It's gotta be our guy."

"See I told you," O'Malley replied, but knew he was one step ahead.

"Keep watch in case the nurse comes back," Patterson instructed O'Malley.

Opening the wooden door again, Patterson shut it softly behind him.

"I told you, I'd be back," he said to Ray, whose eyes were half shut.

Pulling out the cold metal handcuffs from his belt, one attached to the metal bar of the bed and the other to the wrist of Ray.

"It's time to answer some questions." Patterson smiled.

Grabbing the remote from Ray's bed, he turned off the TV. Patterson paced back and forth.

"You aren't going to scare me doing that," Ray said.

"You are in more trouble than you know, pal," Patterson replied. He pulled up a chair from the corner of the room and sat close to the bed.

"Who was with you at the bank?

Patterson opened his notepad.

"Some names would be great, so I can go home."

"Oh yeah? Well, I wasn't even at the bank, so I'm not sure how I can give you any names," Ray replied.

Out of his peripheral, Patterson caught the nurse walking down the hall quickly in her blue scrubs. He stood up to push the chair over to the corner of the room and then pulled the string on the metal blinds.

"Let me ask you again. Who was with you at the bank?"

"I'm telling you, man ... I wasn't there. You aren't going to coerce me into it."

Patterson took his nightstick and pressed it across the throat of Ray. Gasping for air, Ray used his right hand to grab onto the baton and Patterson let off.

"If you hit the call button, I'll kill you before the nurse gets here, so tell me who was with you."

Ray paused, looked around, and felt cornered. The clock across his bed had almost moved half an hour but it felt endless that Patterson was grilling him.

"What's the answer?" Patterson asked.

Before Ray said anything, there was a knock at the door, followed by the nurse peeking her head in.

"Everything going alright in here?" She came in and checked the vital sign monitor quickly.

"Can you order up some food, along with some peace and quiet?" Ray asked her.

She looked over at the clock and saw the hands had crawled around. Taking a menu from the nightstand, she put it on the bed for Ray.

"I'm going to have to ask you guys to leave while I change his bandages."

"We can wait outside." Patterson said while staring Ray directly in the eyes. Ray looked at the nurse to tell her to make them go away.

"It will have to be tomorrow. I let you guys have your time, but you have to give the patient some rest."

Patterson didn't look to have another word and took a step towards the door.

"How bout this handcuff chief?" Ray brashly asked from the bed.

It caused Patterson to pause and turn back.

"They are staying on while you are a suspect."

In the hall, Patterson walked by O'Malley.

"Hold tight."

Back down to the nurse's desks and Patterson took an office chair. The loud rolling of the plastic wheels across the tiles was the only sound in the otherwise silent hallway.

"At least I got you something comfortable."

"Excuse me?" O'Malley replied.

"The early morning shift chair." Patterson said while rolling it across the floor to O'Malley just outside the room.

"Feel free to call in one of the young guns to replace you. I'll be back after some sleep."

Patterson left the hospital and went back to the squad car out front, popping the trunk. He took off his bulletproof vest and utility belt to stow away. Rubbing the back of his neck, he rotated it in a circle to loosen it up. *I'm on the trail and I smell blood.* He closed the car door and thought of himself as a human bloodhound. While it was Patterson's biggest case, his resume had prepared him for this moment. It's a once in a career type case. *I will leave my legacy in this department.* It wasn't enough to catch the robbers but get ahead of them and Patterson had a plan just for that.

Tapping the steering wheel, Patterson made his next move on the way home. He hit the overhead light and pulled out a business card from the center console and dialed on his phone.

"Hello?" a female's groggy voice answered on the other end of the phone.

"Hey Wendy. That story you are always looking for, I have it."

"You have the robbers identified?"

"Not quite yet but close."

"It better be good if you are calling me this late," she replied.

"How about I come by and I'll share it with you?"

"It's three thirty in the morning," she said, while glancing down at the blurry screen on her phone. Wendy sighed. "Yea, that's fine. Come by. When will you be over?"

Patterson looked down at the clock on his radio and then up at the highway signs.

"I'm probably twenty minutes away or so."

"Ok ... I'll see you when you get here but it better be worth my time." She hung up. Wendy's tenacity to always have "the story", made her the best in the business. She had won the reporter of the city two years in a row. The only female to ever do so in Chicago. When others couldn't get a story, she could.

A little while later, Patterson pulled the squad car into the front driveway of a small brick house just on the outskirts of the city. Still in uniform, he went up to the door and rang the bell. The light turned on inside the stairs. Then the living room and finally the foyer.

Opening the door, Wendy took two of her fingers and rubbed her eyes while yawning. She had on an extra-long gray tee shirt that draped down almost to her knees.

"Well, come in," she said, pulling the door back.

Patterson came in and took his boots off.

"Long time, no see," he said while bending over and unlacing his second boot.

"Three-thirty, Mike."

He turned to the stairs to head up but Wendy immediately chimed in.

"No, no. Let's hear what you have to say first. Come on." She led him to the dining to sit down at her large round wood table. Pulling down her shirt, she sat down and grabbed a legal pad and pen that was sitting on the table.

"We have one suspect in custody."

"Go on." She perked up and looked at him. "What is his age and race?"

"Five foot eleven, Caucasian male in about his mid-forties."

"Well, what's his name?"

"We don't have it yet. Should have it in the morning when we run prints."

"Just a mystery man? You think this is good?" Wendy raised her voice and threw down her pen.

"You'll be the first to report we have a suspect in custody." Mike replied.

"I want a bit more than that. You know I only put out the best news, first, the truth."

He stood up and pushed his chair in.

"Where do you think you are going?" she asked. It wasn't in a rude tone but she had the opinion that if she was up, she was going to get the story.

"Shower and bed, of course. If I have something more in the morning, I'll give it to you."

Mike took his shirt off before heading upstairs with Wendy shutting off the living room lights and following closely behind. The light from the bathroom peeped under the door into the master bedroom. Wendy undressed and went back to bed. A moment later, Patterson came through the door, wrapped in a white towel. Hanging it on the back of the door, he climbed into bed too. Well overdue for some much-needed sleep, only after getting what he wanted from Wendy. The deal was done.

A buzzing noise coming from the bathroom woke Mike in the morning. Wendy put her hairdryer on the counter and came through the door in a hurry. Fixing her earrings, she hurried to her closet to pull out a pair of white flats to match the black dress that she had picked out.

Patterson looked over at the clock and rolled back over.

"You know you can sleep in longer ... I'll leave a key here on the dresser," Wendy said while clasping her bra together.

"Just come give it to me downtown later today or drop it by."

"Okay. Thanks," he replied, while watching her dart around the room. "In quite the rush?"

"I gotta get downtown and shoot a bit for the morning news. Anything else on your guy?" she asked.

Grabbing his phone off the nightstand, Patterson lit up the screen. There were three missed calls from O'Malley. *What can this guy want now?*

"Nah, nothing else at the moment," Patterson replied to Wendy.

Almost good for nothing on such a large story. She leaned over the bed, kissing Mike. "I'll see you downtown later."

Patterson waited until he heard the front door close and then dialed O'Malley back.

It rang ...

And rang ...

Then went to voicemail.

Mike dialed back again. After the third ring, O'Malley picked up.

"About time you called back."

"What's up? I'm just seeing your missed calls. Are you at the house?"

"No, no. Got a situation down here at the hospital." He paused.

"Well, what's a situation, O'Malley?"

"A situation is one where your suspect passed away from complications early this morning."

Shifting his body in bed, Mike laid up against the back headboard to process the information.

"Fuck me dead. Are you kidding me? Where were the nurses?"

"Couldn't save him," O'Malley replied. "Anyway I'm rotating off. Someone can sort it out later today."

"Fair enough man. Chat you later." Mike put his phone on the nightstand and walked to the bathroom. Looking down at the whizzing sound of water, he could tell he was dehydrated. Back to square one. He flushed the toilet and ran some hot water on his hands to wake him up.

Throwing on his uniform from the night before, he could smell the sweat on the shirt. Without taking the time to make the bed, Patterson grabbed his things, the key and headed downstairs. Before leaving, he looted the kitchen for a muffin that was on the counter and then locked the door.

The car ride home was silent all except for the wheels on the freeway and the whooshing of passing cars. Mike's mind was focused on his next play, one he didn't have.

The squad car came to a familiar stop in front of the stop sign just at the entrance of his neighborhood. Pulling into his driveway, Patterson was home to his cookie-cutter Chicago suburb home. As he walked in, his son was playing video games on the couch. Gunshots rang out from the TV as Patterson took his shoes off.

"Turn that off and go play outside, man," Patterson said to his son, who was in his early teens. A scrawny kid dwarfed by the large sectional.

"Finally, you are home," his wife called out from the kitchen in a high voice. "I was getting worried about you with all the news."

Patterson walked into the kitchen to see her. His keys jangled off the stone on the granite countertop as he put them on the island.

"You must be exhausted," she said.

"Yeah, I need to go up and get some rest, then head back down to the station as soon as possible," Mike replied and explained.

"Well, are you hungry? I made your favorite egg salad."

"Not now but why don't you pack me one to go here in a little bit."

His wife continued to wash dishes as Patterson went upstairs to shower and change. After rinsing off, Mike closed the shades in the bedroom, set the alarm clock to wake him up back at eleven, and dozed off into a nap.

"Honey!" his wife yelled up the steps almost forty-five minutes later. "Hey Mike!"

There was no response.

"Can you wait here for a minute, please?" Mike's wife asked a gentleman in his late thirties to stay outside. He was wearing a white-collared shirt and blue slacks. He seemed fit and put together. She closed the front door and locked the deadbolt, then jogged up the steps.

"Mike, are you up?" His wife continued down the hall until she opened the master bedroom.

"Hey ... wake up. There's a guy here to see you." She put her hand on Mike's back to wake him.

"To see me?" He was confused. "At our house? Well, who is it?" Mike asked her.

Climbing out of bed, he threw on a white tee shirt over his muscular frame and some black gym shorts. The two headed back downstairs and Mike opened the door to see the tall, skinny, and nicely dressed guy.

Leaning across the doorway, Mike's arm stretched across the entire frame, blocking the entrance to the house.

"Hey, good morning." Mike greeted the guy.

"Morning, and sorry to disturb you. Special agent Rutherford, Chicago FBI." He pulled out a shiny badge in a leather case from his slacks and handed it over to Mike for inspection.

Carefully looking it over, Mike flipped it between his hands. Looking through the opening over Rutherford's shoulder, he saw a black Ford Explorer parked on the street. It seemed to fit the image. Scanning the street, the only other activity was a loud push mower going in front of his neighbor's lawn across the street. A typical Sunday.

He handed back the badge. Rutherford took out a folded white handkerchief from his pocket and wiped down the badge and leather case before putting it back into his pocket.

"I just had a few questions about all the news on TV, if you don't mind."

"Thanks, I'll take it from here," Mike said, turning around to his wife.

"I was thinking I could come in the house and we can have a quick chat. I know we're a day late to the party but you know the bureau likes to get involved in stuff like this."

"No worries, no worries. I'll tell you what, let's set up a bit of time this afternoon and you can meet me in my office downtown. Happy to answer anything then but I do have to run here soon to take care of a few things. You know, with the case and all."

"And to be fair, you kind of caught me off guard here at home."

"Sure." Rutherford nodded his head, sizing up Mike's enormous frame. "That will work out. Let's say two."

"Alright. Will be seeing you then." Mike replied. He turned around to shut the door. "Hey, one more thing, how'd you show up here anyway?"

"The boys downtown said you were leading it. Plus, we're the bureau, Mike. See you in a bit." Rutherford stepped down from the concrete front porch steps and cut across the front yard grass in a beeline to his Explorer. He got inside, took out his handkerchief, wiped down the steering wheel, and then folded it back into a neat square.

Mike watched Rutherford from his doorstep until he got into his car and then shut the front door.

"What was that all about?" his wife asked, coming back down the hall.

"Just business with the case, I guess," Mike replied.

"Can't believe he showed up at the house like that, unannounced and all," she said.

It's not like he disagreed. Heading back upstairs, Mike made a quick change into his blue dress clothes. Debating between the long sleeve and the shoulder length, Mike grabbed the short sleeve to put on.

Jogging down the stairs, he headed to the kitchen to say goodbye to his wife before leaving.

"Here you go. Don't forget your lunch." She handed him a packed brown paper bag with a heavy egg salad sandwich. "Make sure you throw that in the fridge once you get into the office."

"Will do," he said before kissing her.

His son had the video games finally turned off and was eating breakfast on the couch while watching the morning news.

"They now ... one suspect ... custody ..." The TV played out loud.

Standing behind the couch, Mike watched the red banner and white headlines come across the screen. *Man, she's fast.*

"Turn that up, would ya?" he said.

Putting down his bagel, his son turned up the volume on the remote.

"And we are reporting first. The Chicago PD has a suspect at this time and we are told they are actively working to find other involvement."

"Alright, see you guys," Mike said over the broadcaster to his family. The job never slept with a case at hand.

For the seventh day of work in a row, Patterson got into his squad car in the driveway to make his trip downtown. He backed out of his driveway, shaking his head at his overgrown lawn, and headed out of the community. The traffic was light heading into the city just before lunch. While on the freeway, he dialed back home.

"Hello?" his wife answered on the other end.

"Get James off the couch today and outside to mow the lawn," Mike ordered, as if it was one of his subordinates.

"Of course, sweetie. I'll get him to do the lawn this afternoon and have dinner ready this evening."

"Well, I'm not sure when I'll be back. It could be a long day, but yeah, make me a plate."

The first stop Patterson needed to make was back at the bank. Buildings of the skyline towered over him as he navigated through the downtown streets. The sheer amount of hungover drunks from the parade sure does make for a quiet morning, he thought to himself.

As Patterson approached the bank, the entire street was still blocked off with barricades and a cop car at each end. He tucked his squad car in behind a black Ford SUV on the side of the road before the barrier. Patterson took the house key from the center console and slammed his door shut, walking towards the barricades.

The electric window made a noise as it rolled down on Patterson's right as he walked past the black Ford.

"Go get 'em, officer." Rutherford was sitting inside with dark shades on and a cup of coffee in hand. "Surely, if your men can't catch the suspects, our department will. Don't worry." He tipped his cup of coffee and nodded his head while joking with encouragement.

Looking at Rutherford, Patterson didn't even have time to get a word in before the car window rolled back up.

"Morning sir!" A Chicago PD officer greeted Patterson as he walked past the barriers inside the crime scene. The street was lined with multiple news stations, the command center, and squad cars. He walked down the row until he saw Wendy in between shooting a scene. A slight wave was all that was needed to draw her attention.

"Got a sec?" he asked her.

"Well, I'm super busy and you don't always give me the best news, but what's up?"

Pulling the house key out of his pocket, he handed it back over.

"Ah, thanks. You won't be needing that anytime soon. Every other station has the same story as me."

The two continued to walk down the street, away from the other reporters and cops.

"Alright, I have something... but you need to wait until I can confirm it."

"I have a lead that the shooter has passed away from gunshot wounds."

"Now you have news!" she replied while getting excited.

"But I need to confirm it first... so I'll let you know by the late afternoon. Hold off on reporting it until then." Patterson ordered. "By that time, hopefully, we have fingerprints back as well."

"I gotta go, but I'll ring you later." Patterson walked off to go check on the progress inside the bank. To his surprise, when he walked past the two Chicago PD officers at the bank door entrance, it was hard to find any other officers. A flood of guys in blue jackets with yellow writing on the back were walking about. Two of the FBI guys were snapping photos. One in the lobby and one in the safe. The flash blinded Patterson as he walked past the photographer in the lobby.

"Watch out, man!" The photographer ordered Patterson.

"Hey, step aside, officer," another FBI agent with a brash tone chimed in as well.

After collecting his bearings, Patterson spotted one of his detectives.

"When did all these guys come in?" Patterson asked.

"Seesh, early morning or so. Six or seven, give or take. They've been running the show ever since. I don't even know who is in charge of them all." The detective explained.

"I have a meeting with their head later. Just keep on ... Any new leads?"

The detective pulled a small notepad out of his pocket and flipped to the third page, where he had three bullet points.

"We have three areas we are pursuing. It won't be long before the fingerprints come back on the guy up at the hospital. We have traced the getaway truck down to a general area on the west side and we're following up at Presto if they have any stolen trucks."

"Those sounds like good leads. Keep me updated. I gotta run back to the office." Patterson shook the detective's hand and took off.

Chapter Eighteen

Cat and Mouse

"Excuse me, sir!" the officer said again. Tommy was about two feet from the officer who was standing behind him on the sidewalk. The officer was of a fairly average build and had on a vest with the badge shining in the sun. "Would you mind if I check your bag? We have heightened security measures in place due to the parade and the incident downtown earlier."

"Absolutely officer." Tommy sized him up and looked around at both sides. There was a full sidewalk of pedestrians on his left and an intersection with moving traffic on his right. Like a countdown to a race, the light behind him went to yellow. Taking the backpack off, Tommy pulled it around to his chest to hand it to the officer. Hugging the backpack with a full grip, he shoved it into the officer at full force. The hit, like a linebacker, put the officer on his rear end instantly. The split second was enough. Tommy took off like a thoroughbred racehorse out of a starting gate. He swung the bag over his shoulder and took off, weaving between the stopped cars at the intersection on his right.

Dazed, the officer grabbed the radio on his left shoulder and dialed it in.

"White male, about six foot, three inches, mid-thirties, roughly 180 pounds! Green shirt, jeans, sneakers, and carrying a black backpack! Requesting backup! I repeat, requesting backup! Taking pursuit!" shouted the officer.

The officer was back to his feet and across the intersection before the light even changed to green. He could see Tommy in full sprint, fifteen yards ahead.

"Running south on Franklin St, west Adams St."

Bouncing off the shoulders of pedestrians dressed in green, Tommy blended into them like a herd of cattle. He hooked a right on the sidewalk at the next intersection, leaving the officer behind. As the officer caught up to the corner and rounded it, Tommy was running across the street.

"Northwest onto West Jackson Blvd. The individual isn't stopping pursuit!"

An officer just up the block got his eyes on Tommy as well and came down the sidewalk towards him. The fresh legs drew nearer to Tommy, who could feel his heart pumping through his chest. In front of him was a sea of moving cars but he darted out. Beeping ensued in the streets as he barely dodged the cars in full motion. It caused the second officer to come to a stop on the curb, just feet before catching up with Tommy.

The officer waved his arms and badge, bringing a halt to the traffic since the light didn't. The first officer, now down to a jog, couldn't keep up with the pursuit.

Up ahead, people lined the side of the road for the ongoing St. Patrick's street parade. Without hesitation, but down to a steady jog, Tommy ran through the spectators and into the parade. He was in the middle of a tuba section of the parade band that was walking down the street off the main parade over on Columbus Dr. The loud music muffled all the noise from the crowd and the officer who was gaining in. The deep notes blew right into Tommy's ears.

The second officer broke through the crowd and started looking at the faces of the band members, then pants. Out of gas, Tommy walked, then jogged, then walked. Just trying to stay a step ahead. While his green shirt did enough to blend in, his jeans didn't. Spotted, he was about ten yards ahead, then eight, then five. Tommy looked back, then forward. He couldn't get away on the straight street. He looked to the left and the right. The band was crossing a bridge and was just about in the middle. With the cop a few arms' lengths from Tommy's shirt, Tommy cut right and jumped.

His legs dangled in the air for what felt like minutes. Almost instantly, he landed on the upper deck of the sightseeing boat he had spotted. The cop leaned over the edge and contemplated. He couldn't do it. The initial cop caught up and looked over as well. The boat continued down the river where it was docking in the eye's distance, but out of reach.

The cops tried to take off on foot and call it in once more, but they couldn't get there in time. Tommy ran down from the upper deck and was close enough to hop off before the boat even tied up. Jogging up the steps to street level, he grabbed a taxi around the corner.

"Where to, sir?" the cab driver asked.

Breathing heavily and wanting to get out of the city, Tommy gave directions to a couple blocks from his house. His head ducked in the back seat as the taxi passed the policemen standing on the corners downtown but it wasn't long and he was in the clear. The taxi cruised along the highway, with the city dropping back into the distance. Tommy held onto his backpack in his lap for his entire ride.

"This is good enough," Tommy said to the cab driver.

The driver pulled to the side of a quiet residential street lined with a sidewalk and trees. Out of sight from cameras, the drop was just a moment's walk back to Tommy's house.

"$46.75" The driver turned around to Tommy in the back seat, giving him the price for the ride. When the driver turned back around, Tommy reached into his black backpack and tore the strap on a stack of $100 bills.

"Just a $50 for change will do," Tommy said while giving the driver the $100. As Tommy got out and slung the backpack on his shoulder, a $100 bill fell to the floor of the car. Unnoticed, he shut the door.

He waited for the taxi to drive off, checked his surroundings, and took the short walk home. Inside, he hung up his ball cap and walked over to the dining room table, dumping out the backpack. The bricks of bills bounced off the wooden table and paper notes hit the floor with the one broken stack.

"Yesssssss!" Tommy screamed out loud while shaking his fists. He took a moment to relish in the score, then made his way to turn on the TV. The photo of him with his head down played across all the major news outlets. *I don't know if I can show up to work Monday as planned.* Paranoia wrenched through Tommy, who couldn't find a decisive next answer.

He paced from the TV to his stack of money. Then back to the TV. Is it time to take the money and run? He paced.

Tommy picked up his cell, went to his recent calls, and dialed.

It rang and then was answered. "Hello, good evening. Red Dragon Chinese Food."

"An order of the General Tso's, fried rice, and a wonton soup."

After his order, Tommy gave his directions and credit card.

"Yes, yes. Will be there in forty-five minutes," the woman said on the other end of the phone.

"If you have seen this suspect, please call the Chicago crime stoppers." The TV wouldn't stop airing the same photo. Swiping his phone open again, Tommy dialed another number and hit call.

It rang ... and rang some more.

"You have reached Superior Auto and Wheels. It is after our normal hours. Please leave a message and we will get back to you at the earliest."

Tommy hung up and tried again.

"Pick up Donny, pick up," muttered Tommy as it rang.

The call again went to voicemail.

"No!" Tommy shouted and threw his hands to his head. Should I call Jack or Donny's cell? I've already called the shop. Should I go to work or should I flee town?

The doorbell rang. Tommy looked through the peephole and opened the door.

"Alright. Great. Thanks." Tommy took a large brown paper bag with his Chinese goods. He unpacked the white container of fried rice, along with his General Tso's onto the coffee table. He changed the channel up and it was playing the robbery. Clicking down two channels, the robbery was on as well. After eating, Tommy turned off the TV. He had the rest of the restless night and the following day to contemplate his options.

***

The cop from yesterday's chase picked up the Sunday paper and waited for Patterson who was on the phone in his office. The front page of the Chicago Tribune had the black-and-white picture of Tommy coming out of the bank. It also had an excerpt on the rising crime and unrest in the city. He flipped through to the sports section to see the Cubs beating the Padres eight to two. In other news, a Chicago couple was being put on trial for storming the capital earlier in the year. It felt like Patterson would never get off the phone as the officer finished flipping through the paper but he finally hung up and called him in.

"You wanted to see me, sir?" asked the officer as he entered Patterson's office.

The officer put the paper on the desk and sat down.

"I wanted to chat about the suspect you were chasing yesterday. You know, the one that got away."

The officer nodded.

"Did you get any further pictures of the guy?" Patterson asked.

"We're working with some of the businesses down there and should have footage today. It was crowded with the parade and the guy blended in. One of the bars should have some footage that I hope that we can pull. They believe they have a match on the guy."

Patterson leaned back in his chair and stared up at the ceiling to think. Getting up, he walked over and closed the door. He shut the shades to his internal windows facing the hall and sat on top of a long waist-height bookshelf near the door.

"Here's what I need from you," Patterson said with his arms crossed. He pointed towards the officer. "If you get a lead on this guy, give me a call. Let's keep it down low and get a plan of action. You, me, O'Malley, no press. The last thing we ever want is something leaking out to the press."

"Alright, alright. I can do that," the officer replied while nodding his head faster by the second in agreement.

Taking his hand, Patterson smacked the ball cap of a blue baseball bobblehead on the bookcase.

"Dismissed. Take O'Malley with you and get me an update ASAP." He stood up and opened the door for the officer.

The officer went down the hall and to the bay of desks. He looked around for O'Malley, whose head was down, concentrating on a stack of paperwork.

"Let's go." He walked up to his desk. "Cap says we gotta go get the tapes downtown and to bring you with me."

O'Malley's pen dropped to the desk and he looked up in a displeased glare. His eyebrows raised for yet another mission on the case.

"You know this isn't the only thing I'm workin' on, right? Give me ten minutes and pull a car around to the side."

Twenty minutes later, O'Malley came out of the side door of the station carrying a steaming coffee in a to-go mug.

"So what, you were chasing the guy but not quick enough? We wouldn't need these tapes if you had just got him yesterday." O'Malley said, sitting in the passenger seat. There was a feeling of O'Malley being the superior in the car but he and the other officer were the same rank. His brash Irish tone made him the alpha.

"Can't get them all I guess," the officer said while focused on the road. "You know the city needs more of us. That's the issue."

"And you think that is going to happen? Do you not listen to the briefings and watch the news?"

"We're for this city and yet these politicians want to cut our funding, equipment, main power, raises." O'Malley got heated in frustration. "You give me six months running this city and I'd have it turned around. Reunite the people of this city."

"Is that right?" the officer asked.

It was tight but he sandwiched the car between an old truck in front and a box truck behind. The worst parallel parking the city had seen in years.

"You going to leave it like that?" O'Malley asked, waiting for him to fix it.

"I don't see you writing a ticket for this truck in front of us that has its bumper all in our space."

The two left the car with the right two tires about half a foot out onto the street. Traffic was slow, even for a Sunday but any driver would find that parking job a nuisance. A large wooden sign hung above the door as they went inside. As soon as one head turned of the few bar patrons, they all did. Staring eyes watched the blue shirts walk up and lean over the bar.

"Excuse me, you wouldn't happen to be able to point me in the direction of the manager?"

The girl, mid-thirties, slim with brown hair and wearing a red tee shirt, looked back at O'Malley and the officer. She knew why they were there.

"Yeaaa, I'll take you to him."

She came out from behind the bar to lead the guys through the eyes and chatter. Behind the double doors to the kitchen, the bartender knocked on the open door of a small office.

"Hey Mick, these guys are here to see you."

The dark-haired guy looked up from his computer. It was clear he loved the bar, or at least the beer. His gut stuck out in his loosely fitting short-sleeved black dress shirt. The color matched his slicked-back hair. Greasy like the food coming out of the kitchen. His shirt was wrinkled, missing one of the white buttons, and disorganized, like the receipts on his desk.

"What can I do you boys for?" Mick spun his chair towards the officers. Their bodies took up the entire door frame.

"We saw you have some cameras outside. We believe they would have a view of our suspect going down your street yesterday. Afternoon, evening. Around 4:50 p.m. Do you mind checking it for us?" asked the officer.

"I know you guys aren't the most liked in the city right now but let me see what I can do."

The clicking noise of the keyboard cut through the air as the guys waited. Mick went through a dance of dragging windows around on his computer screen. Surprisingly, he was savvier than he looked.

"Alright, check this out, boys." He rolled back his office chair, and the two officers huddled around the monitor.

"Ok. Stop." O'Malley directed. "Play that part again."

"Pause it right there. Can you zoom in?"

Black and white was no quality to be impressed at, but they did have an image, a rather good one at that. The video showed Tommy coming up onto street level from a set of steps before getting a cab.

"Can you send it to this email?" The other officer handed Mick a crisp business card. Mick dragged open another window to send the footage.

"Say, can you pan that thing a bit left to get the rest of that license plate? A87... I can't see the last four digits of that plate."

"She's a straight shooter," Mick replied, of the camera. "I ought to charge you for evidence that good."

Mick leaned back and pointed at them. "You know what? Speaking of charging you, this oughtta qualify for some type of reward, right?"

"We will surely see what we can do and will be in touch."

O'Malley and the officer walked out of the office.

"That's right, and don't forget that money, boys," Mick shouted from his office.

***

Armed with more information than bullets, the officers took the car back to the station. Quitting time on any normal day but the clock was quickly running past five. O'Malley, a man who preached his free time, went down the hall to see if the captain was still in office.

"Got five minutes?" O'Malley asked Patterson, who was a statue in his desk chair, sucked into his computer.

"Yeah, grab the small conference room and I'll be down in a few."

The other officer set up his laptop and O'Malley let him do the explaining. Normally he'd take the lead, but it was past quitting time on a Sunday. He sat back to fill in the gaps.

"And here's where you can see the best shot of his face, coming up to street level," the officer explained to Patterson.

"Um hmm, um hmm. Rewind once more," he ordered.

The clock on the wall kept spinning, closer to five-thirty. Patterson must have seen it four, five, six times by now.

"Let me just summarize, Capt." O'Malley had enough back and forth, cutting into the conversation.

"The workers, they know nothing at the bar. Let's run the face in the system. Hopefully, we get a partial match but get a sketch without the sunglasses."

"And the license plate? I want the full thing," Patterson asked.

"It's a work in progress. I'll have it from the Department of Transportation by the end of the day."

"Ok. Work on it O'Malley and you work on the face ID. Stop by my office in the next few hours." Ordered Patterson. He left the two guys to it.

"Ugh." O'Malley exhaled and put his hand on his temples, seated in the chair. "Give me the room, would ya?" he asked the other officer.

Going through his contacts over at the DOT on his laptop, O'Malley rang one after another. *Any weekday and these people would pick up the phone but no, of course not on a Sunday.* His fifth try got him through.

"Yea, I need you to pull a camera from yesterday, from downtown, 4:52. The taxi plate starts with..." He gave the older woman on the other end of the phone the details.

The lady started to read back the digits, just as the other officer came back into the room.

"O'Malley, I got ..."

"Shut up! Would ya?" He pointed to the phone. He turned around. "Sorry mam, no not you. Yeah, go ahead please... Okay, I got that. Can you tell me who the cab driver is and if there is any phone number on record?"

"Sure, hold just one moment, please."

He set the phone down.

"What do you need?" he asked the other officer, not sitting next to him.

"Alright, no facial match but the sketcher should have a profile done overnight."

O'Malley raised his index finger, signaling one minute to the officer.

"That's great news. Thanks again for all your help." Slamming the phone down on the receiver. His finger held the place on his notepad as he put in the next number, the cab driver. It was impossible to dial it quicker than he did.

If there was one person who always answered the phone in Chicago, it was the cab drivers. O'Malley informed the driver of the reason behind his call, then listened along to decipher the cab driver's Middle Eastern accent as the gentleman vividly recalled the trip. The cab driver said he dropped the passenger on a road in some suburbs just outside Northbrook. Also, he mentioned the money that got left behind on the cab driver's floor.

O'Malley got all the information he needed, took his notepad, and jogged down the hall.

He rapped on Patterson's door with the back of his knuckles. Patterson's head emerged from behind the computer.

"We got our lead." O'Malley made a motion with his head to the left, directing the captain back to the boardroom.

The three of the guys sat down and energy filled the exhausted officers. First, laying out the new details O'Malley recapped that there was no facial match. The captain had his elbow on the table and fist over his mouth, listening intently.

"Well, with a sketch by tomorrow and the drop-off road, I think we have enough to set up the guys." Patterson said.

"I don't want any of this leaving the room tonight. I'll drop an all-hands meeting email tonight, for tomorrow."

"What's the plan?" asked the younger officer.

"That's the point of the meeting tomorrow." O'Malley's attitude showed a clear lack of sleep.

"I'm thinking, as much as I hate to do it." Patterson stopped for a second. "I'm going to have to ask the help of the FBI guys on this one. Get some undercover cars and foot patrols canvasing the neighborhood. Let me sleep on it, but you guys get some sleep too."

It didn't need to be repeated. They turned off the lights to the conference room, which smelled like three unshowered men and coffee. The officers, at least O'Malley got the orders he was looking for all day. He wasted no time in shutting down his computer and getting out of the station because he knew the case was just heating up.

Chapter Nineteen

Rainy Day

For a Monday morning, Jack had to push his body into his normal routine. A test of true mental fortitude challenged by his anxiety. His red truck turned into the Presto Pest parking lot like clockwork. The rain hit his windshield and the squeaky wipers did all but nothing to keep it clean. *Dink ... dink ... dink ...* Large drops peppered the metal hood. Under the cover of the rain that dripped down the windows, Jack put the money under and behind the seat of his truck.

Jack locked up his truck, grabbed the key for the Presto Pest truck, and headed to his first job. His first stop was an office building on the south side. It was a two-person job and Jack pulled his truck into the parking lot next to another Presto Pest truck, already waiting. The pavement didn't even show a sign of the morning rain.

"Did you hear about the robbery downtown this weekend?" his coworker asked while getting a sprayer out of his truck.

"Yeah, man!" Jack shouted back past his open rear van door. Jack's head was stuck deep in his van, sorting out his sprayers.

"What do you think? Who was behind that? Freaking brazen man," asked the coworker. He was a younger guy, in his late twenties, with jacked-up teeth and an always wrinkled uniform.

"I don't know, man. Not the slightest clue." Jack kept it short. "All set?"

"Gosh, I can't fathom that money. Now Presto is in the news. I hear they don't even know if that is one of our trucks. Just crazy." The guy slammed his van doors closed.

"Another day, another dollar, I suppose."

The two walked into the office building with their backpack sprayers on to do a routine spraying.

While Jack made the day look seeming normal, things weren't back at Presto. About the same time the two guys started spraying the office building, a squad car was pulling in back at Presto Pest. The two officers got out of their car at the front of the building and headed towards the side. One was tall and had the build of an athlete, while the other was the complete opposite. Stumpy in stature and wouldn't be able to run down an old lady. With the metal gate wide open, they walked into the lot with all the vans and trucks. Passing the employee parking and Jack's Ranger, there were only four vans left in the lot for the day. Across the street, a news crew was setting up to shoot a piece with the parking lot in the background.

Once the officers finished, which didn't take long, they headed inside. A warm smile from the young receptionist greeted the two officers in blue.

"Can I help you?" she asked kindly.

"Of course you can," the taller of the two replied. "We want to speak with the owner. I'm sure you are aware of the news circulating."

"Just a moment. Let me see if he's available." She picked up the phone and dialed back to Mr. Granger's office. The line beeped with a busy signal. "Hold on just one more moment. Let me go back and see what is going on."

The receptionist took off in a quick stride down the hall, into Susan's office and peered into the window on the door.

"He's on a call," Susan remarked in her crass tone.

She turned the handle and walked in anyway.

"Excuse me." The young girl was either fearless or outright stupid but it did get Mr. Granger's attention. Predictable in nature, he was leaned back in his chair with his feet up on the desk.

He threw his hand high up in the air, signaling one minute with his pointer finger but it wasn't. Seconds later, Mr. Granger put his palm over the mouthpiece of the corded landline.

"Yeah!?" Granger used it as both an acknowledgment and a question.

"Chicago PD is here and wants to see you."

He took his hand off from covering the phone and put it back up to his mouth.

"Jimmy, sorry, I'm going to have to call you back." Mr. Granger said before hanging up.

"Alright, send them back. You have my full attention."

The full attention of Mr. Granger was like capturing the attention of a six-year-old boy. Eager to listen at first but it could die out in a moment.

Going back to the main lobby, the receptionist brought back the two officers. She knocked again before entering Mr. Granger's office.

"Come in, come in," he said. "You can leave them with me. They are in good hands."

"Have a seat, gentlemen." Granger invited them by waving his open palm to the two chairs on the other side of his desk. "What can I do for you?"

"We just want to ask you about that Presto Pest truck. I'm sure you saw one was used in the downtown robbery two days ago." The pudgy cop loved to motion with his hands while talking.

"Ah ... Interestingly enough, that wasn't our truck." Mr. Granger grabbed his die-cast Presto Pest truck and rolled it across the desk in front of him.

"Well, how confident can you be?" the pudgy officer replied.

"I had the guys do a count first thing this morning and none were missing," Granger said confidently. "You won't be able to tell now since most of the trucks are out but you can take my word for it."

The two officers looked at each other and their eyebrows raised a bit.

"Who does the scheduling for Presto Pest? It seems like a coincidence that Presto Pest knew when to show up." The officer moved to his second question.

"Susan does." He pointed through the window. "She's been here fifteen years. You can't accuse me of sending one of my trucks in there without me knowing it! That's ludicrous."

"OK, thanks for that. You got anything?" The officer turned and questioned his partner.

"Yeah, do you know who generally is the team that goes out to the bank?" the taller officer asked.

"Again, that's a question for Susan. Look guys, I don't know much but if I did, I'd tell you. You need to be finding the robbers. This is defaming my business and this is a waste of time. Now, I have a meeting here soon so you are free to ask Susan a few questions on the way out but that will be all for today." Mr. Granger put down his die-cast toy truck, stood up, and showed the officers the door.

"Susan, can you take good care of these officers for a few minutes and get them anything they need?" Mr. Granger escorted them out and closed the door behind them.

Seemingly, it wasn't a few minutes as the officers grilled Susan over the next forty minutes. The shorter officer dug deeper with question after question.

"Can you pull who went to the bank over the past four years?" he asked.

She dug into a silver metal file cabinet behind her desk. It was filled to the brim with colorful folders. Grabbing the bank's folder, Susan slid it on the desk for the guys to look over. She cautioned the officers that some of the guys who used to spray at the bank were no longer with the company and they tried to rotate personnel on the corporate jobs. The officers passed the papers back and forth, looking for any pattern with the names.

"Do you mind if we get a copy of these documents? You know, just to have back at the station."

Although she wasn't great with the machine that looked as old and worn out as her, she managed to run off some copies.

"Who all has access to the scheduling of jobs and how far in advance do the guys know?"

Susan took off her thick glasses and started to clean them. She explained that she was the only one who did the scheduling and the guys know their schedule two weeks in advance.

"I've been here fifteen years. I'm five years away from retirement. Would I like that money? Sure. Did I take it or help take it? No. And I sure as hell didn't move the date of servicing up." She laughed. "I work enough already. I'll leave working on the weekend to the robbers and you guys."

Looking down, she saw her tea was empty and grabbed her mug. "You guys got anything else for me?"

"No mam," the officers kindly replied.

"Well, you know where to find me if you need something." Susan headed down to the hall to the break room as the officers packed up.

Back in the squad car, the officers gave Patterson a call giving the details of their two interviews.

"We just don't have reason to believe that was even a real Presto Pest truck." The shorter officer explained who asked most of the questions.

Patterson fired back a few questions of his own.

"No ... no ... that's not a possibility. Yes, I think one of their workers was involved but no telling who at this time." said the officer.

"What? I lost you for a second, Patterson ..."

"Yeah, sixty-three employees do the spraying for Presto Pest."

"Ok, chat with you later," said the officer as Patterson had to get off for his meeting.

Patterson checked the clock on the wall, and no sign of Rutherford. Moments later, the skinny figure appeared in the office doorway.

"Agent Rutherford, come in," Patterson said in a more commanding than welcoming tone. "Only a few minutes late."

"Special Agent," he said, correcting Patterson. "Well, some of us are out there solving the case."

Rutherford took a seat and put a black leather briefcase on the table, taking out a notepad and pen. Leaning back in the seat across from him, Patterson put his hands behind his head and spread his elbows to the side.

"As you know, we came in just a bit later than your guys on the case. I was hoping you could bring us up to speed on any missing facts and then I'll catch up with my guys. I'm sure you can appreciate we would do a superior job of catching these guys versus the Chicago PD wasting their time but we just need all the facts. Then we will let you get back to the traffic stops and such." Rutherford said.

Taking his arms down and sliding in closer to the table, Patterson made his presence felt. "I think you are confused about what my men can do. We are just going on forty-eight hours and have one in custody."

"Right, right. Anyway, can you give me your account?"

There was a whiteboard on the wall in the office covered in dried-out marker. Washing it down with spray and an eraser, Patterson started to conduct a timeline and put down the key facts.

"We know it was 4 males who entered the bank around 1 p.m. on Saturday for routine pest treatment."

With his chair turned towards the whiteboard, Rutherford nodded intently as the facts were presented in front of him.

"Go on." He instructed.

Estimating that three to six million was stolen, Patterson explained how the people in the bank were sprayed, passed out, and the money was taken.

"Mhmm." Rutherford wrote down notes. "Not to worry, our guys can determine the amount."

Aside from the getaway and speaking to the individuals at Presto Pest, the last piece of information shared was a call about the suspect in custody just before the meeting.

"But we weren't able to get a match of the fingerprints in our databases. We can look into dental records now that he has passed away." Patterson offered.

"We're going to need a copy of the fingerprint samples to run in our systems. Our data analysts have access to quite a few more systems than your boys. You got anything else?"

"There's one last thing," Patterson explained that they had a lead on the individual who fled officers by foot. They had a general drop-off area and money was even left in the taxi. "But we don't have the manpower ... My guys are working in the city mainly."

"I understand. I got ya. So you want to use our boys and budget to put some undercover agents on the streets up there?" Rutherford confirmed he was hearing Patterson correctly.

"I'll get you the men. Send me a copy of the sketch you showed me. This is what we needed though, and I think this has been productive. Keep these open lines of communication and share information with us. Surely we will close in on them." Rutherford closed his notebook with a snap. He got up to shake Patterson's hand, who put the cap on the dry-erase marker and set it down. The handshake was two forces colliding. Patterson gave a strong squeeze and looked Rutherford in the eyes. Rutherford's gaze had a sting stronger than Patterson's handshake.

"Chat soon and send across those documents." Special agent Rutherford tossed a card onto Patterson's desk instead of handing it to him and left.

The rain picked up in the afternoon again as Jack drove his work truck back from his afternoon job. At least the wipers work better than the Ranger. With the heavy rain, he expected a lot of traffic but with his afternoon job ending just past three, there was hardly any traffic to fight. In record time, the truck was pulling back into the lot. Jack headed inside to give the receptionist the keys for the day.

"Thanks." the receptionist said while taking the keys and watching Jack sign the truck back in. "Just an FYI, Mr. Granger is calling an all-hands meeting in the parking lot at 7:30."

Opening the door to leave the front of Presto Pest, buckets of rain were falling and splashing off the sidewalk. Jack made a quick jog to his truck around the side of the building. He fumbled for his keys in his soaked pants and drenched work shirt. They jangled as Jack flipped through wet keys until finding the one for his driver's door. There was a change of clothes in this truck but it had to wait until the truck was out of sight. The afternoon of errands was just starting.

The first stop Jack headed to was the large home improvement store. His truck pulled in under the large orange sign and he walked into the lawn and garden, grabbing a cart. Jack threw a shovel in the cart and headed inside to grab PVC pipe. He grabbed seven, one-foot sections, a bunch of end caps, and some glue.

"$57.37, do you want a bag?" the lady in the register booth at lawn and garden asked.

"Yeah, please for the pipes." Jack handed three, twenty-dollar bills to the older lady in her orange apron.

Wheeling the cart back out into the parking lot, the front right wheel spun around continuously like a floppy, limp leg. Jack pushed the cart right up into the Ranger. It's not like he could beat the truck up any worse. Once everything was thrown in the back, he headed to a sporting goods store across the way in the same strip mall. Looking at his phone, he had all the items on his list except for a handheld GPS and some weatherproof storage bags.

Half an hour later, he was coming out of the store with the items and a tent as well. Back in the truck, Jack tried to call Jen. It rang and rang but there was no answer. Jack put in directions and set his destination to a state park off route eighty, south of the city. The GPS said an hour and forty-five minutes but before Jack started driving, he tried Jen again. Things hadn't been great between the two before the robbery and they weren't getting any better.

Jack left the strip mall with the truck full of cash and newly acquired supplies. Heading down to the state park, he began to question, question everything. *How do I fix this with Jen? Is it even worth fixing now with all this money? Before the robbery, it felt like the money would fix everything.* Now, the money felt like it would fix everything but he questioned if worth it to fix everything for everyone.

The traffic thinned out as Jack got closer to the park. The woods crept up on the side of the road with the trees watching the red truck speed under them. With no traffic in sight, he pulled the truck to the side of the road. Jack pulled off the Presto Pest uniform and put on a black tee shirt and a pair of blue jeans. It was better than his soggy pants from the afternoon rain but his boots were still wet as he laced them up.

After another five minutes of driving, Jack was at the entrance gate. It was a lone brown shack that split the road from cars going in and out.

"Hi sir, it is $7 per car but the park closes at dusk in another two hours or so," a teenage girl in the guard shack said when sliding open the window.

"I was looking to book a camping site. I assume it wouldn't be too busy on a Monday," said Jack.

"Sure, I can do that. I assume you want a tent space? It is fifteen a night."

"That'd be great, with some privacy." Jack requested and handed her a fresh twenty-dollar bill that was not stolen.

"The park is basically emptied out this time of year during the week so you can have your pick." She handed Jack a map with all the unreserved camp spots.

As a kid, Jack used to come to the park with his dad but it had been years since he had been back. Looking at the map, the layout hadn't changed.

"Site thirty-seven please, just one night." He handed back the map.

"Just hang this tag on your rearview mirror and you'll be all set. You are going to go down the road about a mile and you'll see the signs for camping on your left. Follow it up the hill, around the bathhouses and you should see your site." The girl smiled and waved him on his way.

The old truck went down the narrow road until it forked. Camping on the left and a long straight road ahead. The camping sign was almost covered by overgrowth. Jack passed little wooden signs for each campsite, evens on the inside and odds on the outside of the loop. His truck crept around until reaching his site. On the way, he only passed two other sets of campers. One in an RV and another in a tent but they were a fair way down the loop and out of sight.

Backing his truck onto the concrete pad, Jack took out the tent and proceeded to set it up. Once it was all set up, he collected some sticks and larger pieces of wood from the area just behind his campsite. Intricately laying them into a teepee formation inside the campsite fire pit. The dusk sky was quickly settling into darkness as Jack tried to light the wet wood.

After trial, error and inhaling more smoke than a week's worth of cigarettes, Jack had a small campfire. He stoked it with sticks before sitting down on top of a picnic table at the campsite and lit up a cigarette of his own. Looking up he could see the moon coming out and the stars falling into place, for once, being outside of the city. The cool air nipped at Jack's arms and cheeks comparable to a day in early October. There was something to be said for the solitude outside the city, at night, in the outdoors. Taking his last drags on the cigarette, he flicked it into the crackling fire and watched it disintegrate. Quickly, all at once, gone.

The campsite was dark, pitch black aside from the light of the fire. It reflected off the side of the tent and concrete pad, glowing. Jack turned his truck around so his lights illuminated the campsite and trees behind it. Pulling the shovel from the bed of the truck, Jack stomped on it with his boot so it was sticking straight up in the ground. Scanning the tree line behind the tent, a landmark caught his eye. A thick downed oak. Next to it, Jack's blade from the shovel sliced into the soft wet ground from all the rain. The tree looked like it was just uprooted from all the rain.

Digging deeper, Jack made a hole that was a foot wide by about three feet deep. He put the shovel down in it to check the depth and was satisfied. The figure of Jack reemerged from behind the campsite with the glow tracing the outline of his body as he walked back towards the fire. He went up to the truck, pulled out a backpack from under the front seat, and put it in the truck bed. Assembling one of the end caps on the PVC pipes, Jack put $150,000 into the weatherproof bag and then into the pipe.

The black backpack was indistinguishable from the dark bed of the truck. Jack capped the pipe and walked back down to the hole, bringing the handheld GPS too. Logging the coordinates directly over the hole, he set in the pipe and began to cover it. Scoop after scoop of heavy wet dirt was tossed back on top to fill in the hole.

Stomping on top of the loose dirt, he compacted the hole back to solid ground. Just as he was finishing, the woods started to light up with a faint glow. Enough so to make him turn around. His truck was still running, and the fire was still going but over his right shoulder, two headlights were slowly creeping up the park campsite loop.

Slowly, the headlights cast stronger light as they came up the road closer to the campsite. Jack blended in as a shadow in the dark of the woods. He froze, stopping all motion to wait until the truck drove by. The truck inched closer and closer to his campsite. Only to slow down and stop right in front of Jack's truck. It boxed him in with no way to get out.

For no cars or trucks all night, Jack was puzzled by the truck stopping. His mind raced between options to head deeper into the woods or head up and see who was there. He felt like a deer in headlights, blinded.

There was a sound of an opening truck door while the motor was still running. A figure walked towards Jack's Ranger.

Am I being tracked? He continued to stand still.

"Hello? Anyone around?" a loud voice called up from up near his truck. "Park service ranger." The man shouted, introducing himself loud and clear.

"Park service ranger! Anyone here?" he called out again, walking towards the fire pit.

Jack made up his mind.

"Hey, hello there!" Jack called back while walking up from the woods.

The ranger was short and chubby, in his mid-thirties, sporting a wide brim hat and a trimmed outdoorsman beard.

"How many of you are staying with us?" the ranger asked while standing next to the fire.

"Oh, just myself, for tonight. Great to be outside the city." Jack replied.

"What were you doing down there?" The ranger pointed to the woods where Jack had appeared.

"Had to take a leak and the bathhouses sure are mighty far at this time of night," Jack replied.

The ranger went over to the front of the truck and looked at the tag. It looked valid.

He walked to the back closer to his truck and put one arm on the side of the truck while looking at Jack.

"I didn't see anyone here around that burning fire, so just make sure you keep an eye on it."

Antsy, Jack walked towards him to keep the attention of the ranger's eyes. The ranger was an arm's length from the most money he would have ever seen in his life.

"I sure will. You have a good night," Jack replied as he walked over to his passenger door on the ranger. He grabbed the truck's door handle to open it and the park ranger stopped leaning on his truck. Behind a racing heartbeat, Jack was relieved to see the ranger go on his way, disappearing into the darkness around the loop.

Putting the backpack back in the truck, Jack locked it up for the night. He put his shovel into the bed of the truck and sat down again on the picnic table. As the fire worked down to smolders, Jack climbed into his tent, no mattress, a hard night's sleep. The close run-in of the night left him feeling inside that it was more important than ever to hide the rest of the money.

Chapter Twenty

Operation Dog Biscuit

When will any of this get easier? Jack reached his hand behind his back rubbing out a knot in his back. The cold hard ground below the tent did nothing for a good night's sleep. He unzipped the tent and crawled out, looking around. A cool breeze hit his cheeks, sending fresh air into his nose and lungs. The wilderness brought freedom from the shackles of his job. Jack's clothes and skin had a smell of their own, last night's smoke from the fire.

The freedom was enough and Jack wasn't a guy to let down Donny. He checked his phone, Tuesday, 7:30 a.m. it displayed.

"Presto Pest, how may I assist you?" the receptionist answered Jack's call and asked.

"Hey Megan, Jack here. I assume Susan isn't in yet but can you let her know I'll be out sick today?"

"Ah. Sure, she's actually in if you want me to transfer you?"

"No need but if you can let her know, that'd be great."

"I sure will! You get well!" A bubbly attitude was something Jack welcomed but he didn't need Susan to ruin his day.

The campsite was spotless when Jack left and he was back on the road before nine. Quiet roads, a quiet Tuesday, it was welcomed. Jack hadn't had a day off in over two years but this was the first time he didn't have to worry about money, at least earning it. The tires of his old truck rumbled over the pea gravel as he pulled into the nearest gas station to fill up. The station was run down. It had just four pumps and one had an out-of-order sign. After topping up the tank and grabbing a ham sandwich inside, Jack put in the next public land stop in his GPS. Biting into the seemingly cold and disappointing sandwich, Jack was in cruise control himself, even if the truck didn't have it. He made two more stops after, throughout the state. Digging, hiding, and marking the money.

***

There must have been twenty men and women congregating in the small conference room. Patterson looked out into the crowd and saw some officers he knew and others he didn't. His eyes shifted to the clock which closed in on 8 a.m. The young officer helping O'Malley with the case was energetic, bopping around the room and chatting up any officer in sight. O'Malley was nowhere to be seen. Patterson put his index and middle fingers from both hands into his mouth and made a large whistle to settle the officers. Settle or startle was to be debated around the room.

"Alright, alright, have a seat, everyone." Patterson stepped behind a wooden podium at the front. It did little to shield his large frame. The officers sat down and quieted down under the bright lights, many with coffee in hand.

"I want to thank the FBI for the help on this joint task force. I see some new faces out there." Patterson tried to not look Rutherford in the eye but his gaze from the back was strong, relentless. Once their eyes locked, Patterson threw him a little credit with a subtle nod.

"Operation Dog Biscuit." Taking a large sketch from under the podium, Patterson turned around and taped it up onto the whiteboard behind him. He then took out a stack of printed papers and the first officer passed it around one by one.

"Hmmph!" one officer grumbled.

"Interesting." Another took the paper, looked at the face and his head bounced a bit up and down.

"This is our guy," Patterson said proudly. He explained how they got a facial sketch and that the cab driver has money tying him to the bank. "We have the general vicinity. The rest of this week, we are going to flood that neighborhood."

His peripherals caught another officer coming in slickly, but late. O'Malley.

"We will deploy undercover walkers, teams in cars, and a command bus as well, on a rotational basis. Day and night. If this guy is in that area and moves, we'll get him. Any questions?"

A few of the officers and agents hurled questions at the Captain. Nothing he couldn't handle.

"By noon, I want us out on those streets! Assignments will be up on the board after this meeting. We gotta bring him in but remember, this guy is a risk. Be safe!"

Once Patterson concluded, the chatter and excitement ramped up in the room.

"You think we are going to find all that cash?" a greenhorn officer asked the older officer next to him.

"I guess we'll see, but if we do, it's going to be the most I've seen in my lifetime."

To O'Malley's surprise and not to his wish, he was to be a sitter in one of the undercover cars starting the afternoon. Paired with none other than the younger officer that he had been working with for the past few days. There wasn't an ounce of excitement O'Malley had to share with his partner. It was nothing against the guy, the job or the case, but the hours were adding up. A certain stress was looming over catching the perps. One that Patterson could see across the room. The Captain weaved through the other officers, sharing his, "We'll get him", "Be strong out there," and "Thank you, stay safe."

"All good O'Malley?"

"Yea Capt. Exhausted but good."

"That's my guy." Patterson gave a hard slap to O'Malley's shoulder and then a cheeky fist bump. "If you need anything, just give me a shout."

There were days where O'Malley felt like a right-hand man and other days where he felt like a peasant in the field. Today, he just couldn't decide which.

***

After lunch, the weather couldn't have been better for March. The command vehicle, an inconspicuous box truck with "AL's cleaning" on the side, posted up where the taxi driver had dropped off Tommy. There were two FBI agents and two Chicago PD cops inside the cramped space. Patterson set a mile-and-a-half radius border in each direction, with undercover cars sitting on as many corners as possible. Two of the five cops on foot patrol were female. One was pushing a baby stroller through the neighborhood and the other was one of two dog walker patrols walking her German Shepherd.

"What do ya say, O'Malley? Are you a Mauricio's or Giordano's type of deep-dish guy?" the officer asked while sitting in the passenger seat and stuffing a leftover bread stick in his mouth. O'Malley didn't reply to the unwinnable debate. He stared out the window from an unmarked gray Chevy Impala. His eyes examined every car on the two-lane road. There wasn't much traffic and no one was matching the photo on the paper sitting on O'Malley's lap.

They were parked on a quiet main road, opening to a more mature neighborhood with the houses having a bit of grass between them and developed trees. Not like those city neighborhoods with the houses stacked on top of each other. The other officer had a line of sight down into the neighborhood to the right, past the stop sign at the entrance. He could see every person who pulled up to the stop sign, being less than forty feet away. Sidewalks lined the main road and the side street until they disappeared out of sight. For such a nice day, there was only the occasional walker.

From the peak of noon, the sun worked its way down further and further into the afternoon. The command truck radioed out to the officers and agents on the regular but there wasn't even as much as a slight match to the sketch.

The problem wasn't that they weren't in the right place, it was just not enough manpower. Tommy came home from work a little after six. Unbeknown to him were the cops all around his neighborhood but he still got home without any of them seeing him.

Foot patrols were pulled off the streets for the evening. The officer and O'Malley finally got relieved from duty until the next day.

The following day, the pair moved up a street. Same car, same neighborhood, different location.

"This has got to be the spot." The officer told O'Malley as they parked. The view was similar as well. A great perspective of the main street and not a bad one into the neighborhood. From seven to noon, it felt like déjà vu of the previous afternoon. First, the kids got on buses, then there were the moms walking dogs, and finally some joggers. Nothing too out of the ordinary. The other units were seeing the same out on the streets.

"Man, I'm starving. Where the hell is this lunch?" The officer complained to O'Malley. The clock was ticking past twelve thirty but it always seemed like lunch was late on stakeouts.

Not long after, another unmarked car pulled up to O'Malley's window, handing off a bag of greasy burgers and fries.

"Any action here, boys?" the officer delivering the food asked the two.

"Nah, unless you consider the moms and birds," O'Malley remarked. "I see you brought the healthy food. Thanks for considering our orders." He joked while holding the mass order.

"I'm just doing my job and doing what I'm told. Y'all be safe out here."

The two dove in to demolish the bag of food. Once O'Malley put his burger wrapper in the bag, he crumpled it up and tossed it to the foot of the passenger seat.

"Come on, man!" The other officer had enough of any antics in the small space.

Although it was a burger, it felt more like cement in the stomach. Rolling to his side, O'Malley unbuckled his seat belt and got in cozy with the window.

"You're on duty, boss," he said to the other officer. "Wake me if you need me. You know where to find me." His eyes shut as he drifted off into a nap.

The sleeping didn't annoy the other officer but the snoring did. Vibrations in the air felt like a sub-woofer was hitting the windows once O'Malley fell into his deep sleep.

Not to a surprise, the more O'Malley slept, the other officer was more alert. A few times, he almost gave O'Malley a jab to the ribs, thinking he had their man. His lungs were just getting ready to shout with some good news, but it didn't come.

O'Malley woke up past two, asked if they had caught the suspect and went back to sleep. His words, "See you at the end of the shift."

The end of the shift surely seemed in sight before any sign of Tommy. Picking up the picture, giving it a quick stare, and setting it down became a normal every thirty-minute ritual for the officer. His focus was mainly on the stop sign. There were just too many moving cars on the main road for him to see them all with O'Malley sleeping.

A red car pulled up, stopped and drove off. Then a black truck. Then a white van.

The driver of the white van in sunglasses and a hoodie looked promising. More promising than the last 300-plus cars that the officer had seen over the past day. The officer debated the jab. O'Malley returned with a snore. The officer gave the jab. Straight between two ribs of O'Malley, pushing the burger he had eaten into his stomach. That, and a punch to the thigh had him awake quickly.

"Get up, get up! Do your job and follow this white one." The officer requested. He grabbed the radio from the center console and called it into command. "Command, this is unit 319, we're headed east on Chesterfield, following a white van, the possible ID of the suspect."

O'Malley put the car into gear and pulled out of the parallel parking, only two cars behind the van at this point.

"Do something! The officer requested. We're not going to see anything from here." He pleaded with O'Malley who was driving closer to an elderly individual than a cop. "We're two cars back, passing Ashburn Street on our right, still on Chesterfield." Taking his finger off the mic, the message went through.

A quick return came back. "We have an agent with her dog two streets up. She is moving in place to the intersection."

"You better hope you are right on this one," O'Malley said while following along. He belched up the stench of a hot burger into the cab of the car. "Mainly because you woke me up."

The officer could see the undercover cop in the distance. She was jogging around the corner onto the main road. She kept jogging. The white truck zoomed by, followed by the traffic in between and then O'Malley's car.

"Stay on him." The officer in the passenger seat insisted before seconds later it came over the radio.

"Pull off, pull off. Our agent said he looked more Hispanic than Caucasian."

Grabbing the mic to the radio, the officer bit his tongue and threw it against the center console. Surely not convinced.

"That's ridiculous. That could be our guy!"

O'Malley swung a U-turn and headed back to their parking spot for the rest of their shift.

"Look at you giving everyone something to do. No probable cause to stop that guy and not even the right color." O'Malley laughed.

"Not the right color?" He exclaimed. "She's seeing shadows out there, making him look dark. That was our guy!" The officer was adamant.

The right color car, the right color person, it was still up in the air. Sitting back in the passenger seat, the officer just waited for quitting time. For once, seeing eye to eye with O'Malley but not mentioning it. He didn't speak out loud any further of his defeat. The morning motivation was gone and that didn't need to be said either.

***

If the officers weren't already in a waiting game, then the three-car accident on the expressway put them in one. By the time the guys got to their normal stakeout spot on Thursday, much of the morning commuters had already left from the community. They didn't get to the neighborhood until around 9:45 a.m. which was later than they wanted.

"Did Patterson say we were doing this just this week?" the officer asked O'Malley while staring down the side street. The only thing that had changed was the grass that grew a bit longer from yesterday.

"That's what he said. Who knows though? He could always extend it but I think our guy has long fled by now. That's my opinion," O'Malley replied. He turned on the radio to the local morning show as they waited. Waited for something exciting. After politics and gossip, it cut to the news.

"It's been five days since the robbery downtown and we can't say there are any new developments from the police. While there's still no news from their end, we will continue to keep you updated," Wendy Johnson said on the air in her high-pitched voice.

A meaty index finger from O'Malley changed the station to another channel, lowering down rock music into the background.

"This Wendy Johnson, man. I tell you what. Hardly anything good ever comes out of her mouth about the force. If she tried one day in our shoes, she'd see we are trying but she always is putting her media spin on stuff." The other officer was silent. People knew in the station that you can't argue with an O'Malley opinion.

As the minute handmade laps around the clock like a track star, there wasn't much happening except for the rare occasional jogger. The sun slowly drifted high up into the sky, signaling noon.

"You know, I ought to be on foot patrol out there. Back when I was in high school, you know I was a track star?"

"Oh yeah?" O'Malley had heard plenty of stories over the past two days but this had to be the biggest farce. "What'd you run?"

"I was an 800-meter guy. Just think about that if you are trying to catch up in a chase," the officer said with a laugh.

"All units respond ..." A call came out over the microphone from the control unit. "Flatbush and Watercrest Street, suspect is headed East on Flatbush, on foot."

"Here we go again," O'Malley said. The red and blue lights lit up the car so they could speed up all of two streets to Flatbush and cut off the runner. The tires made a loud screeching as the car peeled out of the parking spot.

"Brown hoodie, blue jeans, white sneakers." The control team updated the ID over the radio.

"That's him!" the officer said as O'Malley put the brakes on and stopped at the end of the street to block it. The suspect was running right down the street towards them. Twenty yards back, an undercover CPD foot patrol officer was sprinting down the sidewalk.

Before O'Malley could get the car in park, the officer opened the passenger door and joined in pursuit. If there was one thing O'Malley could see, it was why the officer didn't catch the suspect on the bridge a few days ago. He might be a long-distance runner but clearly not a sprinter.

The officer's chest was pounding after fifteen yards. His lungs burned inside as his heart rate climbed. Never a smoker but probably should have been checked for asthma.

In front and behind, the suspect could hear the officers yelling.

"Get down! Get down! Get on the ground!" But the yelling was too far to concern him. His foot pressed off the hard sidewalk and onto the plush green front lawn of a small brick rancher.

The man's arms were propelling him in perfect form. He opened a wooden gate to a picket fence going around the yard and ran past an empty kids' play set on his right. Just as he jumped over the back of the fence, the two officers were coming through the gate behind him.

"He's going to be running onto Maple!" The first officer called in on her radio while running. It seemed like Christmas would come before they got over the backyard fence but they finally got over.

As the suspect turned the corner onto the front yard of the neighbors, he lost his footing. The officers neared in and O'Malley's partner pulled out his taser. The yellow gun rose. He fired... and missed.

The guy kept running and the two officers couldn't keep up any longer. From another house, two lots up, an agent came out sprinting with her dog. She had cut through the backyard to meet up on Maple.

"Freeze! Get down!" Her aggressive and loud voice cut the air.

Tommy kept running but again was cornered. Front and back.

The German Shepard snarled and barked violently as the agent held him back. The fur from the head to the tail stood up as the dog was at the end of the leash.

Can I make it? Tommy shimmied and made a quick dash to the right, another fence in sight but the agent dropped the leash. It thudded time the ground and the dog was off like a racehorse. The distance between Tommy and the Shepard was cut in half. The fence seemed unreachable. It was.

Ruff! Ruff! Ruff!

The paws sounded like the steps of a giant in Tommy's ears. They kicked up dirt flying across the front lawn until it jumped in the air. Then the bite. A Taser would have been better as it felt like razors cutting into Tommy's right arm.

He screamed a scream that sounded like death for a flesh wound.

"Get it off! Get it off!" Tommy tried to move his right arm but his bicep was pinned into the grass. Seconds later, a knee was on his back by the officer who called it in. His face was pushed nose-first into the dirt. The agent collected her dog and drew her gun.

"Give me your hands!" The officer fought Tommy's squirming until she got the cold handcuffs clasped around his small bony wrists.

"We've got him." The officer reached up to the radio on her shoulder and told the mobile command center.

As she walked Tommy to the curb, O'Malley came down the street. He was one of the first cars on the scene. Rolling down his window, he waved her over with one finger, pointing to the back.

"That looks like our guy! Load him in. I'll take him down." O'Malley knew showing up to the station with a catch this big was like bringing a sport trophy buck.

There wasn't a word out of Tommy. A little mumble and grumble but no clear sentences. The officer pushed his head down into the back of the squad car with her fingers gripping his neck.

"Watch it!" Tommy yelled from the rough shove. He was covered in grass and dirt stains on the front of his clothes.

Once inside the back of the squad car, O'Malley had no words for him. The other officer got into the car for the ride of silence back to the station.

A small recession of cops was waiting for O'Malley's squad car to arrive when he showed up back at the station. Just what he expected.

"You catch him O'Malley?" one cop asked while they pulled Tommy from the car in an excited tone.

"Just assisted. Just doing my job." Throwing every ounce of bravado into his reply.

A few cops and O'Malley led Tommy down a cold but well-lit back hallway in the station, then into a holding room. The jubilee spirits of the cops were the only thing to warm the hall. In the holding room, they chained Tommy to the table.

Patterson and Rutherford were gnawing at their lips to get in there first and ask the first questions. It was Patterson who got the jump on Rutherford, being his station and all.

"You guys can leave." Patterson looked at the two officers inside the holding room. "You stay." He kept O'Malley in there with him.

"Can I get you some water? A doctor?" Patterson looked at Tommy's arm. O'Malley stood off in the corner of the room.

"Nah, I'm just fine, just fine." Tommy's dark eyes gazed up at Patterson.

"You must know why you're here, and it's not just for running away from our officer after lunchtime."

"Yea? Then why's that?"

"We have evidence connecting you to Saturday's robbery. We haven't even gone in your house yet or searched your car but we're going to. So you can work with me now." Patterson demanded and not in a pleasant demeanor.

"The best thing you can do is give us the other three guys. Yea... we've seen 'em on tape. I'll see what I can work out for you when you give me some information." The direction was always led by Patterson. It was clear it wasn't his first rodeo.

"I don't think I can help, but you can help me with one thing." Tommy looked up and paused. "Send me in a lawyer."

Chapter Twenty-One

Carry Jones Jr. Esq.

The driver of the show had been cornered. Patterson didn't like those words, "Send me in a lawyer."

"Oh man! But if you are innocent, you can just tell me!" Patterson joked and gave his closing comment but he knew it wasn't true.

"Do you have a lawyer or need a public defender?" O'Malley asked before leaving the room.

"Do I look rich to you?" Tommy said, in his dirty grass-stained hoodie. "I'm just a construction worker, an honest guy, a hard worker, and you bring me in here. Send me in a public defender."

The two officers left the room and kept Tommy chained by a cold metal handcuff to the desk. As soon as Patterson was outside the holding room door, he was met by Rutherford.

"You think you own this case? Using my agents and you go in there first. Hardly anyone is keeping me in the loop around here. US Feds will be working up a warrant. This isn't state-level stuff anymore." Rutherford wasn't just irritated, he was mad. He wanted to get his hands on this case, tight.

He jawed a bit more at Patterson until finally hearing something to shut him up.

"Well, he's all yours. Why don't you go talk to him yourself?" Patterson offered what seemed like a nice gesture. Only leaving out one key piece of information.

Rutherford brushed past O'Malley and Patterson, yanking open the round metal door handle. He got his first look at Tommy from the back. His brown hoodie and blue jeans were just what he pictured, a blue-collar guy.

"Man, that looks painful. You alright?" Rutherford too, asked about the bloodstains on the bicep of Tommy's hoodie.

Tommy nodded back.

"You know the bureau says white-collar crime is on the up and up and look, here we are." Dragging a chair away from the interrogation desk, across the floor, Rutherford sat down in front of Tommy. He positioned himself a few feet back from the table.

"So tell me, what made you do it?" Rutherford never beat around the bush. He never was the most honest agent but he was a straight talker.

"Didn't those last two tell you? I'm waiting for my lawyer." Tommy looked defeated but there was a little hope that some lawyer could dig him out of the hole he got into.

Of course, those guys didn't tell me that. It wasn't the first time Rutherford had heard the line either and it didn't matter. He was a snake in the grass.

"Let me do the talking and you can listen." Rutherford took note earlier of the no cameras in the room, something for him to take advantage of. Standing up, he pushed in his chair and walked a slow circle around the table.

"Look, we've got you. It doesn't matter when your lawyer gets here or not. Our evidence is going to tie you to the crime, whether you like it or not."

There was a bit of disbelief on Tommy's face. Stone-like, but inside something was telling him it was possible.

"Now we haven't executed our search warrants but that will be soon. As soon as the judge signs. We're going to go into your house, your vehicle, your phone, and tear it apart. We will find any money you stole and you will go to jail, so it's best to work with me."

There were no words from Tommy.

"Here's where I help you when you help me. I'm not like these cops that are looking to make you the poster of Chicago. I don't like what you did but I like what you have. I don't even care so much about who you did it with."

Rutherford sat back down in the metal chair and rolled up his white dress shirt sleeves.

"Let's make a deal!"

"You can tell me where the money is. I'll take my cut. I'll hide your portion before the warrant and life is good."

Tommy went to move his hands from the desk, realizing they were still chained as the shackles clinked together. It was the first time Tommy had spoken since his silence.

"What's your take?"

"See, that's where I get you. You are scared, you want the money, but you now told me you have it. I take eighty percent and you keep twenty percent."

"Eighty percent!" Tommy let out a loud laugh. "Absurd. I didn't even say I was involved."

"Look, I'm not going to play games with you. We have you connected to the crime. I can gladly lock you up but you can work with me here. I'll even lobby that you were just an accomplice when the time comes. You are going to have to do some time regardless for the media and CPD but I'm here to help you."

Adjusting his watch on his left wrist, Rutherford drew attention to it with a long stare.

"I reckon you have twenty minutes before your lawyer shows up and then I don't see how I can help you."

It was less, as there was a hard knock at the door. "Carry Jones Jr. Esq, at your service," the tall blond-haired man announced loudly as he walked into the room. His neat cut faded haircut didn't match the oversized gray suit he was wearing. The extra fabric bunched up over his brown dress shoes and the cuffs came too far up on the wrists. By the looks of being in his mid-thirties, Rutherford gave a look questioning why Carry's fashion sense wasn't refined for his age.

"Mr. ..." Carry put out his hand that wasn't carrying his brown brief-case to greet Tommy, reaching over from the side of the table.

"Tommy."

"I hope you haven't said much to the cops or the agents?" He gave Tommy a questioning look, raising his eyebrows, with Rutherford's back towards him.

"Not yet. Been quiet. I do want to entertain listening to a few minutes of special agent's ramblings here. Can you give us five? He'll call you in when we are done."

An even more surprised look came across Carry's face as he willingly agreed and left the room.

"Ok, I'll trust you a bit more than this half-wit, crock of shit lawyer. I understand I'm ousted by the rest of the guys I did the job with, but I still can't give them up to you."

"That's ok, that's ok." There was a calmer and friendlier tone in Rutherford's conning voice. "We already have a guy up at Kindred who was suspected on the job. A strong-built guy, dark hair."

"Ray?" questioned Tommy, looking stunned.

"Yeah, if that's his name? Last time I checked, we didn't have it. Any-way, that guy is dead. He'll surely take the fall for you. I could pin this thing on him right now if I wanted."

Tommy's head sunk into his chained-up hands. "He was a good guy. Man. He was fine when I left."

"Yeah, security guard smoked him with a hot round on the way out. Shame, but lucky for you. This is your break if you play it right."

"He was just an accomplice too," Tommy said through his hands.

"Wrong answer. If you aren't going to pin it on anyone else, you are the mastermind for all I know. Now look, I need your address and I need to know where the money is."

It was painful but Tommy pulled the directions out of his mouth. His bargaining chip was gone, hoping to be recovered later, later in life.

Rutherford took note of the address, location of the money, and Tommy's spare key outside his house.

"Alright, we're partners." Rutherford went over to shake Tommy's shackled hands. "You just made a better deal than you could have with any lawyer. You now have the law on your side. Rest easy."

Opening the door, Rutherford held it like a gentleman for Carry to enter.

"You making friends with these cops?" Carry let out a quick laugh. "I'm only kidding. You know, as a public defender, I don't even like these guys that much. Did you tell him anything? What was he trying to sell you on?"

"Nah, still didn't tell him anything. I guess just the usual, telling me I am guilty and all."

"Well, did you do it? It's confidential under client privilege but it's going to help me when I build a case for you."

"Yeah ..." Tommy sighed. "Yeah, I did it and he said they have stuff linking me to the crime."

"Well, not to worry, he might just be bluffing us."

"So what is next?"

"They are going to finish up this booking and then we'll have the initial hearing within the next forty-eight hours. I reckon they hold you here until the initial hearing and then either bail or county."

"That agent, he mentioned getting me a good plea deal if... if well, I pin it on my partner Ray."

"Alright, well, let's get through this initial hearing and we can go from there." As dim-witted as Carry looked, he wasn't a guy to waste time on a losing case. This one surely seemed headed that way. He grabbed his briefcase off of the metal desk and let Tommy know he'd see him soon.

Two officers came back in to get Tommy. The rest of his day was spent between the cold cinderblock walls of the police department where he was led around like an animal with no rights. He was taken to get a mugshot, fingerprints and his information recorded.

Time was ticking. Rutherford knew he had to get back out to Tommy's house before putting in a search warrant if he wanted the cash. He drove with the speed as if he was cashing in a lottery ticket. It would seem as if he had pulled similar stunts on helpless criminals, even if he hadn't. An hour later, and with the sun coming down, Rutherford made it back to the now much quieter neighborhood. Parking his car up the block, he changed inside it into jeans, a black tee shirt, and a black ball cap. From his glove box, he took a black handkerchief and squeezed it into his tight jeans pockets, along with a pair of black leather gloves. It was fair to say Rutherford looked like any other dad walking down the sidewalk as he got to Tommy's house. The only thing that made him look suspicious was the checking under multiple planters in front of the house, to which no one saw, even if it felt like everyone was watching.

He said it was under the planter but it doesn't help there are like seven of these damn things. Lifting yet another red-hued clay pot with his gloved hands, Rutherford snatched up a lone silver key. He was quicker to the door than even grabbing the key. Inside, it was right where Tommy said it was going to be. Next to his living room chair, Rutherford grabbed the black backpack. All of the apparent cash he could see was still on the dining room table. Bagging it all except for a few scattered bills on the floor, Rutherford left the place clean. *That's how you do a robbery.*

Taking out his handkerchief, Rutherford wiped down the table and the light switches. He took the remote to the living room fan and slid it into his pocket. Finally, wiping down the door handle, he left. A heist that took Tommy hours was gone in mere minutes. Rutherford was on edge as he headed back to his car and put his gloves into his back pocket. His shifty eyes were rapidly checking to the left and the right of the sidewalk. When he passed a mother walking her toddler down the sidewalk and pushing a stroller, he smiled and kept walking at a fast clip. Once back in his car, he put the backpack in the trunk immediately but heard his cell phone on the front seat. Slamming the trunk, Rutherford grabbed the phone before it went to voice mail.

"My guys said you left the station a bit back. Did you get that warrant written up?" Patterson asked on the other end of the phone, as he insisted on building a stronger case.

"The guys at the field office were working on it. I checked in with them just a few minutes ago and it was still in progress. It should be wrapped up in the next hour or two. Patience. Patience Patterson."

Rutherford kept him at bay with lies until he called in the warrant. The two went on to talk about the next steps for Tommy but Patterson took it back to the talk of the warrant.

"I'm sure we can get up there tonight if you plan on executing it."

"Yeah, we're going to get in there tonight but we don't need this as a joint operation. I have seven to eight good guys who can help hit the house... I'll catch up with you tomorrow and fill you in with the details."

It was what it was. Patterson only had so much say in the matter with the Feds on the case. He offered all the assistance he could but was starting to get turned away. As they had closed in on Tommy, his work almost felt done even if his interest wasn't yet. Until justice was served for his city, Patterson wouldn't put any case down. Even though the bank was back to normal operations.

On the way driving back to the field office, Rutherford called in the warrant to some of the junior agents.

"Yeah... I want a warrant worked up for the bank case. Get the house, phone, car. I want it all on there. I'll be back in one hour at six and I want to be able to take it over to the judge."

The officer on the other end of the phone agreed with Rutherford, his superior. One hour wasn't enough time to get back home so Rutherford headed directly to the field office, money and all. He stopped on the way, hitting a drive-through to grab some grub and an oversized coffee in a tall Styrofoam cup. An addict to the black brew, it burnt his lips on the first sip. Once he parked and ate, he did a quick change in the small space of the car back into his dress clothes. Using the flip-down mirror on the visor, Rutherford inspected his face, turning it side to side, lifting it up and down, stuck out, and lifted his tongue before finally rubbing the circles under his eyes.

"You are the case closer. You will close this case." He spoke to himself while closing the sun visor back up to the ceiling. In the past, Rutherford had used criminals to facilitate his own personal scores but this was the largest. His priority was always to close and pin the case.

Back on the road and driving another fifteen minutes, he circled up the ramps of the parking garage to the field office downtown. The cold breeze coming through the garage was enough to make Rutherford grab his long coat out of his truck before heading inside. After swiping his badge and waving to the guard, he smashed the plastic button on the elevator and rode it up to the twelfth floor before it made its loud ding. Steeping out with his massive coffee in hand, Rutherford navigated the rows of cubicles, lit with a bright white hue. Although the office was pretty empty, the team was excited to see Rutherford.

"You got it?"

"Sure do." A young action-hungry agent in his late twenties with an athletic build handed the paper over.

It took a few minutes to read and review, but Rutherford gave his approval.

"Fax it over to Judge Abbot. I'll let him know it's on the way to his house. The rest of you, head down to the staging bay and check over your gear. Check the rifles, armor, and breacher."

"Any information if anyone is in the house?" an agent asked Rutherford in front of the group.

"Not that our intel would suggest but get those rifles ready. We gotta be ready for anything tonight."

Energy picked up with the agents as they headed down to the bay. Tired but excited for some proper fieldwork as some of the guys saw it as a welcome change to pushing paper.

Setting into his office, Rutherford shut the door and gave the judge a call. The older man on the other end with a scratchy voice promised to have a look and get the document back within the next two hours. That was as long as the technology of the fax machine didn't give him any trouble.

Tapping a pencil on his desk, Rutherford took his time to start typing up the conclusion for search warrant which hadn't even happened yet. He carefully crafted his on story of events to come. Getting to the end of the second page, he added the names of his team members who were going to be executing it. There was a knock on Rutherford's office. An agent walked in and sat with his back facing the wall. The back of the computer screen faced him and another agent stood in the doorway.

"Sir, just wanted to let you know the guys are ready to go. Guns are checked. Ammo is in the trucks. Do you have the green light yet?"

"It should be any minute now. That's good work." As soon as he finished his sentence, his phone was ringing.

"Special Agent Rutherford speaking... Yes, Judge Abbot... Sounds good... Yes, we will be executing before 10 p.m. OK, thanks."

The fax machine in the hallway just outside his office made a whirling noise, spitting out seven sheets of paper.

"Can you grab it?"

The agent brought it back into Rutherford's office. Again, Rutherford dragged his clean finger across it for his scrupulous review. He flipped to the back and saw the large signature where the Judge signed.

"Let me change into a polo and we'll head down to the boys." A moment later Rutherford came out, 8:07 p.m., black polo, tactical pants and high laced-up boots. A fitting outfit to be breaking down doors.

Down in the staging bay, the men gathered around a whiteboard to listen to instructions. The eight men were to split into two pods of four. Each pod had a blacked-out F250 to take to the scene, fitted with push bars on the front and light bars on the top.

"Quiet down, quiet down."

"You four will fan out in a U shape at the back of the house. Two covering the back and two with visibility on the sides." Rutherford drew a diagram like a football coach at halftime.

"The rest of us are hitting the front. Jaxon, you're on the ram with Lou. Pete in behind, then me." The guys did a quick communications and buddy check before Rutherford gave the departing words.

"Load up! Let's be safe out there!"

The agents split off to the two heavy-duty trucks and pulled out of the bay door. It was a clear night as the trucks punched it out of the city and up the highway. The driver put some music on the radio to keep the energy high. There was little chatter among the agents while Rutherford scrolled through his phone, disengaged from the group. Once they got to the neighborhood, Rutherford grabbed the walkie-talkie in the center console, directing the second truck to pull in behind them. The agents were two blocks up from the house when they parked on the long, narrow street. Aside from a few houses with their lights on the second floors, the street was dark and quiet. Sprinklers were rattling around in a few yards as the two pods started to make their way down the street.

Disbursing around the target house, the first four agents in black all were carrying long rifles in addition to the pistols on their hips. Fittingly like the other houses on the street, the target house was quiet and dark too.

The main pod including Rutherford lined up at the front of the house. The third agent got behind a shield and steadied it with his pistol on the side. Rutherford was the only agent without nerves before the door got rammed. He crouched down in the back behind the flowerpots. In front, the two lead guys had a heavy battering ram with "the bull" written on it. Jaxon, the lead agent, held his hands up in his black gloves to count down. Three, two, one, bringing his last finger down.

"FBI search warrant open up! FBI search warrant open up! FBI search warrant open up!" The living room light came on.

Chapter Twenty-Two

Search Warrant

"FBI search warrant open up!" Lou repeated one last time. They didn't hear any footsteps with the light on. "Cover the back. We have lights on in the premises," Rutherford called out over the radio.

"Go! Go! Go!" Jaxon yelled as he and Lou started swinging the bull battering ram in a rhythmic motion. The heavy thuds were enough to wake any sleeping neighbors as they echoed down the street. Just before the hinges fell onto the concrete, Rutherford slyly reached into his pocket, turning off the living room lights using the remote he had taken earlier before leaving. The door crashed onto the floor and Pete pulled the pin on a flash bang. Chucking it inside, he yelled, holding his radio, "Lights back off, flash bag deployed!" His pistol was the first in, sticking out to the side of the shield, with Pete crouched behind. Once through the puff of smoke, his red laser dot hit the back wall of the living room, illuminated by a flashlight. The sights from Jaxon and Lou's guns followed suit.

"Clear!" Pete yelled after quickly working through the living room and into the kitchen. His back was to the walls, shield out in front, checking every corner. "Clear!" He yelled again once through the kitchen. The team worked through the first floor, up to the second, and gave the all-clear for the entire house on the radio. The Bravo team came inside, gathering with the other guys in the living room.

"Good work on that, guys. I think we all saw those lights. Can't explain what that was about, but good job nonetheless." Rutherford told the team. Bravo team, head upstairs to get the search underway and we will start down here. We are looking for money, evidence, laptops, phones, and anything else that links this guy to the crime." Rutherford ended the huddle and headed to the sofa. Taking out his pocketknife, he cut into all the cushions, slicing them like butter. In the background, he could hear Pete and Jaxon pulling open the kitchen cabinets and doors. Lou was bagging money that was on the floor near the dining room table.

Forty-five minutes later, an agent came down from upstairs and was explaining to Rutherford that the team wasn't finding much. They recovered a computer from the upstairs office and a cell phone charging on a nightstand.

"It's our guy." Lou overheard the conversation and held up a bag of money to show the other officers.

"Give us another strong hour. Comb it all over and then we will reconvene," ordered Rutherford.

Upstairs, the carpeted steps were a scene of chaos. Doing a few search warrants with Rutherford, his team knew anything was fair play and he wouldn't complain. Mattresses were flipped in the two bedrooms. Drawers were hanging out of all the dressers and nightstands. Pictures, mirrors, and a few pieces of imitation art were pulled from the walls.

Downstairs was a similar scene. Pete found a small safe in the hall closet and set it aside to open later. Rutherford was like a bull in a china shop ripping furniture apart, even if he knew he would find nothing.

"Any more luck Lou ... Pete ... Jax?"

They shouted back in sequence but it was a resounding no.

"Must have hid it off-site aside from this bit," Lou added. "We have enough with this cash though. A simple case to close."

Music to Rutherford's ears. The team of agents from upstairs came down shortly thereafter with again nothing new to report. They closed up the house and put a yellow flier on the propped-up front door that a search warrant was conducted. Meanwhile, two of the guys fetched the black trucks from up the street. A little past midnight, the street had quieted back down. All the early-on lookers from a few hours back were asleep. Pete came out and threw the battering ram into the back of the truck.

"Good job in there, Lou. See you all back at headquarters." Rutherford got in the passenger seat and shut the door.

The next morning Rutherford was first to the office. He must have only owned white shirts because he showed up in the same thing every day. Simple yet efficient in his blue dress pants. The outfit was more fitting of an accountant than an agent but he dressed well. The clock said office hours but the empty cubicles said otherwise as Rutherford passed them on the way to his office. He fired up the computer and made an Americano in the break room. By the time he was back, his brick of a computer had started, allowing him to pick up where he left off the night before.

Slowly but surely over the next hour, the guys made it into the office. It was questionable if the adrenaline had worn off on a few of them as they recounted busting down the door. Rutherford could see Pete, Lou, and Jax, chests above the cubicles chatting until he broke it up.

"Jax, let me see you in here."

Wearing a relaxed polo, blue jeans, and a dark pair of sneakers, Jax stood at the door.

"Have a seat." Rutherford slid his chair to the side of the monitors so he could look Jax eye to eye.

"Great job out there last night, and I mean that. Today, I want you to review this report I wrote up on the search warrant after taking the lead we found on the cell phone and computer. Let me know if you are seeing anything by the afternoon. I'll be out at lunch but let's catch up after that."

Thanking him, Jax promised he would deliver a thorough review of all three tasks. Sitting in contemplation, Rutherford seemed to watch the clock spin circles until lunch. A retirement on the water in Seattle or maybe a ranch in Texas. Material goods populated his head. One after crime-fighting, an easier life. Locking up his door, Rutherford prepared to head across town on his lunch hour.

There was a struggle to get the black agency SUV through the down-town lunch traffic. Forty minutes later, hindered by too many stoplights, the SUV pulled into the police station. Rutherford buzzed into the side door and stepped up to the sterile white counter to ask to see Tommy. The officer went down the hall to the row of holding cells and checked with Tommy if he would see Rutherford. Moments later, the officer came back with the answer Rutherford was looking for. He followed the officer down the hall to a small room and waited for Tommy to be brought in. The room had two chairs separated by a table in the middle.

"Do you want the shackles on or off?" the officer asked when he walked Tommy into the room.

Tommy rotated both wrists in the air and told Agent Rutherford with his eyes to take them off. Rutherford did a once-over look and didn't feel a threat.

"You can take them off."

The officer slid the key into the handcuffs, took them off, and put them back on his belt. Tommy took up a seat in a metal chair at the table.

"Give us ten minutes," Rutherford instructed the officer.

"Shall I let Patterson know you are here? He's running the case on our end."

"No need. I'll be in and out before he could even walk down the hall."

The officer left and Tommy quickly opened his mouth.

"Well, what brought you back here?"

"I came to let you know I secured our money and it is safe."

"My money. The money you are taking from me."

"No, no. Not your money. The banks, but now ours." Rutherford corrected him. Tommy's face stiffened up a bit when hearing the words "ours".

"Last night, my men and I executed a search warrant at your house. As expected, we found some of the money, enough to tie you to the crime. My guys are also going through your computer and phone."

"That's fine. They won't find anything." Tommy said with confidence.

"Is your initial hearing scheduled?"

"Yeah, my lawyer Carry told the guard it is for two this afternoon."

"Ok, go hear out the judge but I'll let him know you are cooperating and gave us as much information on Ray as possible. I don't care about your other two accomplices. The sooner I wrap this case up, the better. Sound ok?"

"I guess that's the only choice for the time being."

"It is but we are wrapping this thing up to everyone's benefit. The court, the city, you, me. It will all be over before you know it and I'll have your cut on the outside." Rutherford explained in a calm and convincing demeanor.

The plan sounded like the best thing to Tommy. At least the agent stopped down for an update. *Seems like a stand-up type of guy in all this shit.*

Rutherford knocked at the door to end their conversation and get let back out.

"Good to go Tommy?" The officer put the handcuffs back on Tommy.

"Tommy, I'll call you later once I speak to the U.S. attorney on the case."

On the way back to the bureau, Rutherford stopped in a local sub shop just outside the police station to grab a late lunch. After waiting in a deep line to place his order, he sat down and waited at the table when a group of three CPD officers came in. Overhearing them from his table, they stood on the other side of a half wall in the order line. Rutherford could make out pieces of their conversation but not the whole thing. They were going on to criticize the FBI and say they could have had a quicker conclusion to the bank job.

His towering sub arrived and Rutherford ate half. He wrapped the other half and took it to go. Getting up, he saw the CPD guys were at a table near the door. Tempted to say something and generally he would, Rutherford took his paper wrapper from the half of the sub he ate, threw it out in the trash, gave a glance at the guys, and left.

Pulling his SUV into the bureau, the hope was Jax hadn't found anything to keep the case going. When Rutherford sat down with him at 1 p.m. the case took another turn. An unexpected extension for the guys to wrap it up.

"Jax, what is the word, man?" Sipping on a fresh Americano as a caffeine crutch, Rutherford opened a notepad and flipped to clean page after page of case notes. The aroma of the freshly ground beans filled up the office as the door was shut.

"Well, there was nothing on the computer that furthered the case, but the phone had some suspicious activity that we should probably look into a bit further."

"Oh, yeah?" His voice pitched a bit high.

"We took the liberty to trace some of the numbers and there was a pattern to dialing a tire shop across town. The amount of calls and the timing after the robbery seem to line up."

"I gotta call the judge on this plea arrangement but if you want to head over there with one of the guys, Lou or Pete, feel free."

Excited to get some more fieldwork, Jax thanked Rutherford who inside wasn't thrilled on approving the assignment. He could hear Jax asking Pete if he wanted to make a quick run over to the shop and surveil from the streets. If it wasn't for Pete having to attend a school function, he would have but instead, Lou offered to join.

"You good for four?" Jax asked Lou, who obliged.

Two hours later, he bugged him again. Lou was working on his computer when Jax stuck his mug over his cubical. "Ready?"

Following him down to the car lot, Lou got in the passenger seat of a black Crown Vic, Jax driving. Jax knew his way around on that side of town but it still wasn't somewhere he went often. They beat the intercity five o'clock rush hour and got over to the industrial park quarter till five.

Parking just up the street on the side, the two had a good view down to the auto shop. One of the white bay doors was down but the other on the left was rolled up.

"Hand me a pair of those binoculars, would ya?" Lou grabbed it from behind his seat and passed it over to Jax. They were heavy with extra thick glass lenses. Lifting them to his eyes, it felt like Jax was almost standing in the shop.

From a black case, Lou took out a camera and screwed on a telephoto lens.

"You seeing anything interesting?"

"Looks like three guys in the shop. Hard to say if they are all employees or what the deal is. A few cars out front and one on the lift ... Let me try my regular play." Jax put down the binoculars and picked up his cell.

"Yes, I was calling to see what time you guys are open till. Six? That's terrific. I wanted to speak to the owner ... oh, this is him?" Jax motioned, clicking the camera's button with his free hand to tell Lou to start taking pictures of the guy behind the desk on the phone. The shutter snapped into a fast burst as Jax put his hand over the mic of the phone.

"Terrific, yea, I just wanted to ask if there was a warranty on my wife's Honda Accord's engine work that was completed at your shop. It's a blue one and she brought it in last week but it's still having issues ... oh, you can't recall that car? My fault, let me ask my wife again. I was sure she told me Superior Auto but I might be wrong. I'll call you back, if need be, after speaking to her again. Thanks." Jax hung up the phone.

"Did you get them?" he asked Lou.

"Of course I did." He laughed. "I got the owner and pictures of both employees. You are a smooth talker on that phone, boy."

The shop was getting ready to close-up and the guys left the street before the employees started heading home. Even though they could have kept at the case, when they got back to headquarters, they called it a day.

***

While things weren't on the up and up for Tommy, all had cooled off for Jack. Even the wife was coming back to her senses with Jack home at normal times. She was almost encouraging him to go see Donny for a few nights, just to get Jack out of the house a bit. In his head though, he was adamant to stick to the plan and had no contact with Donny.

Boasting of finally getting a raise at work, the bickering stopped between Jack and his wife.

"We don't need to worry about these mortgage payments. Mr. Granger finally came to his senses," he told her. Jack planned to take a bit of the cash and launder it through the casino and then into his bank before the mortgage. Not something he needed to share with her. Internally, he made a promise to not gamble it away. He didn't need to make money, he had it.

While the girls would play on the living room floor at night, Jack scanned the TV for any new word on the robbery but it seemed like the news had mainly moved on to the latest crashes on the highway, as well as the latest weather developments. Anything was better than heat on himself, he thought.

***

Jax and Lou were chomping at the opportunity to get into the office the next day. They beat Rutherford in by a few hours. Lou was already hard at work on the pictures before Rutherford or Jax arrived at the office. When Jax arrived, he already had news.

"You aren't going to believe this one," Lou exclaimed. Jax hadn't even had time to set down his brown briefcase that he showed up with every day.

"Give me five and I'll be back around." Jax requested.

It was more like seven minutes before he brought his coffee and stood behind Lou's desk. The picture of the left side of the screen was an enlarged facial picture they took the evening before. On the right side of the screen was a match to their database.

"Donny Macintosh, robbery, theft, and carjacking. Looks like the carjacking was when he was seventeen."

Jax leaned in and read the previous charges.

"Looks like he came out and is just looking to go back into a cell. What's his connection to Tommy or Ray?"

Lou turned around in his chair to face Jax and leaned back. He explained he didn't know ... yet.

Once Rutherford got to the bureau around 8:30 and stepped foot into his office, Lou was right behind him. Rutherford would have thought it was his own shadow if he was outside on a sunny day.

"You got a few?" Lou generally wasn't the type to pop into Rutherford's office so early, or even at all, so he knew something was up. Rutherford entertained Lou by offering him a chair and the floor to speak.

"That lead we picked up on last night. It's gotta be related somehow. The guy just got out recently. He's a regular at the jail."

"Oh, yeah?" Rutherford was a bit interested but equally annoyed. Just when he wanted it to be a closed case, his guys created another open end.

"We need a day or two to explore this. You might be able to tie this into Tommy as well."

"I'm proposing a plea deal on Tommy today, if not tomorrow. We need to show this city that we don't stand for crime and are doing our jobs." Rutherford sounded like a politician to Lou. More so a liar and less for the people.

"So currently you have nothing but you want me to wait? I can't do that but I'll work with you if you dig something up."

"Have Tommy ID the guy," Lou suggested. "He's giving you information after all... Should be easy if he's on our side and this guy was involved."

Inside, Rutherford hated it. On the outside, he squeezed out an "Ok, print me off a lineup of photos."

That was the answer Lou was looking for. He went back to share the small victory with Jax who wasn't impressed because he knew it was the right thing to do all along. Lou printed off three pictures and Jax two. Each picture consisted of a full body image and a picture of their face. The lineup consisted of a short-looking Hispanic guy, two other bald white guys that were similar to Donny's age and build, a tall black man and a fat mixed-race man with some number tattooed on his neck.

With their lineup assembled and the clock approaching lunch, the guys were ready to head across town. It so happened that Rutherford owed Tommy a call or visit anyway. Neither of which he had delivered. Lou knocked again on Rutherford's door.

"We are headed out in thirty. You coming?"

Rutherford didn't like the question. It felt like orders, and he was the one to give orders. He asked to see the lineup that they had prepared. The Hispanic guy just didn't do it for Rutherford.

"Switch him. Too short. It's like you didn't watch the surveillance tapes at all. Once you sort that out, be ready to go in forty-five."

Lou walked out and then raised his eyebrows, unimpressed. You switch it out. He thought.

Soon enough though, the three of them were in an SUV headed across town to see Tommy. Rutherford wasn't too sure why Jax needed to come along but didn't argue the point. Jax sat in the back while Rutherford was driving. Lou was in the passenger seat with a stack of folders on his lap. The dynamic in the car could be felt. Even though Rutherford may have not been the biggest guy, his personality felt like it.

The same officer was working from the day before when Rutherford buzzed in the side door at the police station but he was surprised to see two more agents.

"Bringing your whole office with you today?" the officer asked Rutherford.

"Something like that."

"You seeing the same guy today?"

Rutherford acknowledged the officer told them they could head down to the waiting room. He went in and waited for Tommy but told Lou and Jax to wait outside for a few minutes. His excuse was to chat on the plea deal. It was partially true.

The clinking of the chains proceeded to introduce Tommy even before he was in the room. Jax stared him down like he was a bomber when he walked by. When he came through the door, Rutherford smiled at him. A smile that said the chips were stacked in his favor and not Tommy's.

"I'll leave you two lovebirds together." The CPD officer unlocked Tommy's handcuffs and left the room. Rutherford asked how he was getting on and if everything was ok. Not the best thing to ask a guy who is locked up. The initial hearing wasn't good. Judge Abbot wanted to put a twenty-five-year sentence on Tommy and was in no mood to hear anything Carry Jones said to him.

"Well, I have good news and I suppose bad news," Rutherford said. "I'll be speaking with the prosecutor on a plea deal and calling the judge, so that is still intact. But my men... After the raid, they went through the phone and laptop. You told me it was all good... They tracked down a Donny Macintosh?" Pausing, he looked to see if it rang a bell with Tommy.

He could see it in his eyes that it did. "Not to worry, it's something we can handle but my men are sitting outside. They are going to come in and show you a photo lineup here shortly. If you want this plea deal, you are going to have to ID him. Also, give me the location of the truck. CPD will want that for a presser."

Tommy had a look of disgust on his face with Rutherford. He was convinced he wasn't a rat but also a wanted guy to face twenty-five years. That would put him out at fifty-six. There was no way he would survive on the garbage-tasting jail food for that long.

"What are my other options?"

"You can go crying back to Carry and have him try to beat your case or you can take the twenty-five years."

It was all too much for Tommy to think about and process at once. His demeanor was stoic in the orange jumpsuit as Rutherford looked on. Rutherford knew Jax and Lou were getting antsy outside in the hallway so he broke the last piece of important information to him.

"I know we said we would pin this on Ray, and we still will but I'll need you to testify in open court against Donny."

Tommy let out a sarcastic laugh while Rutherford got up to get his men.

Chapter Twenty-Three

Decisions

"You think he will ever finish up in there?" Jax asked Lou while waiting in the hallway. He wasn't mad that his time was being wasted but did want to get a crack at grilling Tommy. At least he thought that's what Rutherford must have been doing.

Lou was the more patient type, seated in a chair, looking at the pictures in his folder while Jax stood next to him. Anytime a CPD officer walked by, Jax liked to give them a cocky nod that he was an agent and they were just an officer to him. Many times, the look in return from the officers at the station was one of not caring at all.

Rutherford popped his head out the door with his clean crew-cut hair leading the way. He looked to the right but then found the guys to the left of the door.

"You guys coming or what?" he said, acting like they were late. Although they knew they couldn't have gone in without permission.

Inside the sterile room, it felt crowded. *Why is this guy unchained?* Was Lou's first thought but it quickly passed as he realized there were three agents in the room. Rutherford walked over to a corner of the room and started to check emails on his phone while letting his guys get to work. He turned away his eyes but kept his ears on.

"Tommy, glad you could work with us on this one. We know Special Agent Rutherford will get you the best deal possible and we appreciate your help on this one." Lou said while opening the conversation.

Tommy wanted to say stuff back. It was eating inside him and boiling up, but he kept his mouth shut. It was unlike him but he realized it wouldn't improve the situation.

The sound of the thick flopping pieces of paper was the only noise in the room as Lou laid out the five pictures in front of Tommy. He laid Donny out first, on the far left of Tommy, and then the four others in a row after it.

Staring at Tommy from just behind Lou's shoulder, Jax focused in on his head movement. It scanned side to side several times quite slowly. Jax couldn't see his eyes as Tommy's head was tilted down but if he did, he would have saw Tommy focused in on Donny's picture multiple times.

"Which one was your accomplice?" Lou asked.

"Is this really necessary? Don't you guys already know who it is?"

"Yea it's necessary and you work for us on a plea deal. Now, which one was it?"

Lifting his head, Tommy looked up at Rutherford but he was paying no attention back. He slid forward a picture of Donny.

"See, that wasn't so hard, was it? How'd Donny Macintosh get in touch with you in the first place?"

Lou gave him his typical stare-down. Rutherford's ears even caught wind as he turned around to listen.

"Ah, I've known him from his garage. He's got a garage over on the other side of town, Superior Tire and Wheels."

It wasn't new information to the agents, clearly. Jax and Lou looked at each other, knowing they had enough to use.

"Rutherford, you need anything else? We're sitting pretty good here."

"I just need that one last piece of information. Where'd you guys stow the truck, Tommy?"

He went on to tell the guys. There were a few other important details to the heist Rutherford didn't know but Tommy gave most of the key ones. If it wasn't for Tommy, they were never going to find that truck. Rutherford knew that too.

After every last word was out of Tommy, Jax left to get the officer in charge.

"Thanks for your help today. Once I speak to the prosecutor and judge on your sentence, I'll get in touch with your lawyer."

Rutherford and his men reconvened in the SUV to discuss the next steps on the way back to headquarters. Ready to pick up Donny, Jax and Lou knew they had to push through another warrant. Not that Rutherford was going to stay in office but he told the guys to have it ready to deliver to the judge by morning. He didn't even want to stay in the office for the rest of the afternoon and said he'd have to go home early. High stress, long hours and low sleep would cause someone to burn out, but not Rutherford. He just wanted to get home to his money.

It was a little after six when he returned home. Rutherford never favored the commute to the outskirts west of the city but he valued the privacy. When he used to live in a condo downtown, it always felt like building personnel was in his condo. He owned that place and didn't see his condo as a common area. Once he sold that five years back, he moved to the commuter lifestyle. It was a bonus that he worked weird hours and usually didn't get caught in the city traffic.

He pulled into his paved driveway, parking his unmarked SUV from the bureau. Rutherford didn't own any other cars. The brand-new blacked-out SUV would make neighbors think he had a lot of money but that was the only giveaway. The small brick house needed work and that was more visible than the shiny car. The front door on the porch and the side door near the car both needed repainting. The awning on the white porch needed to be mended as it was slouched down. Rutherford had two patio chairs that he bought when he moved in a long time ago but they were rusting too. His house wasn't a reflection of the neighborhood as a whole.

The trunk popped open as Rutherford grabbed the black backpack and took it inside. His senses had him lock the door behind him and lower the curtains to any eyes. The other instinct he had was to pour a glass of chardonnay. That was a daily habit.

He took the bottle out from the fridge and it had a little less than a glass left in it but that was ok, he always had more. His wine-drinking habits were defined by quantity and not quality. Once the bottle was poured and emptied, it was tossed into a large, open blue recycling bin near his side door. The loud clang of an empty bottle rang out every two to three days as he tossed one in. Sometimes earlier.

Rutherford changed out of his white dress shirt and blue pants into a pair of jogging shorts and no shirt. He rehung his dress shirt and pants methodically inside his walk-in closet. There were six other white dress shirts and blue pants hanging up in the closet. It was one area in his life that was easy. Not just because he wore the same style every day but he would often wear the same clothes for three or four days before washing them.

Back in the kitchen, he unzipped the backpack, admiring his take. One of his better takes in recent years. It was always a wonder how he could keep passing the annual lie detector tests at the bureau.

Filling up his pockets with the money, Rutherford went and sat down on the couch with his glass of wine. He put on some bachata music on the stereo and relaxed in the moment. His head swung slowly from side to side with the rhythm of the music. As the second song ended, he noted his lips were sipping from an empty wine glass.

Filling the glass up, the music filled the kitchen too. One hand-held the stem of the glass in a sophisticated fashion while the other took the bag of money. Twirling back into the living room, Rutherford dumped the bag onto his orange carpet. That old carpet looked like it had never been changed since building the house and had an eighties era to it. Closing his eyes, he danced.

The more he drank, the more he turned the music up. Classic Spanish sounds set the rhythm of his dance moves. His hips moved across the living room while his feet kicked around the money. He liked the feeling of being on top of it and frankly, he felt on top of the world.

When there was enough alcohol in him that it wasn't just his dance making him dizzy, Rutherford sat down for a minute to collect himself. He wasn't incoherent but rather in a state of happiness. It took him time to collect this money but then he put it into two piles. One for himself and one for Tommy. He took them both back to a safe in his walk-in closet. A trophy case was more accurate to Rutherford than a safe.

The bills filled almost two shelves in the large safe. They were accompanied by other trophies that Rutherford kept including a few Rolexes, small stacks of cash, rings and necklaces. It was never the value of an item that drew his interest but rather that act itself. Anytime he was doing a search warrant, his eyes were on the lookout for the next thing.

He double-checked that the safe was locked when he shut it, giving the handle a swift pull. When Rutherford got up off his knees, a crippling dizziness hit his head. He went straight to the toilet and leaned his head over to get rid of three-quarters of the bottle of wine. The no dinner didn't help.

After spending the next few hours crippled to the bathroom floor tiles, he made his way to bed for the night.

The next day when he woke up it was clear he forgot to set his alarm. Eight thirty-seven, and he was still in bed. The only time Rutherford saved was not having to pick out his clothes but he showed up to the office late.

Jax already had a search warrant slid under Rutherford's door by the time he got to the office.

They were able to get the search warrant back from Judge Abbott within three hours after Rutherford looked it over. The old judge made time between his court cases and before his mid-day nap to sign it. With the paper in hand, Rutherford rounded up his men once again.

He advised them this game of cops and robbers would likely be over in the next week, after which they would be back at desk jobs. The guys were probably fine with that though as the case seemed to cause a missed lunch hour every day.

Down in the staging bay, Rutherford let Jax and Lou take the lead on briefing the execution of the warrant. On the large whiteboard, Lou put the pictures from the night before showing the target and the auto shop. They figured it would be best to pick Donny up at the shop and not his house, to take him off guard.

The plan was to have Jax drive in as a regular customer in plain clothes and Lou would provide backup close-up the street. The remaining six guys would set a perimeter and stand by. It was routine work for the guys, simple enough.

Lou asked if everyone understood the plan and there were no questions. Even Rutherford was on board and his face said he was quite impressed with the plan. Jax got into a red Toyota Corolla that was in the bay, and Lou took a dark blue Mustang. The rest of the guys dressed in their vests took the two trucks.

When they got to the industrial zone, Rutherford's truck took the street behind Superior Tire and Wheels. Through a line of sparse trees, they could see the metal fence and back lot of the shop. It looked more like a junkyard than customers' cars. Some that Donny kept were decrepit with rust.

One agent stayed in the truck while Rutherford took the far end of the street and the other agent took the close end. The truck was in the middle between both.

The other truck dropped a guy off to the street on the right of the building and one to the left, parking the truck way down the street in front of the shop. They had built a four-sided perimeter for the strike.

With the go signal on the radio, Jax led the way down the one way. The Mustang followed inconspicuously and parked fifty yards up the street. As Jax approached the shop, only the left bay door was open. A few cars sat out front, including Donny's black Mustang.

Blocking the door on the left, Jax got out of the Corolla and walked into the shop. One guy with a greasy shirt was on a tire machine putting a new tire on a rim. The other employee was working on a truck raised on the second lift. Jax stood at the counter until Donny came out of his office. He wasn't wearing a blue striped uniform shirt like his two employees, instead just a black tee shirt. His biceps protruded out from the sleeves.

"Hello, I was at the stop light up on the main road and there started to be a knocking noise in my engine. Can you come outside and have a quick look?" Jax asked.

"If there's a knocking sound, it's best to leave it here and we will check it out."

Donny wouldn't budge from behind his desk for some guessing work.

"Hey Donny, can you give me a hand for a second!" the workers on the second lift yelled.

"Just a sec." Donny told Jax as he went over and helped with a stuck bolt. His biceps looked like they could rip through his shirt when he muscled the wrench. Donny came back over and carried it in his right hand.

"So, do you want to leave your car here or what?"

"I have a scratch on the back bumper as well. Can you have a look at that and see if you can fix it?"

Donny obliged and followed Jax out to the Corolla. He saw the Mustang up the street with Lou sitting in it and something didn't feel right. The street hardly ever had sitting cars.

"So where's this scratch?" Donny asked, standing on the left side of Jax. There was nothing too visible.

"These little ones here." Jax pointed with his finger to some tiny knicks.

Getting onto a knee, Donny had a closer look and rubbed his left hand across the bumper.

A familiar sound went into Donny's ears as he heard a gun being drawn behind him.

"FBI lay down on the ground!" Jax shouted.

Immediately, Donny knew the scratches on the bumper were too small for anyone to fix. He had been made. Signaling over his radio, Jax said they got him. It wasn't true.

Slowly, Donny stood up.

"Get down on the ground!" Jax tried to kick the back of Donny's knee. It did push him a little off balance but not enough. Turning around quickly, Donny pushed the gun with his left hand and swung the wrench to Jax's temple with his right.

Immediately, it sent Jax to the parking lot. Blood was flowing out just to the left of his eye. He saw Donny step over him and pick up the gun between flashes of light, then blacking out.

"Move in! Move in! Agent down!" Lou yelled over the radio as soon as Jax's body hit the ground. The Mustang rumbled as he turned it on and made the quick sprint down the street toward the auto shop.

Donny put the gun in his waistband and sprinted to his own Mustang. Donny and Jax could both hear Lou's car coming but they didn't know who he was coming for. Groaning, Jax rolled onto his side on the pavement, covered in blood.

The thunderous roar of Donny's Mustang dwarfed the exhaust of Lou's stock car. Hopping up into the right side of the parking lot, sparks kicked off the undercarriage of Lou's car. Donny flew out to the left.

Lou couldn't ignore Jax lying between them in the middle of the parking lot and pulled in next to him.

"Damn it, what's the location, Lou?" Rutherford yelled over the radio. The officer at the far end of the street and himself were sprinting back to the truck.

"He's going to come out the end of the street. He passed me in a blacked-out Mustang, going north toward the other truck."

Throwing his door open, Lou knelt next to Jax. He was conscious but still bleeding. Running back to the car, Lou had a first aid kit in the trunk. Grabbing it, he went back to put a wrap of gauze around Jax's head. He looked like a wounded soldier, laid out on the pavement.

The other agent saw Donny flying up the street in his Mustang and tried to meet him on the road with his truck. He knew the push bar on the front would stop Donny like hitting a brick wall.

Donny swerved to the right, inches from the truck barreling at him. His right wheel drove up on the sidewalk for a brief second to avoid the agent. The two guys locked eye contact as Donny drove past him.

There was something about the adrenaline rush that Donny loved. His heart was pumping through his chest and his freedom was on the line, but this was his zone. Everything seemed to slow down as he looked in the rearview mirror and saw the light bar of the truck flashing red, blue, and white.

At the end of the street, Donny made a quick left. There wasn't much traffic when he peeled out. He couldn't decide between taking the back streets to lose the agents or putting the pedal to the floor on the highway. Halfway to the highway, his decision didn't matter.

He saw it in his peripherals and in a split second, couldn't believe it was getting closer. The metal from the front of Rutherford's truck collided with the Mustang on the passenger side. The noise could be heard around the block.

The impact shook Donny up and slammed his head into the driver's side window. There was blood coming down his forehead from his hair-line. He looked over and could see Rutherford behind the wheel. Rutherford put his truck in reverse and backed up ten yards to create some space. Instinctively, Donny climbed out as quickly as he could. Falling to his knees, he got back up and started running.

There was a sharp pain in his ribs when he inhaled and exhaled. Donny could hear his breath and the shouting of the agents in the background.

It was the first time Donny was scared. He dodged the traffic on the street and ducked behind a silver car parked along the sidewalk. Donny hugged it tight with his body. Rutherford opened his door and took cover. The other two agents did the same.

Raising his hand, Rutherford signed his agent from the back to fan out on the left and take cover behind a car across from Donny. The agent sprinted over to the better shooting angle.

Behind the car, Donny wiped the warm blood from his face and then checked the magazine in the pistol. It was full.

Donny couldn't even imagine the time for this one. Twenty-five years at least. Maybe life with his priors. This wasn't a spot he thought he'd be in. He chambered a round. If a shoot-off is what it came to, Donny wasn't scared. Heck, it might have even been better than jail again.

Instead of engaging, Donny slid the pistol under the car onto the street. It made a loud scrape across the pavement but it was muffled by the sirens. Next came Donny's hands. They were straight up into the air as he started to stand up. Clearly, he was no visible threat but Rutherford thought he could be to his money.

As Donny emerged from behind the car, three shots rang out. They were quick and all from Rutherford's gun.

"Pop! Pop! Pop!"

The lead sunk into Donny's chest in a triangle pattern. Two bullets ripped into his lungs and one into his sternum. His black tee shirt filled up with liquid and he couldn't stop it. The force sent Donny back onto the ground.

Rutherford holstered his weapon and yelled for the other agent to call an ambulance. He knew it was too late though. The shooting was calculated, meticulous, self-defense, he'd say if asked. Donny's fingerprints were all over an agent's gun. Rutherford knew it was too easy to close the case. Better than leaving it open, that was for sure.

The other truck of Rutherford's agents showed up on the scene. Then the ambulance got there five minutes later as the police went over first to the body. They couldn't confirm it but the ambulance personnel had the qualification to say, he was dead.

"These criminals always think they have a good run until they are caught," Rutherford told his other agents who were looking at Donny. "That was a justified shoot. It was us or him. Remember that guys."

Local police set up yellow tape around the area of the shooting and were taking pictures. The tape was barely enough to hold back the reporters who were showing up on the scene not long after by listening to the police broadband.

"You guys ok?" an older police officer with no hair up the middle of his head asked. His tone was like a monk, so the haircut was fitting but it was due to age and not a haircut.

"We're fine thankfully," Rutherford replied while rounding up his men.

"That was some good shooting," another agent commended Rutherford.

The comment had no merit, as the only time that agent took his gun out of his holster was to polish it. While Rutherford stood around waiting for a formal interview with the local police, Lou rang over the phone. He said Jax was in the hospital's hands but would be fine.

"Did you get him?" Lou asked.

"Of course we did. We served justice."

"Jax is going to appreciate that. I'll let him know. I'm going to head down to the hospital and check in on him."

"Sounds good. Hey if you need to take a day off, feel free to take one tomorrow. It should be pretty slow in the office and I'll write up this report with the guys."

Lou thanked Rutherford before getting off the phone. Then one of Rutherford's other men came up to get his attention.

"Sir, Nine News is asking if they can get an interview over at their truck."

Nodding, Rutherford ducked his tall body under the yellow caution tape and went over to the large white van. It had a large dish on top for broadcasting the news. Their signature red writing logo was on the side of the van.

Wendy was fixing her hair as Rutherford walked over. He knew of her. Everyone in Chicago did. Generally, Rutherford would get an interview approved or not do one at all but he did want to set the facts on this one.

Letting him look over the questions, Wendy asked if he was ready to go live. As soon as Rutherford gave the ok, the cameraman threw his hand up in the air to start counting down with his fingers. Five. Four. Three. Two. One.

Anyone watching at home saw the red banner fly across the screen with breaking news and the signature intro.

"We're going live with Nine News now! Reporting on the latest developments in Chicago." Wendy shouted with passion into the mic. She described the scene and location as the crew played shots of the agent's truck and Donny's car smashed together in the middle of the street.

"We're here with Special Agent Rutherford of the Chicago FBI field office. How would you describe the scene here today?"

"Thanks, Wendy, it's been a chaotic day. I can't say much of the ongoing investigation. We had a good lead, went to make the arrest, and took fire from the suspect. Fortunately, none of our guys were hurt. The suspect is seeking medical treatment at this time."

After Wendy highlighted the suspect was armed and shot at the agents to her viewers, she closed the segment, thanking Rutherford for the exclusive, off-camera.

There was a flatbed already pulling up to take Donny's car out of the street. It was a wreck, but salvageable with a good mechanic.

Chapter Twenty-Four

Aftermath

It was a week before an investigation into the shooting of Donny was concluded. Jack was notified as part of the family Donny had. Rutherford had to attend multiple questioning sessions with the local police but reaffirmed his stance that he thought the suspect shot first. The ballistics team easily told otherwise and that Rutherford was the only shooter. With the gun at the scene, the chase, and evidence linking Donny to the robbery, it was hard to argue with Rutherford or a dead man. He didn't have much to say.

The investigation into the fourth accomplice dried up while the team put together more pieces. They finished the search warrant on Donny's house and shop. There wasn't much to be found in terms of money. The agent's biggest break was Ray's motorcycle still in Donny's shop. It was never moved since the robbery and the license plate was a direct link.

Records in Donny's office went on to show the shop was short on cash as the agents sifted through them. Some of the machines were new on the floor and more was being spent than coming in the door. He kept an unregistered firearm in his desk drawer but that wasn't much help to the investigation. The shop ended up closing for a while.

In the weeks after Donny's death, the agents also hit the warehouse which made Tommy good on his word. The owner of the warehouse, a frail man in his late seventies, couldn't give any information of use to the agents when they arrived at his home. He just collected his money and was happy every month. If anything, he was most disappointed to hear they shot his tenant and the money would stop coming in.

The CPD police assisted in the warehouse search and even Patterson got another press conference. At that rate, he was setting himself up to be the future chief of police.

A team from the bureau took apart the truck looking for fingerprints or any clues but they were impressed with the job done by the crew. The truck was spotless, even to the best agents. The only holes in it were the bullet holes. It took the team time, but they were able to alert the bakery they had found their stolen truck. One thing they could not sort out was the link to Presto Pest. The large logo of the roach stared at them. Jax had a photographer snap pictures to take back to a war room set up inside the bureau.

Inside the war room, on the right side of a corkboard, hung pictures of the three guys, Ray, Donny, and Tommy. Rutherford and Lou let Jax take a red Sharpie and put it through Donny's picture. Ray and Tommy were already crossed off. White string connected Ray's photo to the two other guys. They had him pinned as the leader. A picture of a question mark was on the board as well. On the left were crime scene pictures. The vault, the parking garage, Donny's shop, Tommy's house, and the warehouse were all scattered.

Jax was finally healing up, although he had a scar on the side of his head from the impact. He spread out photos of the guys' vehicles on the wood table, looked at the Presto Pest truck, and then looked at the whiteboard beside the corkboard. For weeks, it had a running list of the same names of persons of interest. Mr. Granger, Susan, a few Presto Pest employees, the two men who worked at Donny's shop, and two bank security guards. The guards had black strikeouts on their names. Jack's name was still on the list as they had linked him as Donny's cousin.

Susan stood out to them as the scheduler but clearly she wouldn't have been able to waddle into the bank. The guys were all linked by Donny's phone records. There were outgoing calls to each of the guys and incoming calls as well same.

"I reckon we pay Presto Pest a visit, along with the guys at the shop," Lou suggested.

If it was up to Rutherford, he would close the case without the fourth member but the CCTV footage on the news networks showed four guys again and again. The city wanted four guys.

"Yeah, I want to get back out there and put this to bed. What are your guys' feelings?" Jax asked.

"I have none," Rutherford said, while holding a picture of the vault at the table. He wasn't going to share his feelings that he would have liked all that money in the vault and only had some.

"I'm thinking it couldn't have been the guys at the shop. They would have run in all the commotion."

Jax cocked his head to the side and supposed that could be true.

The next day, Lou and Jax took a black unmarked squad car out to Presto Pest. Parking on the sidewalk in front of the building, they were there before any other employees. Lou had worked on cases before with blue-collar workers, they just worked too much and could be hard to track down. It wasn't long before the first technician drove up into the side parking lot and grabbed his keys from the lockbox.

The white box truck came flying out of the parking lot, almost taking the mirror off the squad car. Four more trucks came out of the parking lot and the lights were still off in the main office as it approached half past seven. Lou and Jax were specifically looking for Jack's red truck to pull in or Susan's car. Both of which they were beginning to think of as people who show up late.

Just as they thought that they saw movement at the front door. The receptionist let herself in, turned on the lights, and not long after, Susan arrived. Even from afar in the car, the guys had no trouble telling it was her and matching her up to the pictures in the war room. She was almost as wide as the front door and her hair looked grayer by the day.

"Head in and I'll wait for Jack."

"You sure?" Jax asked.

Lou didn't know Jack but he felt a woman almost in her retirement age would be less of a fight for Jax. Slamming the car door, Jax headed up the concrete front steps and pulled open the door.

"Excuse me, I'm here to see Susan Ritchie."

"And you are?" The receptionist was kind but frank. She looked over Jax in his black polo and dress pants. Not a typical pest control interview candidate that she often saw.

He leaned over the counter to show her his badge. "FBI."

"There sure have been a lot of you coming around the past few weeks. Let me see if Ms. Ritchie can see you." She stepped away and walked down the hall. *A lot of us?* Jax thought to himself, perplexed.

She came back a moment later. "I don't think she wants to see you now, but she can. Go down the hall and you can't miss the large opening on the right."

Thanking her, Jax walked down the hall cautiously. He wasn't in the mood to put up with this lady he had heard about but rounding the corner he had to.

"I heard you are from the FBI. You guys still haven't closed the case? What's it going to take you, years?" And she was serious.

"Well, thanks for taking the time to meet with me today, mam. I just have a few additional questions from, I guess, the last time you spoke to some agents."

"Yeah, I wouldn't even be talking to you unless it was for Mr. Granger, who advised me I should cooperate."

The two went back and forth for the next twenty minutes. In walked Mr. Granger to his office and stopped.

"Ah, another one," he said to Susan. "Well, keep him entertained for a bit." He smiled, but she didn't find it funny. The conversation went on another twenty minutes before he was convinced that the old lady didn't have a part in it. Frankly, they weren't going to figure out who moved up the date. Jax had come to the realization. Susan wanted confirmation they wouldn't come back and interrupt her again at work and he gave her that promise.

Jax expected to find Lou in the car waiting for him but when he walked out the front doors, he saw the car was empty. Heading around to the side lot, he found Jack and Lou talking next to the chain-link fence. It looked like Lou had caught Jack as soon as he parked his car.

Expressive with his hands, Jax could see Lou was explaining something important to Jack but he was too far to hear. As he got closer to the two, Lou gave Jack and card and reassured him, "Call me if you know anything". Lou stuck out his hand for a shake. His goal was to make Jack feel like they were on the same team. Jack didn't feel that way when he shook Lou's cold large hand that housed a crushing grip.

"What was that all about?" Jax asked as they walked back to his car.

"I put a little fear in him but told him we're on the same team. The guy explained he had an alibi. The guy swears he didn't leave his house that day and his wife can verify."

"Yeah? Ha!" Jax laughed aloud. "Like he's going to fall for your fear-mongering. We'll have to check out his alibi. Man, that Susan is a dead end. There ain't no way that she's connected. I'd say take her off the board." They both opened the car doors and headed back to the bureau with much of the day left.

Rutherford was around at mid-lunch while the guys were putting sandwiches down their throats. He rapped on Jax's cubical from behind. The guy really couldn't catch some lunch break peace to save his life. The remainder was for qualifications at the indoor range in the afternoon. One that had completely slipped Jax's mind. Sure enough, it was on the calendar that Lou pulled up. Rutherford made a pistol symbol with his pointer finger and thumb. After firing off a couple imaginary rounds into the air, he told them he'd see them at the elevators in forty.

They all met and rode the elevator down seven floors to the basement. Due to the size of their small office, Rutherford had the keys to the shooting range since he was the most senior agent. He lived for qualifications and would often go shooting many nights after work. Jax wasn't a fan of the biannual requirement to score at least eighty percent of five hundred points. It's why the team usually put him on the breacher.

Flipping up the lights, Rutherford illuminated the two shooting lanes. They had clean paper targets with the outlines of bad guys. The paper men had pictures of fake guns shooting down the lane.

"Alright, who wants to go first?" Rutherford challenged the guys, standing with score sheets in hand. Lou took the offer. He took a pair of earmuffs from a table in the shooting lane then handed pairs to the other guys. His stance was shoulder width apart in the booth as he readied for Rutherford to hit the buzzer.

Buzz! A green light lit up on the lane.

Rutherford smashed his thumb on a timer as Lou emptied the thirteen-round clip into the paper target. It was an impressive time but what was even more impressive was the shot grouping at twenty-five yards. Ten shots were to the chest and three to the head, all shedding the paper. Rutherford applied a complex formula that multiplied the time taken against the points for the area and came out to 437.

"Nice shooting Lou. That might be the best we'll see all day."

Lou took out the magazine and began filling it up with more bullets. Stepping up to the range, Jax fired off his rounds and scored 405.

"Not bad, not bad. So how'd you guys make out this morning?" asked Rutherford as he handed off the clipboard, pen, and stopwatch to Lou. Chiming in, Jax explained it was pretty much a dead end. There were no slip-ups that led to it being anyone but the most convincing was Jack.

"At the same time, I couldn't get around his demeanor. His body language wasn't giving me any signs when I mentioned the heist to him and his connection to Donny Macintosh," said Lou.

"Yeah ... that is a strange one if he's our guy. Do we have enough for a warrant with any of these four?" Rutherford asked and then put his hand up for silence. He was ready to show the guys how to shoot.

The light came on and his gun went off, over and over. Seconds from a record time, Rutherford holstered his weapon and hit a buzzer signaling an all-clear on the range.

"How was that?" he said with a cocky smile on his face. "How are we going to close this case out, boys?" It was a reoccurring theme but

Rutherford knew only three things ever closed a case. A bigger case, the right suspect or the wrong one. None of which it seemed like they could get to fall their way.

Lou came back with the calculation of his score, 455, announcing it was the highest one all day. Rutherford wasn't surprised. He often said he was one of the fastest shooters in the FBI. Being the competitor that he was, he asked if the guys wanted another crack at a better score. They were just there for the qualification and didn't care as long as they passed.

The three headed back up the elevator and with only a few hours left in the day, Rutherford gave them the last hour off. Now and then he did nice things like that. It wasn't like he was a bad guy to work for. People just found it best to be on his good side.

Inside his office, he sat down and there was a white sealed mailer on his keyboard. The outside read, "Federal Bureau of Prisons". Taking a metal letter opener off his desk, Rutherford cut into the mailer. It was a notice of prison transfer for Tommy Fox.

Rutherford hadn't heard of Tommy since he was sentenced to eight years with possible parole after five. It was the best plea deal that Rutherford could arrange. At least that was all the effort he put in. He wasn't motivated to do any better and frankly, that was better than twenty-five years.

In Rutherford's eyes, everyone was a winner. Carry Jones never had to go to trial. He was bound to lose anyway for Tommy. Tommy wouldn't rot in prison forever, just a long time.

The further that Rutherford inspected the letter, he didn't like it. A transfer was set to take place from the Metropolitan Correctional Center in Chicago to the Federal Correctional Institute - Perkin. Rutherford knew some of the correctional officers at the Metro Center from outside work. There were a few inmates there that Rutherford liked to keep tabs on. As for FCI Perkin, he just didn't have the leverage.

Any notice to appeal the transfer by any parties was due in five days. Five days, thought Rutherford... He didn't know what he could use to block the transfer within that short of a time. The letter stated the reasoning was for overcrowding in the city at MCC. Overcrowding... that's no excuse, he thought. All the jails were crowded in this day and age. It also read that they believed Tommy was a lower risk as he took a plea deal and had no prior convictions.

The transfer wasn't something Rutherford was going to solve at five on a Thursday. He took the paper and headed home. On his way, he made a call to which he thought would help him. The ringer buzzed over the speakers of the SUV as he sat at a stoplight. Then the person picked up.

"Hello? Yes, this is him."

"Can you stop by my office tomorrow? There is something I want to discuss."

The person on the other end said they had plans but could do the afternoon. That was fine with Rutherford as long as they came in.

***

Rutherford had stayed up late to think of how he could stop the transfer. He didn't want Tommy to just stay in prison for years, he wanted to own Tommy in prison.

That afternoon, Carry Jones came in to meet with Rutherford after lunch. Carry was in a gray suit and always tried to look the part, even if he was a C-grade lawyer. They took a conference room aside from the war room. Now that Tommy had agreed to a plea deal, Rutherford didn't find a need to pick separate sides. He wanted Carry on his team.

"I don't have much but I can offer you water if you want," Rutherford said while pouring himself a glass from the glass pitcher on the long wood table. The two guys sat across from each other with the pitcher in between.

"I'm fine." Carry sat with his hands folded. He didn't know what to think of the meeting before Rutherford got into it.

He took a swig of his water and began. "So, Tommy. I think he has a pretty good deal with his time that we worked on together but I hear there is a transfer to Perkin Correctional Institution on the cards."

"Yeah, I heard that. It should be good. Get him out of the city. Hopefully not as crazy there."

"Well, that's what I was going to ask you. See if we can have Tommy stay in the city. I think I can be more invested in him when his parole hearings come up."

"That's too far away to worry about now. It's irrelevant. Plus, MCC is for short stays only. Tommy is in for a while."

Carry wouldn't budge even after a few more tries. What could this guy want? thought Rutherford. It couldn't come over as direct but there had to be something this guy wanted.

"I'll tell you what, we both work for the public. Isn't that right?" Rutherford asked.

"Yeah."

"Well, you support me on this one case, and next big one, I'll throw the judge your name."

Even that didn't mean much to Jones. He already had enough cases to defend that he needed an extra year of work to catch up.

"Nah, that doesn't work. I'm happy to see Tommy get transferred. It's best for him."

Rutherford couldn't comprehend this guy's issue. They were both on the same side, so why did it matter? The personal dislike could be felt in both seats.

Carry scooted out of his chair and stood up. He told Rutherford if this was all he brought him down to the bureau for, then it was a waste of his time. To be fair, at least he had some honor in his role.

Showing him to the door, Rutherford didn't want to have to resort to his backup plan but he always had a contingency. Shutting the conference room door, he rang a connection at Metro Corrections. To say that the guy owed Rutherford a favor was an understatement. The only person that got him off the hook for beating his wife was Rutherford.

Charlie Wood answered the phone.

"I'm on shift. What's up Rut?"

Rutherford went on to tell him what he needed. It was between a big ask and a small ask. The two guys saw it on opposite ends of the spectrum.

"Can you do that for me? You know you…"

"I owe you one. I know, I know but after this, we are even. No more favors, man."

Agreeing, Rutherford asked for Charlie to give word when he had news, then hung up.

Jen was cleaning the house during the day when she became part of the criminals too. She had just finished vacuuming, the dishes and dusting. The last item on her list of chores was to clean the toilets.

One thing Jack did like about her was she was much cleaner than him and she didn't rag on him generally for how dirty he was. After cleaning the upstairs bathroom, she took a toilet bowl brush and cleaned the brown scummy ring off the downstairs toilet. The crud looked like it hadn't been cleaned in months but the bathroom hardly was used anyway. After a weak flush, brown gook still was dripping into the bowl.

She took the lid off which revealed a build-up of mold and iron but also a bag. The bag was a clear plastic freezer bag that she pulled out. It dropped water across the floor until she put it into the sink to dry off.

What the hell is that? She thought.

It was green, money green. Opening the bag, that is exactly what it was. $3,000 worth to be exact, when she counted the hundred-dollar bills. She couldn't believe her eyes and gasped.

Jen had never seen money like that in her life, let alone in her own house. If not her, then Jack put it there. *But why?* She wondered. *And how?*

Even if it was the raise from work, who in their right mind puts it in the tank of the toilet she asked herself.

It was still four to five hours until Jack got home but she was determined to ask him some questions. What was he not telling her? She wanted to know. Putting the money back where she found it, she left it until she could get more information.

When Jack walked in, in the evening, it was to his surprise who he saw in the living room. The girls were playing on the floor as usual with Jen supervising but Jen's mom Alice was also watching the girls.

Alice was in her mid-seventies and a heavy smoker. That gave her the look of being in her eighties with the wrinkles on her face and hands. Jack knew the only time she was over was to babysit and that hadn't been in five months. It was cheap to have Alice babysit for free but Jen and Jack weren't able to have a date in the past months regardless with no money.

Having Alice come over always worried Jack. When he left his kids with her, he just hoped she'd be alive still at the end of the night. He could never tell with people her age.

"Hon, I was thinking, we go out tonight. Change things up for a bit and get a night off.

"It's ladies' night at Lucky's. I was thinking we could get some food and drinks there," Jenn said.

While Jack was skeptical, it's not like he was going to turn down Lucky's on a Thursday night. Ladies' night meant at least there would be a lot for him to look at. It wasn't a no-brainer since they had Alice but Jack figured she could only do a few hours.

Chapter Twenty-Five

Lucky's or Unlucky

Although Jen appeared like she wanted a night out, she was livid the entire ride to Lucky's. Feelings that she kept inside. They stirred inside her stomach as all she wanted was the truth.

Jack parked the Ranger which was starting to have a whirling noise coming from a belt. He was glad to shut it off because it was a head-turner. Embarrassing. At least Jen didn't judge Jack's truck, partially because it was their only vehicle. He just wondered how he'd fix it now with Donny gone.

The two walked into Lucky's and Jen picked a wood high-top table in the corner. It gave them some privacy from the bar and the pool tables.

For Lucky's to call it Ladies' Night was a joke. There were three men for every single woman, with a total of three women in the bar. The bartender who looked like he hadn't shaved in a week doubled as the waiter. He came over and laid two sticky menus on the table while he took drink orders. Jen stared Jack in the eyes devilishly and smiled a little.

"Hon, what haven't you been telling me?" She grabbed Jack's hand to hold.

"There's nothing on my mind. I think you know everything about our relationship, babe."

"Today I found money in the downstairs toilet tank. When were you going to tell me about that? Where is it from?" She started to get worked up but then the waiter brought over drinks.

"Will you two be ordering food?"

Jack went for a burger as he usually did and Jen took the grilled chicken salad.

"Answer me," she said when the waiter was out of hearing distance.

"I don't know what you mean, Jen."

"Don't play stupid with me, Jack. The girls didn't put it there and I wouldn't be asking if I did!"

Why the hell did she look there? Jack wondered. "That pay increase from Mr. Granger, well there, you found it."

Jen leaned back in her chair. She wasn't believing it or buying it. Her face was squinted in confusion. "He gives you cash? And you shove that cash in the toilet tank?"

"It's confusing, I know."

"No, Jack! Confusing is one thing. A lie is another. Tell me the truth. I think you were wrapped up with all that shit Donny was into before he died."

Jack felt trapped. Was it even worth it to continue the lies? Out of respect for Donny, he didn't. He leaned over the table closer to Jen and lowered his voice. It didn't stop his angry tone.

"Yeah, I was with Donny and yeah, I don't want to lose the roof over our head. I want our girls to go to good schools when they grow up and not have to worry about money."

"Well, what does that entail, Jack."

She hadn't figured it all out but she was led that something had changed.

"I helped Donny a bit with that bank downtown."

"You what?" Jen's eyes popped out larger but more from shock than anger. Then the food arrived. She couldn't wait for the waiter to walk away. Her mind couldn't comprehend what her ears had just heard.

"I knew... I just knew when I saw the Presto Pest truck on TV."

"That wasn't a Presto Pest truck," Jack said calmly.

"Well, it sure looked like it!" She could hardly control her emotions. Flustered, flabbergasted, she was a bit of everything. He explained that the truck was stolen and they had put the wrap on it, so technically it wasn't a Presto truck.

"I'm done." She pushed her plate forward. "I can't eat."

"You are being overdramatic," Jack said while taking another bite of his burger.

"Dramatic? Coming from a guy who robbed a bank, my husband, of all things."

Her attitude was so bad that no one would have wanted to be subjected to it. To their left, two guys cracked a white billiards ball into a racked set to start a game. Jack always knew there was going to be a catch for Lucky's on a Thursday night and Alice at their house, come on.

The attitude didn't scare him though. It may have been before all this but he wasn't the same person as before. He could care less about her mood and judgments. The waiter came around to check in and see if the food was ok but he could tell the meal wasn't. Jack politely asked for the tab.

They settled up and went outside. Once Jack lit up a cigarette, Jen refused to get into the truck until it was out, so they stood there. There were as many stars in the sky as questions she still had. The colder air calmed her mood and she finally came to her senses.

Pulling down the worn-out red tailgate to his Ranger, Jack offered her a seat.

"What do you want to know? The less is probably for the better," he said while flicking red ash onto the ground. Then she realized it was over two weeks after the robbery and he still wasn't caught.

"Will they, are they going to arrest you?" she leaned against his shoulder.

"I don't know. I spoke to the cops recently as they came to Presto Pest and told them I was home all day. They may call to verify my alibi." He shook his head back and forth slowly. His hands gave the remark that he didn't care. "You and the girls will be set for life. It doesn't matter anymore but it was never the plan for it to fall out like it did." Jack stared off into the distance. She didn't ask any more about the money and agreed to stick with his story. He watched the C, in Lucky's neon sign flicker. At any moment, he figured it would die but maybe it was luck that kept it on.

"I know it is a lot to process, I know it is late and I was going to tell you... eventually, but for now, I wanted you to be safe." Laying back on his back in the bed of the truck, Jack stared up at the stars in the parking lot. The view would have been better with his pickup truck in the middle of a field, on a farm. Maybe one day, he thought.

"The money was just for the mortgage and stuff. I never thought that you would find it."

"Well, I guess better me than a cop." She gave a little laugh and smile and rolled on top of him with the cold metal button of her blue jeans pressing into him. Something got in her to make her happy. It was just hard to tell if the happiness came from the money, Jack being out of jail, or that the truth was shared. At least Jack had the feeling that she wouldn't be calling the cops tomorrow to report him.

"I've been thinking about one more thing."

"What's that?" she asked as she rolled back over next to him.

"I was thinking I get the guys at the shop to fix up Donny's car. I'm sure they would be more than happy to. He built that thing with those guys. It'd mean a lot to me."

He didn't have to convince her. Jen was for it without a doubt and wanted him to get rid of his truck for so long anyway.

"Let's do it. I think that's the best we can do right now." She smiled as her mood had come full circle.

***

The orange jumpsuit just wasn't a fitting look for Tommy. He laid in bed, staring up at the bunk above him, wishing he had a pair of blue jeans and a tee shirt. Boy, the money he'd pay for more comfortable underwear.

Days started to mesh together in Tommy's mind as every day seemed the same. Wake up, eat. Yard, eat. Nap, eat. Sleep. His cellmate, a credit card fraudster, had run out of stories to tell him and it had only been weeks together. At least he was a similar build and not threatening to Tommy.

Twenty stories up, the concrete jungle of the yard was a far cry from where he wanted to be. He spent most of his time walking around. The real hunt was to find a blade of grass that would have landed on top of the building, somehow, some way.

Tommy wondered how much the razor wire would cut him if he climbed to the top or if the fall would hurt more. Or would the fall be painless? He had too much time to think. The officer blew a whistle to line the guys up and take them back inside.

As the metal cell door slammed behind him, Tommy couldn't think of anything except a proper hamburger, proper fries, and a proper soda. Carry Jones wasn't kidding him when he had told Tommy to consider not taking a plea deal since the food was so bad. Every meal seemed to be mush, slop or goop and of course a slice of cheap white bread. Everything went into Tommy the same way it came out.

Although Tommy usually went to the cafeteria for food, there was some sort of lockdown. He heard word that there was a fight in the adjacent ward and there'd be no cafeteria for the day.

A fellow prisoner was delivering food to all the cells but it didn't come to Tommy. Even the cells on either side of them got food. Tommy asked the prisoner who was bringing the food to the other cells and his response was simply, "Charlie is bringing it."

That was fine with the guys. Inside the prison, Charlie was one of the more liked guards. Tommy liked to think he could tell when a guard was crooked and he would never have thought that of Charlie. His mustache and beer belly just didn't make him as intimidating as some of the other guards. It was a wonder how he passed the physical test every year but then again, Charlie seemed to slim up come every October. Being it was April, he was still overweight.

It was strange though to Tommy and the cellmate. They had never been skipped when it came to their food.

The metal keys on Charlie's duty belt announced him before he got to their cell. Then he hit the metal bars with his baton to give it a knock.

"Gentlemen," he greeted them as they opened the metal flap to the cell.

"Complements of Rutherford."

Charlie handed a heavy tray to Tommy and then a separate one to his cellmate. The guys inspected the food.

"Who is this Rutherford guy?" his cellmate asked.

Tommy didn't want to explain he took a plea deal with an FBI agent so he lied and said he had connections inside the jail.

Taking off the lid, Tommy revealed three tacos, a burrito, and cilantro lime rice. His cellmate's tray had eight pieces of pizza on it, four different types. It was the best food they had seen since getting in there.

"You know it should all be mine, right? You better save me two pieces." Tommy said to his cellmate. "You will owe me for this."

"Can't be, so they just would have brought me no food?" the guy remarked from the top bunk. He had already finished a slice of pizza, which in Tommy's mind, they only got because of his connection to Rutherford. For a split second, Tommy had thought about offering some food from his plate but in reality, he didn't know how many years until he saw food this good again. It was five-star, even for fast food compared to the stuff MCC was serving every day.

Once Tommy finished his rice, he demolished two tacos. If Rutherford had only sent Irish food, but he wasn't complaining. He'd give an arm for some corned beef. Saving a taco for later, he did eat the burrito even though he was practically already full. It was so much food that he had to lie down with his stomach hurting.

Rolling to his side, a knot went through his stomach. A loud gargle made him grip his lower stomach.

"Man, you eat all this prison food, and look at you. Can't handle the good stuff anymore. I'm not even sure you'll want that pizza I saved for you."

Tommy didn't reply. He could only wince in pain on his bed. He wondered if his body was only used to the subpar food or if he ate too much. Trying to rest it off, he couldn't sleep. His cellmate went to the yard when it was their time but Tommy stayed behind in his cell, hugging the bed with his body.

An hour later, the sweats hit him. He put the back of his hand to his forehead and could feel a fever coming on. The only way to the toilet was a crawl over the chilly concrete floor and it felt far. Tommy went for it on his hands and knees. The cold concrete radiated up through his hot palms providing a bit of relief. What seemed like a mile crawl was just feet. Then he was able to stick his head over the uncleaned toilet bowl.

Puking up what seemed like all the food, Tommy felt weak. He laid on his back and stared up at the cell ceiling as a headache rushed in. There was no average food poisoning that could come in that fast. Especially with his cellmate still in good health.

The thoughts that ran through Tommy's head weren't great. *Will the pain get any worse? Can I make it out of this?* He seriously didn't know. Then he heard footsteps and keys jangling. He rolled over onto his stomach to see who was walking by.

"Excuse me. I need to see a nurse."

Looking at his pale face, the guard saw he wasn't making it up. Through his couple weeks at MCC, Tommy had seen guys faking stuff to go to the infirmary but not him. The pain ripped through his abdomen.

"Ok, ok. Well, can you stand?" the guard asked while unlocking his cell. The way Tommy stood up was like an eighty-five-year-old man with a hunchback. He leaned forward gripping his stomach the entire way to the infirmary.

Inside the small waiting room, a guard sat at a desk and the inmate chairs were spread apart on the outside of the small room with four feet in between. It gave the guard a few seconds to react when there was a rare stabbing between inmates. At least they were already at the infirmary when that happened.

Taking a seat, Tommy was sandwiched between a fat white guy with a bald head on his right and a skinny black guy on the left. Instead of hair, the white guy had a spiderweb tattoo on his head. A real art lover, Tommy thought while assessing the terrifying-looking man. He could probably snap Tommy's twig body in half.

The guy on the left was less scary. He was in his late twenties and looked like any other individual who would be in on a petty crime. Probably locked up for more time than what he committed, Tommy figured. Then Tommy's name was called.

He went to the back room and was greeted by another guard giving him a serious stare. The nurse was kind though. She wasn't as pretty as the prison nurses Tommy had seen in movies and was a little older than he liked but any female was better than no females.

She asked him to lie down as she pushed on his abdomen. Nothing seemed strange. The only strange thing was that the pain started after eating lunch, which she found out from questioning him. The nurse asked if his cellmate was having complications too but it was only Tommy.

With all the throwing up that Tommy did before getting to the infirmary, her hunch was that whatever it was, was now out of his system. She put a cool ice pack on his head and hooked up an IV, then drew the curtains around the bed closed.

Before moving on to the next patient, she filled out paperwork for Tommy's folder. Marking down his sickness meant no transfer for thirty days. A rule Tommy wasn't aware of.

Chapter Twenty-Six

New Beginnings

Sitting on the phone with a song that kept saying to hold, Jack's lunch hour was almost up. *Do these government workers even work?* After a maze of a touch-tone directory and waiting for twenty minutes, he finally got through.

Once he verified himself, the lady on the other end of the phone gave the shop where the tow company had taken Donny's car. Luckily, it was just a few blocks from Donny's shop at a tow yard. He could make it over before work if he just showed up a bit late to work.

Stopping by Superior first on Jack's way to work, the garage doors were up so rightfully he stuck his head inside. He had known Pete for some years, Donny's right-hand mechanic. The guy was skinny with a long ginger beard that couldn't be missed.

"Hey!" Jack yelled over the playing music.

"You doing alright man?"

Pete turned around and wiped as much dirt off his hand as he could before giving Jack a crushing handshake. Working with his tools every day made Pete's handshake like a vise grip.

He said they were getting on just fine but things weren't the same at the shop. The other mechanic and he were keeping it going but even the cars were backing up a bit since they were a man down.

"I need a favor from you if you have time."

"Of course, man, whatcha need?"

"Can we borrow a flatbed? Donny's Mustang is just up the road over at City Collision Center. I was hoping you could look it over and see if it's possible to fix it up for me ... Of course, I'll cover all the costs and labor. I just wanted it since it is sentimental."

"Yeah, no worries at all, man. Let me grab one of these trucks. I'll tell Spencer to watch the shop and we can take a ride up there to check it out."

As the guys left the shop, Jack could see the black rubber marks on the road and scrapes on the sidewalk where Donny drove up onto it. He could only imagine how hectic the scene was when the agents were after him. His phone rang on the way. Jen was on the line, calmer than a person would expect. She told him that she had just got off the phone with the police and confirmed his alibi to them.

A few blocks over and the guys pulled into City Collision Center, the specialists in collisions, so the place said. Pete knew the people working there including the lady behind the desk and some of the mechanics. The lady called a mechanic up who took the guys to the back lot of salvage cars.

"There she is. If you need anything, I'll be just inside there," said the mechanic before leaving Pete and Jack to look it over.

"Wow." Jack had no other words. He walked around it. Every single window was shattered. There were a few bullet holes in the front quarter panel and hood. The front bumper was hanging off on the left side and barely hanging on, on the right.

The worst part was the passenger door side which had been slammed by the push bar of the truck. Donny would have been better off in the passenger seat where the impact would have killed him instantly. Both airbags had deployed and there was glass all over what remained of the passenger seat.

"What do you think?" Pete said as he was lying on the pavement looking up at the underbelly of the car.

"Gosh, I don't know man, I'm not a mechanic. Looks horrible to me. Maybe this was a bad idea."

"Nothing that a little body work and paint can't fix. Might need a seat, axle, drive shaft, or engine work but I can do it for you. Battery looks fine." Pete slammed close the hood. "Let me grab the truck."

Pete backed in the flatbed and winched up the beat-up Mustang onto the bed. The winch cable made a whirling noise and the metal from the car screeched as it was drug up.

When they drove back to the shop, Jack asked how long Pete thought it would take to fix. He said to at least give him a month but he'd try for sooner.

Chapter Twenty-Seven

Yard Bird

"It's done," said Charlie in his deep voice to Rutherford over the phone. Rutherford told him he'd take care of him the next time they saw each other.

It wasn't until the next day that Tommy made it back to his cell. The nurse gave him the news that he would at least be at MCC for another thirty days. His cellmate was lying on the top bunk reading a book when Tommy was let in by the guard. He moved it to the side and was surprised to see Tommy.

"I thought you died and I was going to get another cellmate."

Tommy didn't find it funny. He'd have been tempted to punch the guy but didn't need to start anything with the one guy he lived with.

"So what'd you have?"

"They said it was food poisoning," Tommy said while lying down.

"Well, don't worry, I ate the last two pieces of pizza so you won't have to eat those. I didn't want them to go to waste if you weren't coming back."

Tommy laid there on his back feeling trapped. He had been put in by Rutherford and had minimal contact with the outside. What could he do next? He wondered. Meanwhile, Rutherford was thinking of his next chess move to keep his pawn Tommy in check.

Rutherford knew the clock would tick quickly over the next thirty days and then Tommy would be up for a move again. He thought about labeling

Tommy as a critical informant. That would have kept him in Chicago for a while but he had a better plan up his sleeve.

Later that week, he met up with Charlie when they were both off work in the evening at the Silver Keg Emporium. The brew house had rooftop seating, one of the reasons Rutherford liked the place so much. Charlie was there early, the only place he was timely to was to bars. He had already finished a pint when Rutherford showed up at the picnic table. There was still fresh foam in Charlie's mustache as he greeted Rutherford. His body dwarfed Rutherford who was half his size in width.

Rutherford shook his hand and smiled at him. He sat down and handed Charlie a white envelope. Inside, two thousand dollars in crisp one-hundred-dollar bills. Charlie didn't even care to look inside it, he just put it inside his coat against his chest.

"All is good down there?" Rutherford asked Charlie, referring to the jail. "How's the wife?"

"Just keeping the scum in line. The wife is good though. We have a second little one on the way."

They shot the shit for a while as more beer came to the table. Charlie and Rutherford went way back. Before Rutherford ever got to the FBI, they did a short stint in the police force together. Charlie was honorably discharged although he was removed for use of excessive force while policing. Nothing that the public ever had to know.

"Man, a long way you've come since a young cop in the streets." Charlie laughed and then sipped his beer.

"I suppose but you too! We're keeping this city under control." Rutherford looked around. It was quite empty with mainly just people at the bar sitting under the outdoor string lights. "I have one more favor that I need your help on."

A third round of beers came out since Rutherford arrived as he explained what was needed from Charlie. Luckily, Rutherford was walking distance home because his head started to get a little cloudy sipping on the third beer. He didn't have the tolerance of Charlie who was on his fifth.

"Well, that's going to cost you."

"It always does," said Rutherford. "But you know I'm good for it."

"Twice as much as the last time and that is the rate for friends."

Agreeing, Rutherford reached across the table and shook Charlie's fat hands. He then gave him a second envelope with a thousand dollars.

"The rest when the job is done," he said.

The two went back to the normal chat and Rutherford gestured for the bill. He took it when the waitress brought it and handed his card over. Generally, they'd split but it was a gesture of good faith now that Rutherford was a little richer anyway.

"We should do this more often," Rutherford said when standing up. It was like a sailor trying to find his sea legs. His thin legs wobbled under him and barely kept his torso upright.

Charlie agreed and wanted to but knew it probably wouldn't happen, especially with a kid on the way. He was the only one to think he might not see Rutherford for a long, long time.

***

Jen shouted from the kitchen for Jack to hurry up in the bathroom and get ready. She didn't want them late to Donny's funeral but the way Jack was getting ready; they were surely going to be a few minutes late.

They pulled into the cemetery and walked down quickly to the gravesite as the priest was saying some last words for Donny. He was a younger priest, probably younger than Donny even.

"And he will be remembered by the many great people in his family, his coworkers, and his friends. Donny lived a full life of memories and was a gift to the people around him."

There weren't many people at the funeral so it was good Jack made it. The two guys from the auto shop were there, some close friends and one of Donny's ex-girlfriends. He probably had more friends in jail than ones who could attend the funeral.

Most of the men were somber but Jen had an eye full of tears. She knew most of the time that Donny was a bad influence on Jack and that couldn't have been more true. Her heart still missed him. The priest closed his Bible, and the funeral ended.

Jack and Jen didn't stay to see Donny's coffin get lowered down into the dug-out piece of ground. They took one final look at his headstone and Jen left some flowers.

"Donny Macintosh. February 6, 1981 - April 5, 2023. Gone But Never Forgotten," it read.

Walking up to the truck, the grass was freshly cut and manicured. The spot where Donny was to be buried was peaceful and had oak trees to watch over him.

When they got back to the truck, Jack noticed a black SUV was parked behind them which wasn't there when they left. He was ten yards away when the door opened and a man in a black suit appeared.

"I'm sorry for your loss. Let me know if there is anything I can do at all." Rutherford held out a business card in his hand to Jack but he didn't take it. Instead, Jack ushered Jen into the truck. There was a sinister smile on Rutherford's face and nothing about it showed remorse.

It was a good thing the funeral finished up when it did because the gray skies turned into rain on their way home. Jen asked who the guy was near the truck in between her sobbing. Jack didn't think she had the stomach to hear it was the man who shot Donny. He told her it was just one of Donny's old friends.

When the truck finally got home to the driveway, Jen didn't want to get out. She didn't want the kids to see her as such a mess. At least when she went in, the raindrops on her face hid some of the tears.

***

The work days got tough for Jack with Donny gone. He had all the money he wanted but would have traded it back in a heartbeat. The price was just too much paid in blood between Ray and Donny. Working at Presto Pest became more monotonous than before. At what point could he quit this and be a free man, free from society? He thought. All Jack wanted was to move out to a quiet piece of land and not be bothered anymore, maybe even get a new truck.

His phone rang with a Chicago number as he was putting his sprayer back into his truck.

"You have a collect call from the Metropolitan Correctional Center. Would you like to accept?" Jack declined. It was the third call from that number in two weeks. It had to be Tommy, he thought. He had seen the high-profile news reports when Tommy took a plea deal. Nine News had nothing new to roll on TV for four days.

Jack was conflicted even with the first call. It was worse that this was the third. Donny would have told Jack that taking the front door out of the bank sealed Tommy's fate but they were friends for years. Jack wanted to write Tommy off ever since then but still couldn't. He just hadn't answered.

Walking down the middle of the cell block, Charlie whistled Sittin' On The Dock of the Bay while taking a roll of the prisoners. He got to the second to last cell on the block and opened it up.

"Pipsqueak Jonesss." Charlie said, drawing out his last name. His first name was Anton but no guard had called him that since he entered MCC. Pipsqueak was the only inmate on the cell block to have his own cell, he was also the shortest. His cell was shorter than the rest of the cells due to a few construction errors a long time ago. The guards always rewarded the shortest guy in the cell block with the solo cell.

Pipsqueak had the rein of that small cell for over a year. He was in jail for a spree of armed carjacking and was not due to see freedom for another twelve years. The nail in his crime spree was when he tried to take an undercover agent's car by accident. The agent let him have the car but there were two other agents on him in other cars within seconds.

"What do you want?" Pipsqueak asked while lying on his bed and looking at Charlie. He had a gritty-looking face like a Pitbull that had been in many fights. No one knew if his head had hair because he was always wearing a bright orange beanie. Always. For Pipsqueak, the only amusement he had in weeks was seeing Charlie wedged into the tiny cell.

"I gotta job for you. Pays better than working in the kitchen."

"I'm interested. Let's hear it."

Anything was better than making gallons and gallons of bean soup every day, thought Pipsqueak. He heard out Charlie and gave a resounding yes. It was just the job for his type.

"I'll have it done by the end of the week," Pipsqueak said while Charlie locked the door.

"If you squeak or squeal, then no pay."

Tommy walked around the yard on the top of MCC with one thought. He wished he could see downtown Chicago. Not just through the fence but really walking and seeing downtown Chicago again. Freedom felt like it was taken from the fresh air.

During his time at MCC, he had made friends with two guys who had the same yard time as him, Liam Martin and Patrick Caffrey. Both were fellow Irishmen who were waiting for their transfer around the state.

Liam Martin was a repeat offender. A lot of other inmates in MCC knew him as he had been in and out three times. Mostly petty stuff like stealing phones and purses. He was a pleasant guy in his early forties who kept in shape with a routine of one hundred push-ups every day. His hair was always well trimmed, even if he hadn't seen a barber in weeks. He sat on the left side of Tommy on the bleachers in the yard.

To Liam's further left was Patrick. He was an old Irish man who had grown up in the city all his life. His stories, if not prison stories mainly consisted of telling how the city went up. This building and that building. Most of his stories were told time and time again.

Thinking he was going to live his last twenty years outside the jail didn't become a reality. He was back in on a parole violation when he went out of state for one weekend. Even though Patrick seemed wise, it was only over prison knowledge that he had gained over twenty years in jail.

The guys sat in the top row of the bleachers due to some special sort of status Patrick had for being old in prison that Tommy just didn't understand. He hoped he would never be in prison at that age to find out.

Hispanics had a section in the middle of the bleachers and further down on the other end were the blacks. If you stepped back, there was a clear color gradient across the bleachers from light to dark. The only place in the yard where it was mixed was at the one basketball hoop.

Spending his time between his people and the basketball court, Pipsqueak started to keep an unsuspecting eye on Tommy. Patrick, Liam, and Tommy took a lap around the yard. Pipsqueak kept an eye.

As the guys walked behind the basketball court, Pipsqueak ran to the three-point line and screamed for the ball. Catching it, he took two quick dribbles inside and threw a hard pass past the baseline. There was a player but the intentional miss hit Liam in the shoulder, just missing his head. The ball ricocheted off and back onto the court.

Pipsqueak stood there grinning and waiting for a reaction. He didn't get it from the guys walking but a large bald-headed white guy picked him up by his collar on the court. His feet were dangling six inches above the ground. Two black guys swarmed in, one punching him in the liver and another to the back of his head. Pipsqueak's feet hit the ground and then he threw in one punch of his own to the guy's large gut before the guards rushed in to break it up.

Just as the guards were breaking up the scuffle, a group of inmates started running to the opposite fence line. "Oohs and ahhs," were being shouted by the inmates, along with a lot of whistling.

More guards had to come up to the yard and started to take control of the crowd. The inmates were all focused on a parking garage across the street that they could see down onto. An exotic dancer moved herself around on one of the levels to give the guys a show. Her beaded yellow thong and bra sparkled to the onlooking animals.

Tommy and his friends steered clear and lined up to go inside. Once the performer finished her dance, she packed up and drove away. It was hard to say who was more shocked, the guards or the inmates.

The next day wasn't as exciting for the inmates in the yard, but it was for the guards. A few inmates were on the lookout to see if the girl would come back but she didn't. Things were back to normal.

Pipsqueak was back on the court as Liam, Patrick, and Tommy were walking a few laps. When he got the ball, the guys were just rounding the corner to walk behind the basket. This time, Pipsqueak threw it at Tommy as hard as he could.

Catching it like a dodgeball, Tommy dropped it onto the ground and charged Pipsqueak. He intended to tackle him into the pavement but couldn't. In the split second that Tommy ran at him, Pipsqueak pulled out a shank from his back waistband. The next thing Tommy felt was a scolding sharp pain in his abdomen. It wasn't anything like the poisoning stomach cramps.

"How do you like that one!" Pipsqueak grinned through his teeth at Tommy who had fallen onto one knee. His hands no longer went after Pipsqueak as he laid down and grabbed his side. Pipsqueak dropped the shank and took a punch to the face by Liam.

Liam then bent down to Tommy as Patrick stood back and watched the guards swoop in again.

"Ugh, fuck me!" Tommy cried out. There was a puddle of blood on his right side. Patrick took his shirt off and put pressure on the puncture.

"What issue did you have with that guy?" Liam asked while pushing down harder.

"None, I haven't caused any trouble here." Tommy winced. At this rate, he thought he was going to be the next to go behind Ray and Donny. He also thought he'd never see the end of his sentence if this was just the start.

He stared up at the cloudy sky as two paramedics put him on a stretcher, getting ready to take him to the hospital. Tommy was carted off as the guards called an end to the yard time for the day.

Liam jumped in line behind Patrick who shook his head at the whole situation. He was too old to be getting into fights.

"Man, that was out of nowhere," Liam said. He was still heated about the whole situation.

"It's never out of nowhere Liam," Patrick replied, all the wiser as they walked inside.

Chapter Twenty-Eight

Common Enemies

The gurney rushed off from the back of the ambulance and took Tommy in for surgery. Luckily, the doctor informed him they were not life-threatening stab wounds after he was stitched up. The doctor ordered a two-day mandatory rest at the hospital.

Now he knew how Ray must have felt having a cold handcuff around his wrist and attached to the gurney. Still, it was better than being in jail. He had a full room to himself and a cable TV.

They assigned a single guard from the jail to watch over Tommy as he lay there. It was an older guard who occasionally fell asleep in a blue corner chair. Only to wake up when the nurse would come in and check on Tommy.

"Can I use the phone?" Tommy asked the guard after the nurse had left. It was out of reach on the left side of the room but a tease was in sight.

"Nah," muttered the guard. "Just stay put."

"Anything you want to watch?"

The guard thought for a second and Tommy tossed him the remote, gritting the quick pain. Flipping around through the channels, the guard settled on Seinfeld. There weren't any sports on and Tommy wasn't going to complain at that choice.

Tommy nodded off to some of the pain meds with laugh tracks playing in the background.

A few hours later, he woke up with a nurse asking him to take a Clindamycin and Ciprofloxacin. She wanted to have a look at the bandage and Tommy really couldn't refuse.

"What time is it?" he asked her. The clock was out of his view on the right side of the wall when he was laid back. It was just above the guard.

"It's just past 7:40," the guard answered for the nurse. "You in a rush to get somewhere?"

During his time at the jail, Tommy had found that these older guards felt more entitled to say stuff like that. They thought of themselves as veterans of the jail and "had seen it all" if you'd asked them.

"Excuse me, ma'am, do you mind handing me the phone on your way out?" Tommy asked as the nurse was just throwing a few things in the garbage can. She looked at the guard for his approval. His eyebrows quickly raised, as if to say whatever. The protocol was that it wasn't allowed. Moving the side table within reach of his left hand, she put the phone in reach. Tommy thanked her before she said she would be back again in a little bit to check on him.

Making all the moves with his left hand, Tommy picked up the receiver and stabbed at the dial pad numbers with his pointer finger. He cocked his head to the left in bed to sandwich the phone between his ear and shoulder.

It rang and rang but eventually Jack picked up.

"Hello?" He wasn't familiar with the number but he was with the voice.

"It's me, Tommy. I'm over at Stroger Hospital."

"Oh yeah? Is everything alright?" Jack didn't want to say too much and he surely was hoping Tommy wasn't stupid enough to say anything about the robbery either.

"Yeah, yeah, I got picked up and put into MCC in town. I've tried to call you a few times from the jail but haven't got through. You think you could come down and visit one of these days? Of course, after I get better."

Part of Jack wanted to know what was going on and why Tommy was even at the hospital if he was supposed to be at jail. The other part was furious with Tommy. Just the sound of his voice pissed off Jack after

Donny's death. He didn't promise anything, just that he had to get off and have dinner with Jen but he'd think about it.

Back in the jail, Liam and Patrick started to learn a bit more. News traveled quickly through the cells. It's not like the inmates had anything to talk about.

At lunch they were sitting two tables away from Pipsqueak and Liam was looking at him directly. If it wasn't for the other three large black guys at his table, Liam considered walking over and breaking the lunch tray over his head.

"I heard he was paid by that crooked guard, Charlie, through a few of my sources," Patrick said while stirring some watery green beans with his fork. There was more water than beans.

"Oh yeah? Well, I wonder if Tommy knows anything about that." Liam gave Patrick a stern look.

"Well, I wouldn't get wrapped up in something that could be much bigger than you know," said Patrick. The guys finished up their meals and took back their trays. Liam waited anxiously for Tommy to get back from the hospital. He wanted to get to the bottom of it and had nothing else to do.

That afternoon, Tommy was ushered back into the cell block. The first cell on his left was Pipsqueak's, who caught eye of him walking through the first set of cell doors. He got up and stuck his face into the bars while Tommy walked by.

"Next time I'll kill you, boy. That was just the warning!"

The guard put Tommy back in his cell and the door slammed behind him. His cellmate looked happy to see him.

"Gee, I heard about that one. You can't keep on anyone's good side around here," he remarked. Tommy didn't disagree because frankly, he was starting to think the same.

"You ought to just lie low for a few days." The guy suggested like he had the whole situation figured out. No one could call him an expert though. This was the first time he had ever even seen a jail.

What does this guy think? Is he some sort of preacher or counselor? I'd hit him in the face if I wasn't busted up myself thought Tommy as he sat down.

Over the next couple of days, he took the advice. Tommy stayed inside during yard time, only going to the cafeteria once feeling a bit better. He survived on commissary ramen noodles until then. It was better than what they were serving in the cafeteria.

Liam slid over to make space as Tommy finally came to lunch and joined the guys at the table. Patrick was happy to see him. He knew how fast a guy could come and go in prison. Over his time, he had seen multiple stabbings and not everyone would return.

"I hope this juice stays in your stomach today," Patrick said, welcoming back Tommy.

"Yeah, they sewed it all back up. Hope to keep it that way."

"Man, what was the cause of that one in the first place?" Liam asked and looked at Patrick.

"I don't know. I never spoke to that Pipsqueak before."

The guys ate their food and Tommy couldn't help but look up and see Pipsqueak. When they made eye contact, Pipsqueak motioned with his knife that he was going to cut Tommy's throat. It didn't faze him since he knew where the threat was coming from.

"I heard that Charlie had paid Pipsqueak for that little number on you." Liam said to Tommy. "Any reason he'd be after you?" Patrick exchanged a disappointed look with Liam for stirring the table.

"Hmm. Nope. Nothing I can think of."

The news was alarming to his ears. *Again, the same guard?* Rutherford is using him like a puppet, he thought.

"What are you going to do, Tommy?" Liam was curious to see if he would retaliate. He wanted to see what kind of man Tommy was deep down.

"I'm going to go about my own business and heal up."

"Wise decision, kid," Patrick said as they finished up lunch.

He liked having the three of them back together. It was the closest thing Patrick ever had to kids in life.

***

The rapping of Charlie's baton on Tommy's metal cell woke him up from a mid-afternoon nap. He shoved the baton back in his holster and announced to Tommy that he had a visitor.

There weren't many people on Tommy's visitor list so anyone was better than no one. Especially with almost two months gone in jail and no outside contact. Tommy popped up like a spring off the bed and followed Charlie down to the visitor rooms.

"Glad to see you are alive and well," Charlie said as they walked down the hallway.

"You have fifteen minutes."

Charlie opened the door and greeted another guard in the sterile room. There were seven white round tables spaced out in the room that the guard watched over. He took custody of Tommy and led him over to a table where Jack was sitting. Tommy had the biggest smile since he entered the jail.

"Man, you came." It took him a second to gather more words.

"You look good. Lost some weight and the clean shave is a nice touch." Tommy laughed at Jack. The five o'clock shadow on Tommy was begging to be shaved. His face hadn't been cleaned up since before the stabbing.

"How are you getting on in here? What's all this with you at the hospital?" Jack asked.

The question soured Tommy's face a bit but it was mainly the reason he wanted to see Jack. It was just hard for him to talk about.

"It couldn't be going worse and to be fair, I don't know if I'll make it out of this sentence. I was poisoned when I got in and then stabbed just a few days ago. Worst of all, it's not the inmates giving me all this grief."

Jack thought he understood but he didn't. He continued to listen and started to feel bad he hadn't visited earlier. He could read the pain on Tommy's face.

"There is this Special Agent. Special Agent Rutherford was the guy behind my plea deal. He got to my portion of the cut hence the lesser sentence. But, ever since inside he's been using one of the guards to get to me."

"Well, why would he do that?" Jack asked.

"Probably to silence me like I heard they got to Donny."

"Don't you speak his name. I know your plea deal couldn't be just from that agent getting some of your ..." He quieted down before saying money. Jack wanted to tell Tommy that he could only blame him for not sticking with the guys and going out the front door. It was just too quiet in the room to do such a thing.

"I'm telling you, man, after being stabbed, what's next? He kills me whenever he wants? A dead man tells no lies and Rutherford knows that."

"I don't think there's much I can do for you, man. You kinda put yourself in this position. You gotta own up to it."

"Five minutes!" the guard in the room shouted. He held up his hand with a visual cue as well.

"Put myself in this? You better not talk like that because I could have you sitting here right next to me," Tommy said in a threatening tone.

"I don't even know why I came down here. When you went out that front door, it showed who you were." Jack stood up to leave.

"You figure something out or you might be my cellmate. I'm not going to die in here alone."

Jack had heard him but was already walking to the metal door. He nodded to the guard who opened it and politely thanked him as well. Left at the table was Tommy. The thought crossed his mind that he wouldn't see Jack visiting him again after that.

His thoughts were broken with a stern, "Get up!" from Charlie, who tightly grabbed his right tricep. Tommy walked in front as Charlie marched him back to his cell. He hoped that enough would go into Jack's head to help him.

***

The whole situation was a lot to think about for Jack. With his relationship getting better with Jen, maybe she could offer some insight. She was a great ear when Jack faced challenges, generally. The foreclosure notices were a bit much when they were getting those but that was out of the way. Plus, who wouldn't be stressed getting those? Jack thought to himself.

After dinner, he stepped out back for his nightly smoke. His habit never broke. Now, he could just afford it easier than before. It was true though that the cancer sticks were addictive because it was the single habit Jack never broke. He could take a work sick day and still smoke a bunch of cigarettes.

At least the weather was getting warmer for standing out there in the evenings. The stress though was different from a month or two ago. Even with more money, he was stressed. He wondered what would have Donny done if he got shot to death instead of him.

Staying out a little longer than normal, Jack had two cigarettes vs his normal one. Jen stuck her head out from the back door to check on him.

"Everything alright?" she asked. She was much sweeter since they were comfortable with money. More than eighty percent of their arguments before were about not having enough money to bring up the girls.

"Why don't you join me? It's nice out."

"I don't really want to get smoke in my hair..." she remarked but stepped outside anyway. They both sat down at a clear plastic table. It needed a wash between the ashes that had blown out of the ashtray and the bird poop.

"What if I told you the guy that shot Donny was also trying to murder Tommy... What would you think? What would you do?"

Jen looked shocked. She didn't really know Tommy and knew more from the news stations than from Jack.

"I guess I'd think, can't you go to the police?"

"Mmm, I can't do that. They could kill Tommy. I stopped by to visit him today and he is just recovering from a stab wound. If I can't do anything for Donny, I think I should for Tommy."

"No Jack. What do you owe him? It's his fault for the situation he's in... Life is finally good."

"Well, he threatened me..."

Again Jen couldn't believe it. "After all this? He has the nerve?"

"Yeah, his ultimatum was to do something about this agent or go join him."

"Well, do you think he meant it?" Jen asked with concern in her voice.

"I couldn't tell."

Adding his cigarette to the collection in the ashtray on the table, Jack stood up to head inside. Sure, life was good for Jen, he thought, but she wasn't the one still on the line to go to jail. For the time being, Jack figured he would just wait it out and let Tommy cool off a bit.

The weekend came and went with no calls from Tommy. Although Jack had a creepy feeling of people closing in on him. He went to the grocery store with Jen and it felt like everyone was staring at him. What if Tommy does rat me out? His biggest fear was someone who just showed up and carted him off to jail.

The consequences didn't scare Jack as much as the anxiety. He didn't have feelings of guilt but rather just wanted to live a normal life.

Halfway through the week, his phone rang. It was a familiar number from MCC. Jack ignored it and stuffed the phone back into his pocket.

Two days later. The same number popped up while he was on his lunch break. Being controlled by an inmate. What a feeling it was ... Jack answered and asked how Tommy was doing. Tommy didn't want the small talk.

"Were you able to help me out, bud?" Tommy asked.

Jack considered giving him a lie, in hopes that he would stop calling but figured Tommy would find out one way or another.

"Hey man, I've been busy with work."

"Do you know why I have fewer years, Jack?"

"I know you took a plea deal."

"Do you know why I have fewer years?"

Jack didn't have an answer. All he knew was stuff from TV and they never said.

"I'm the guy. I sold out Donny and lowered my sentence. I didn't want for him to get shot but what are you going to do? Look at the situation I'm in."

He didn't say it but Jack knew it was a threat. Promising to see what he could do, Jack said he had to get back to work and could chat more in the coming days.

Chapter Twenty-Nine

Can't Beat Em, Join Em

After speaking with Tommy, there was nothing more than Jack wanted to do than strangle his throat. That would solve half of his problems, so he thought.

On his way home from work, Jack took a detour to solve his problems. He parked his truck in front of a sub shop at a strip mall and went into the pawnshop next store. The door chimed as he opened the door covered in bars.

The shop was dingy but well fitting for the run-down strip mall. A few light bulbs needed to be changed in the ceiling that lit up old computers, power tools, stereos, and some used video game systems. There was a wrap-around jewelry case in the back of the shop with cash registers on top of it and guns on the back wall. Jack doubted that all the jewelry was real.

Just aside from the pawned-off diamond engagement rings were the handguns. Most of the long guns were hunting shotguns and not rifles to Jack's disappointment. He had always liked the AR-15 even though he had never owned a gun.

"Can I help you?" a guy with a large gut covered by a white tee shirt asked. He had a heavy gold neck chain and a few rings on his fingers which gave Jack the impression he was the owner.

"Just browsing. I wanted to see a few of your handguns." Jack said while crouching down and peering into the case.

"So, you want to exercise your second amendment. Well, you came to the right place. Luckily, we have some good ones in stock right now." He bent down to unlock the case and his curly dark hair bounced on his head. It took him a second to adjust his thick glasses and see what he had pulled out.

"This one here is the Glock 19, great for personal defense. S&W Shield is a true workhorse. Finally, a P226, you'll never get a jam with this one," the guy said as he set the three down on the glass countertop. They each made a loud clunk as the heavy bodies of the guns lay down on the glass.

He seems to know what he's talking about. Jack picked up the one in the middle and pointed it at the wall off to the left. Frankly, all three looked the same to him and as long as they fired, that was all he cared about.

"That's a good choice there," said the shop owner, who was happy to make any kind of sale.

Just holding the gun, Jack could feel the power. It was a strange feeling, an invincible one. *So, this is why everyone loves these things.* He flipped over the white hanging tag to see the price: $349.

"Can you do $280?" Jack asked as he set it back down.

The guy eyed Jack over and knew by the way he had held it up that he had never held a gun in his life.

"That's almost an insult. $330 is the best I can do and that's a bargain." The owner started to put the other two pistols away as Jack thought it over. He told him that he'd take it and they headed to the register for some paperwork.

Just in a matter of an hour, Jack was a new gun owner. He put the Smith and Wesson into the glove box and drove over to the sports store to pick up some ammo.

A voice in his head from Donny was saying it was a bad idea but then he heard Tommy in his head saying to do it. His mind was made up. He had already got the gun so there was no turning back, at least in Jack's mind.

Over dinner, once the girls finished up and went off to play, Jack thought about telling Jen of his new purchase but decided against it. She would have only told him to get rid of it or something. There wouldn't have been any encouragement from her end, he thought.

***

Loud beeping, followed by a knock on the door the next morning had Jen shouting for Jack's attention.

"The door is for you," she yelled as he was just finishing up breakfast.

When he came down, Pete was at the door with the keys in his hands. Behind him on the street was the black Mustang. From afar, it looked better than ever. The excitement couldn't hide behind the big smile on Jack's face as he shook Pete's hand.

"Let's go take a look," Pete said as he led Jack outside.

From closer inspection, it was even better. The lines were straight as an arrow and the fresh wax job shined in the morning sun. There wasn't a single scratch to be seen on the car and it looked like it had just come off the showroom floor.

"What do you think?"

"It's incredible man."

"It was a lot of long nights, sweat, and beers to get this one fixed. Also, I couldn't have done it without Spencer down at the shop." Pete said.

Opening the door, Jack sat inside and admired the steering wheel. He remembered when he used to ride in the passenger seat with Donny at the wheel. That guy used to love punching it at every red light when they rode together.

"What do you say? Take it for a spin around the block and put it in the driveway?" Pete handed Jack the keys and climbed into the passenger seat for Jack's first drive.

When they got back, Jack carefully backed it into the driveway next to the Ranger. He now had both the nicest and crappiest car in the neighborhood.

"You oughta think about getting rid of that truck. They just don't look great together." Pete laughed and walked back over to the flatbed. "I'll see you down at the shop sometime."

The surprise was just the motivation Jack needed for the workday to beat the slump. Although he was afraid to take it to work though and left it at home. Plus, he didn't need all his coworkers to see a sixty-thousand-dollar car in the employee parking lot. That was almost twice what he made in a year.

Around lunch, the happiness wore off. Jack stopped at the gas station between jobs and grabbed a hot dog. "Special Agent Michael Rutherford" read the top line of the business card that stared him in the face. It was still sandwiched between the folded bills in his wallet.

He took his hot dog back to his work van and flipped the card between his hands then picked up his phone to give it a ring.

"Special Agent Rutherford speaking."

"Hey Rutherford, it's Jack, Donny Macintosh's cousin. You gave me your card at his funeral. I was hoping we could meet up and chat about the case. There were a few things about Tommy Fox I wanted to share with you."

"Oh yeah? Not a problem. Why don't you come down to the office this Thursday and I'll see that I make time."

There was no way Jack was going to drive into the city to meet Rutherford. The cameras, the parking situation and the amount of people, no chance.

"I was thinking we meet somewhere like Roadhouse 38. Thursday works though, I can do seven o'clock. I don't get into the city much and we can chat over a beer. This isn't really on the books sort of conversation, if you know what I mean."

"Oh yeah? Is that right? Well, what did Tommy tell you that isn't by the books?"

"I can't say it over the phone. I just wanted to give you a chance to speak in person before I use the proper channels."

The proper channels? Who does this guy think he is talking to a special agent like that?

"Ok, if you want me to drive all the way out there for some information I probably already know, on my time off, I can do it but this better be worth my time."

Rutherford had heard plenty of people complain about bad policing this and bad policing that. Any talk of that from Jack wasn't going to be anything new to him. Maybe he'd bring up the money, thought Rutherford, but then again, he thought Jack wouldn't have the balls for that in a public place.

Chapter Thirty

Making Peace

The glove box snapped shut as Jack made sure his gun was inside. He felt naked as he left his phone at home, purposefully. His hand flipped on the lights as he backed out of the driveway. The lights of the Ranger weren't great at lighting up the evening sky.

Roadhouse 38 was a dive bar. If there was ever a place to have an off-the-books conversation, it was there. Just off the highway, Roadhouse 38 was a frequent stop for the bikers, blue-collared workers, and rough crowds. It was along the gateway to the countryside, just outside the city.

Jack hadn't been to the bar in a few years since Donny took him one weekend. He'd never been back as the one time, Donny got into a fist-fight. It was almost another assault charge post his prison stint. The nine, two-dollar beers were enough liquid courage to have any man throwing fists. It wasn't an unusual scene at the roadhouse that night.

Forty minutes later, Jack slowed down as he cruised by the roadhouse. It was on a main two-lane road with sparse traffic. His clock said six-forty as he made a pass by the bar. He could feel his heartbeat in his chest, largely driven by anger.

It was dimly lit and some of the exterior wood needed repair. The gravel parking lot wrapped around the front and two sides. Jack saw a couple of motorcycles and a few old trucks that were as bad as his but nothing that would look like a special agent's vehicle.

He continued driving down the road to burn up some time until swinging a U-turn. There was an intent about Jack that just wasn't there when he went into the bank. The parking lot was pitch black but filled with Thursday drinkers. The clearly out-of-place, clean black SUV parked in front of Roadhouse 38 had to be Rutherford, thought Jack.

Parking across the way in between two older trucks, Jack backed in the Ranger and turned off his lights. He waited.

It was impossible to see him in the cab under the dark shadows of the night. His sight line was clear to the front door in front of the SUV. There was a good ten yards from what appeared to be Rutherford's SUV and the front door.

The clock ticked around to quarter past seven and everything was still. A few people came in, a few came out and Jack waited. Moments later, a few guys in their leather jackets got on their motorcycles and roared off.

Jack kept his eyes on the door, his heart was pumping, just waiting for Rutherford. Two men and a female came out of the bar for a smoke and Jack could hear them quarreling even across the parking lot. Surely, if Rutherford was in there, Jack's cell at home had a few missed calls. There was no way Jack could see him fitting in with that crowd.

He was right. After a forty-five-minute wait, a tall skinny figure came out of the door. The light above the door lit up the side of Rutherford's face towards Jack. Rutherford looked to the left and to the right before walking to the SUV. He got in but didn't start it up.

What the hell is he doing? Jack didn't have a clue. The air felt tense as every minute felt like two.

The lights came into the black SUV and blinded Jack. It felt like forever as the beams of light sliced through the windshield into the cab. Jack pressed his body back against the seat. He was sure that Rutherford must have seen him.

Rutherford made a left in the parking lot and waited to turn onto the road. A few seconds after he left the gravel parking lot onto the pavement, Jack started up his truck. He kept his headlights turned off and pulled out quickly to follow.

The red taillights were lit up at least one hundred yards in front of Jack as Rutherford drove down the road. It was so dark that Jack was looking ahead to use the SUV's taillights as a guide. He pressed on the accelerator to get the Ranger closer. His old truck was soon going fifty in a thirty-mph zone and closing distance fast.

Just ahead, Jack knew the road. They were approaching a section lined by trees and ditches big enough to swallow any car. He gripped the steering wheel as hard as he could with both hands, holding on for control.

It wasn't until the Ranger was five feet from Rutherford's bumper that he saw the truck in the rearview mirror. The eerie shadow had no warning. It was followed by a smash into the back left corner panel and a screech of brakes from the SUV. The impact shattered the Ranger's front right headlight and dented the bumper.

Come on!

Rutherford tried to regain control and was shaken up. Jack put on his high beams as he rammed the SUV again. The wheel rattled between his hands. He was ruthless and reckless. Oncoming headlights skimmed by both of the vehicles.

With a final hit, it was enough to send the SUV off the road.

Try me!

The two flips of the vehicle kicked up a cloud of dry dirt. Jack pulled on the shoulder just in front of the wreck and opened his glove box.

He shut off his truck, put on a pair of gloves, and walked down the embankment with the Smith and Wesson in hand. The SUV stopped rolling as it was wedged against a tree. Upside down headlights lit up the grass in front of the SUV and a bit of the woods.

Jack stepped out of the blinding light and took a wide loop around the car to approach it from behind. Walking up to the passenger side, the first thing he saw was that the airbags had gone off for both front seats. There was an outline of an upside-down head but no movement. Jack wanted to execute him.

Pointing his gun at the window and with his heart pumping, Jack looked inside the vehicle. Rutherford was still in his seatbelt but hanging upside down in the driver's seat. Blood was running down his face and dripping onto the ceiling of the car which was wedged into the ground.

Ready to pump him full of bullets with any move, Jack saw that Rutherford was motionless. A branch was impaled into his ribs and his right arm was mangled into the wreckage. He walked around to the driver's side, bent in, and turned off the headlights.

Above on the road, Jack's ears could hear a vehicle zoom by, then it was back to silence. He went back up to his Ranger and looked at the front-end damage. It was bad, but not as bad as Rutherford's SUV.

Jack started the Ranger and knew he'd need Pete to do a bit more bodywork on the truck after hitting this deer. That was Jack's story, anyway. The darkness gave him solitude after a scene of chaos. He knew the agent who solved cases would now be a case of his own.

Thank you for reading Sprayed! If you enjoyed this book, please consider writing a review with your honest impressions on Amazon, Goodreads, or the platform where you purchased this novel. Your feedback is incredibly valuable for helping independent authors like me reach a wider audience.

Check out David Dabbs's other books at www.daviddabbs.com

For movie rights, please use the contact form on the website above.

www.ingramcontent.com/pod-product-compliance
Lightning Source LLC
Chambersburg PA
CBHW062124020426
42335CB00013B/1083